The

Wild Sensitive

Unlocking the Power of the Highly Sensitive Sensation Seeker

Written By
Randy Grasser
&
Annet van Duinen

Published by

If you would like to inquire about the authors' availability to speak at your event, contact info@thewildsensitive.com. Examples of topics they can speak on are:

- **The Power of Being A Wild Sensitive:** Understanding and harnessing emotional depth in a chaotic world.
- **Thriving as a High Sensation Seeker:** How adventure, challenge, and self-discovery fuel a meaningful life.
- **Emotional Intelligence & Mental Resilience:** Understanding how thoughts, emotions, and beliefs shape reality.

Cover designed by: M. Waqas
First Edition July 2025
Paperback - ISBN 979-8-9928422-3-4
EBook - ISBN 979-8-9928422-4-1

General Disclaimer

The information in The Wild Sensitive is intended for educational and inspirational purposes only. While we share insights based on research, lived experience, and professional practice, this book is not a substitute for medical, psychological, or psychiatric advice, diagnosis, or treatment. We encourage readers to use their own judgment and to seek guidance from qualified healthcare professionals for any mental health or medical concerns. The authors and publishers are not responsible for any outcomes resulting from the application of information presented in this book. You are the expert of your own experience. Please take what resonates and always prioritize your well-being with the appropriate support.

To the fullest extent permitted by law, the authors, publishers, and any affiliated representatives of The Wild Sensitive disclaim all liability for any direct, indirect, incidental, consequential, or special damages arising from the use, interpretation, or application of the book, its content, or related discussions. This includes, but is not limited to, personal decisions, psychological effects, or any perceived emotional impact resulting from reading or engaging with the material.

Dedications

To Randy, we share a love so intense and fiery, it allows us to see each other fully and fiercely. You brought forth the missing pieces in me I didn't know I was still searching for. Together, we've discovered what it means to live with both tenderness and intensity as strengths, and to start living as Wild Sensitives. Without you, this book would have remained unwritten.

And to my two amazing and beautiful daughters, Louise and Sofia. With this book, I hope to inspire you, and all other young people like you to live your best lives possible, with the tools and awareness I didn't have growing up. You don't have to struggle or piece it all together alone, the way I once did. You are my heart's reason for every wild sensitive step I take.

To Dr. Elaine Aron, Jacquelyn Strickland, and Barbara Allen,
Without your pioneering work and unwavering dedication to the HSP trait, this book would never have existed. For years, I lived in quiet struggle, unaware that high sensitivity was a gift, and even less aware of how powerfully it could intertwine with the fire of being a High Sensation Seeker. You taught, mentored, and supported me as I grew my wings. Because of you, I found the strength to understand myself and embrace who I truly am. Now, I have the honor of paying this immense gift forward, helping others grow their wings and soar.

With love,
Annet

To Annet, my partner, my mirror, and the light in my wildness, thank you for giving me a home in your heart. You've not only made me whole, you've amplified everything good in me. Because of you, I know what it means to belong.

To my sons, Josh and Alex, there is not a day that goes by when you are not in my heart. You are my greatest adventure, my deepest why, and the quiet strength beneath every word of this book. I hope you always feel the fierce love and pride I carry for you, no matter the distance or the years.

To my mom, Barbara Grasser, raising a Highly Sensitive, High Sensation Seeking son wasn't easy, especially without the tools we have today. But you did it with love, and I wouldn't be who I am without you. I love you deeply.

To William Allen, thank you for being a brother and a voice for men like us. You opened a door that had been shut for too long, and your integrity and heart continue to inspire.

To Dr. Tracy Cooper, your groundbreaking research gave language to what once felt like contradiction. You helped us see that our dual nature is not only valid, it's also powerful.

To every Highly Sensitive, High Sensation Seeking man, this is for you. For the boys who felt too deeply, the men who learned to dim their light to survive, those who crave both thrill and stillness, and the fathers watching their children face the same inherited beliefs they fought to unlearn, you are not alone. This book was born from the struggle of existing in a world that often misunderstands men like us, and from the quiet triumph of building a life that finally does. Within these pages, may you find tools, purpose, and a reflection of your truth. Be wild. Be sensitive. Be yourself.

This is our beginning. Our wild, sensitive revolution starts now.
With the deepest admiration and respect to you all,
Randy

Table of Content

Foreword

It's a rare Thrill to introduce a book that unapologetically challenges the status quo. The Wild Sensitive is that book, a wake-up call for anyone who's ever felt too much and wanted more, all at once. Written by two remarkable people I have known for some time, now partners in life and in their mission to illuminate the experience of those who are both highly sensitive and high in sensation seeking, I met Randy Grasser and Annet van Duinen at different times, each encounter leaving a strong impression.

I first met Annet at a workshop for what would become the international consultants on high sensitivity, a cadre of professionals deeply familiar with Dr. Elaine Aron's research. Annet's openness about her identity as an HSS/HSP was inspiring, and little did I know she would later join forces with Randy Grasser, another Sensitive Sensation Seeker. My introduction to Randy came while Will Harper and I were creating the documentary Sensitive Men Rising. Randy's unwavering support and encouragement were invaluable, as he recognized how sorely needed the film was for highly sensitive men. Randy is impressive not only as a genuine world-traveling adventurer but also for his warmth and compassion; he's the kind of guy who pushes you to go further, think bigger, and refuse to settle. Over time, I grew fond of both Randy and Annet, and I was delighted to learn they were writing a book on HSS/HSPs.

What sets The Wild Sensitive apart is its unique blend of cutting-edge research, practical strategies, and deeply personal storytelling. Randy and Annet are passionate champions and emerging thought-leaders in the field of high sensitivity advocacy, bringing years of combined experience to this work. Their book fills a critical gap in the literature, offering not just understanding but a toolkit for transformation, especially for those who have struggled to see both their sensitivity and their craving for adventure reflected in existing resources.

As you turn these pages, you'll discover not only the science behind sensitivity and sensation seeking, but also the lived wisdom of two people who have walked this path. They're not just talking about high sensitivity and sensation seeking, they're living it full-on. Whether you're seeking validation, practical tools, or simply a sense of belonging, this book is for you.

The Wild Sensitive embodies what it feels like to be both a high sensation seeker and a highly sensitive person. The "wildness" of HSS/HSPs is something I sought to capture in my own book, Thrill: The High Sensation Seeking Highly Sensitive Person, in 2016. The more I have advocated for recognition of HSS/HSPs within the overall HSP population, up to half, as we now know thanks to our 2023 study, the more I have seen the need for works like this, which truly reflect how we Wild Sensitives experience life and how we might align our dual needs for stimulation and for reflection and rest.

Randy and Annet's care and commitment shine through every page. This book is especially helpful for HSPs who are also High Sensation Seekers, but may not yet realize how these two powerful traits live inside them at the same time. For those who feel both deeply and restlessly, The Wild Sensitive offers clarity, comfort, and direction. Drawing from their own real-life experiences, Randy and Annet have created a guide that fills a gap in both research and everyday tools, something the sensitive world has needed for a long time. Their stories and insights make complex ideas feel personal, practical, and empowering.

There is a gap in the wealth of books, articles, blogs, podcasts, and films, where the focus tends to be on the highly sensitive trait, no doubt due to the lack of support many HSPs experience throughout life. Yet, there is a need for strategies and models for HSS/HSPs to move beyond the initial stage of identifying as an HSS/HSP to phases of growth that can be transformative. This is where The Wild Sensitive truly shines, presenting cumulative reflections on the lived application of both traits. The deeply personal narratives of Randy and Annet further imbue the book with the warmth of their collaborative expertise and their unfolding story together.

Strategies like the Adventure Triskelion offer a new way of envisioning an empowered pathway to align mind, heart, and body, encapsulating the somatic, emotional, and cognitive, to holistically navigate a sustainable sense of well-being. Likewise, the 7P Rule will resonate with most HSPs, as it promotes the kind of thorough planning the trait is known for. The book is replete with useful tools you will find yourself returning to again and again, as the practical nature of Randy and Annet's work inspires you to try their techniques for understanding emotions, setting boundaries, and deescalating from states of overwhelm.

Whether you are a coach, therapist, Wild Sensitive, or know and love someone who is, this book presents The Wild Sensitive path as one of gentle practice and adaptation. If you are caught between craving depth or intensity of experience, struggling with the dynamic push and pull of trying to satisfy both traits, you'll find this book inspiring and illuminating of this lesser-known or less acknowledged half of the HSP population.

On a personal note, I remember the first time I recognized both my need for deep reflection and my craving for new experiences. It was only when I met others like Randy and Annet, people who had not just survived but thrived by embracing both sides of their nature, that I realized I wasn't alone. Their stories, and now this book, offer that same reassurance and guidance to you.

By doing the tough inner work of getting to know ourselves, and the tools in this book will certainly help, you will, in time, develop a greater sense of personal sovereignty and appreciate how the differences in HSS/HSPs beautifully complement the strengths of HSPs. This book is your permission slip to be both. If you're caught in the tug-of-war between craving depth and chasing intensity, you'll find not just understanding here, but a call to action.

As a long-time advocate and mentor for HSS/HSPs, it is rare to see a book written with such passion and belief in the expansive, connecting nature of our two traits. Randy and Annet have done an incredible job of owning what it means to be high in sensation seeking and high in sensitivity. As society increasingly embraces new possibilities in careers, relationships, and creative culture, it is precisely the Wild Sensitives, in my view, who are the vanguard of an emerging transformation of what it means to be human and alive in our time.

May The Wild Sensitive inspire you to embrace your contradictions, break your own rules, and show up fully, wild, sensitive, and unapologetically you. Randy Grasser and Annet van Duinen are shining examples of personal courage, fueled by the unique combination of two powerful traits, and their book is a gift to all of us who walk this path.

Tracy Cooper, PhD

Introduction

The Wild Sensitive

Unlocking the Power of the

Highly Sensitive and Sensation Seeker

Some of us were never meant to live quietly. Not because we fear the world, but because something in us pulses with raw aliveness, a way of feeling that refuses to stay contained. We cry at sunsets. We shiver at music. We read the room before a word is spoken. And we ache, not just for peace, but for possibility. For movement. For meaning.

This book doesn't begin in a lab, though research grounds it. It begins where real transformation starts: in the tension of being human. In the ache of trying to live fully in a world that keeps asking you to shrink. To choose between sensitivity and boldness. But what if you are both?

This is the story of two souls, Randy and Annet, who lived that paradox long before they could name it. A man and a woman from different continents, different cultures, both wired with the rare blend of High Sensitivity and High Sensation Seeking. Deeply feeling, fiercely curious. Misunderstood, mislabeled, too emotional, too intense, too restless. But they weren't too much. They were made for more.

Each of them walked alone for years, trying to make sense of themselves while navigating a world that couldn't quite make sense of them. Adapting. Hiding. Longing. Until they found each other, not to complete one another, but to expand together. Two whole people, joining forces to create something honest, wild, and liberating. Their meeting wasn't coincidence. It was what happens when people stop pretending and start living true. Their journey isn't just a love story. It's an invitation to live as a Wild Sensitive, fully, freely, without apology.

This book is the result of everything they've learned: from decades of coaching, traveling, and exploring the internal and external worlds of HSP-HSS life. It's a roadmap for those who feel too much and want too much, and who are ready to turn that into power.

Because sensitivity is not a weakness. Craving life is not a flaw. You were never meant to simply fit in. You were meant to awaken, to feel deeply, to grow wisely, and to live wildly. This is where your journey begins. This is where you become a Wild Sensitive.

Annet's Story... The Wild Tangle of Sensitivity and Sensation
Long before Annet knew the words, *Highly Sensitive Person* or *High Sensation Seeker*, she was already living both truths in her bones. Not as traits on a page, but as forces in her nervous system, shaping every breath, every choice, every ache, and awakening.

She was two years old the first time the wild called her. Not through storybooks or parental permission, but through instinct. While the world around her rested in quiet predictability, Annet slipped out through a garden gate she'd never opened before, answering the call to explore the empty construction site near her home in the Netherlands. There, among towering concrete sewer pipes, relics of a strange and mysterious world being built, she discovered a pipe laying horizontally, just big enough to crawl inside. And in that still, cool tunnel, she curled up and fell asleep, hidden from the noise of the world. Her parents searched frantically for hours, hearts pounding with fear. When they finally found her, she was serene. Untouched by panic. Completely at peace.

That moment would become a mirror for the rest of her life: the need for stillness tucked inside the hunger for edge. A child who craved sanctuary… and secretly loved the unknown.

As she grew, Annet became very good at reading the room. She could walk into a space and sense every aspect, who was hurting, who was pretending, who wasn't saying what they meant. She didn't just read the atmosphere. She absorbed it. Emotions moved through her like weather crossing the sky, full-body experiences that no one else seemed to notice. And yet, for all that sensitivity, she also carried an unrelenting fire.

While others craved routine, Annet's heart beat to a different rhythm, one that demanded realness, aliveness, more. She was labeled "too much," "too dreamy," "too intense." Teachers praised her imagination but quietly wished she'd just color inside the lines. She never had many friends, they never quite understood the depths she longed to swim in. She was the quiet girl who secretly wrote fantasy stories at recess and the one who once launched herself so high on a swing that adults begged for her to stop. But she didn't. She flew.

Because she felt so different, Annet often felt excluded, as though she existed just slightly out of sync with the world around her. The noise of childhood games felt too loud, the chatter too shallow. So, she did what many sensitive souls do to survive: she began to disappear. It felt safer not to be seen. Attention, even well-meaning, brought discomfort. So slowly, almost imperceptibly, she became a master at invisibility. She learned how to blend in, to not disrupt, to read a room so well that she could adjust her presence to near-transparency.

In her twenties, she passed a bookstore window and saw a title that seemed to reach straight into her chest: *The Highly Sensitive Person* by Dr. Elaine Aron. She bought it, devoured it in one night, and that moment, something clicked. She realized then there was nothing wrong with her and that there was a name for the way her whole system responded to life. There was a clear explanation for the overwhelming empathy, the rich inner world, the deep processing. With this new understanding, a sense of quiet validation washed over her.

But naming that part of her was just the beginning.

Even with that revelation, life still didn't fit. She cycled through educational programs and jobs like ill-fitting clothes, each one stifling her just enough to make her feel so uncomfortable, she left. While less sensitive people saw her as being flaky, she sensed a calling for something greater, something far more meaningful, the calling to feel alive. Back then, the world didn't know what to do with someone who refused to trade aliveness for stability, and in many ways, it still holds onto that misunderstanding. Eventually, she stumbled upon an article from Dr. Elaine Aron on the research by Dr. Marvin Zuckerman and later, Dr. Tracy Cooper, about another rare trait: High Sensation Seeking. And things began to make far more sense.

Annet is not one who is satisfied just following the herd, those who feel less and fear more. She was designed by nature to lead. And though she didn't yet know how to take that lead, and often felt an unshakable discomfort in doing so, something deep inside her knew she was born for it. She wasn't indecisive. She was naturally dual-wired, for both exploration and reflection, softness, and speed. She wasn't scattered. She was whole, in a way most others hadn't yet learned, nor were they willing to understand. And beneath it all, she carried a deep empathy and intuitive understanding of others, a quiet ability to see and hold what many couldn't even name.

Annet's adventures became bolder. Hitchhiking to distant cities she'd never seen. Riding on trains to visit new countries where even the language was foreign to her. She would say yes to experiences that scared most, not because they were dangerous or reckless, because she was born a *Wild Sensitive* designed to discover the unknown.

Each wild step she took was a reclamation. A slow re-conditioning that social expectations placed upon her. A morphing of limiting beliefs into affirming facts that only a Highly Sensitive Sensation Seeker understands.

Eventually, however, her sense of adventure would give in to the expectations of society, trading bigger dreams for the more accepted path of settling down, marrying, and motherhood. When her children were born, a new magic filled Annet's soul. She was now a guide for two curious and beautiful daughters. Every new experience they had, from tasting new food, to learning to walk, helped Annet fill the deep desires that High Sensing High Sensation Seekers need. Yet, as children grow, a parent's need for guidance becomes less and less, yet the natural call within her still called out.

By her forties, Annet was living a life that looked stable on the outside, marriage, and motherhood, but inside, something had begun to break. Her marriage, while full of experiences and shared love, had become too small for the woman she was inside. She then dove headfirst into life coach training, not to fix herself, but to find herself. A quiet boldness began returning to her bones. Week by week, she practiced being seen again, not as a performance, but as a reclamation. Coaching wasn't just a profession, it became a rite of passage. She was stepping out from behind the veil, not to be loud, but to be real. To show up in what is called her authentic self, kind, compassionate, fully felt, and fully visible.

She became a certified coach through one of the world's top coaching programs, iPEC. And eventually, she earned the rare honor of being selected by Dr. Elaine Aron herself to join a small group of international experts specializing in High Sensitivity. She is now one of the few *International Consultants on High Sensitivity.*

From there, Annet became a leader for other sensitive, seeking souls. She spoke to rooms that once would have overwhelmed her. She coached clients across continents. And her name grew within the Highly

Sensitive Community. And behind that visibility was a woman who never stopped. A perpetual learner, Annet followed every spark of curiosity with devotion. Over the years, she completed many trainings, from Mindfulness-Based Cognitive Therapy (MBCT) and stress counseling to teen and kids coaching, confidence coaching, interpersonal neurobiology, and Positive Intelligence® (PQ). She wasn't collecting certificates; she was gathering tools for understanding the human heart. And yet… there was still something very unfulfilling in her chest. Something calling her to go beyond.

While she was helping so many sensitive souls find their inner truth, her own soul was whispering louder each day:

"You're not done. You are destined for more."

Annet carefully looked at her life, as a Highly Sensitive High Sensation Seeker does. Her sensitivity to the subtleties and depth of processing began to expose a truth unfolding within her. As her daughters became more and more independent, a deep emotional emptiness began to emerge. As they began finding their own way, needing shorter moments of connection, the home slowly shifted. The marriage, once a shared structure, was dissolving quietly, more absence than presence, more routine than relationship.

And so, with trembling hands and an aching heart, Annet made the hardest choice of her life. She left that existence, the marriage and answered her desire to explore herself again. In this growth, Annet wanted, more than anything, to show her daughters what it meant to choose truth over tradition. To be true to herself over conformity. To show them, life isn't about just accepting the status quo, it was about living fully. She wanted them to see what wholeness looked like.

That single act of courage changed everything, while testing the precious bond she had with her daughters, as a Highly Sensitive Person, which can be the biggest risk of all.

As Annet was planning her new life, she came across the profile of another Highly Sensitive Person. Someone who dared to challenge the stereotypical picture that was painted about Highly Sensitive People. He was bold, daring, sensitive and adventurous. She wondered, would he make a good guest on her podcast, *Sensitive and Strong*?

Sitting back in her chair, she sent this stranger an invitation. Little did she know that message would grow into a first spark of love, a partnership, and a purpose far beyond anything she could have imagined, for wild wasn't done with her yet, it had just begun.

Randy's Story... The Sensitive Seeker Who Refused to Go Numb

Randy's story begins in structure, not the kind that brings stability, but the kind that cages. Born into a world where silence was demanded and the rules changed without warning, he learned early that safety was just an illusion, that even a subtle shift in the environment could trigger emotional outrage. As a result of this, he became a master of reading the room. A six-year-old with the eyes of an old soul, scanning, tracking, predicting. Not to manipulate, but to simply survive.

His sensitivity wasn't welcomed, embraced, or encouraged. It was weaponized. Seen as too emotional. Too intense. A threat that needed strict control. Because Randy scores extremely high on the Sensitivity Spectrum, the very traits that made him extraordinary were framed as flaws by everyone around him. So, like many Highly Sensitive children, he learned to adapt, not by simply hiding his emotions as society expected all boys do, but by becoming extremely vigilant to the world around him. Learning to pick up on the smallest details that would indicate a risk to his survival.

Randy, a Highly Sensitive boy, didn't become 'Hypervigilant' as less sensitive children do when facing trauma. He tapped into his natural sensitivity to detect the subtitles others overlooked while building an even deeper ability to adapt to his environment.

To help you understand this, let's imagine Highly Sensitive People (HSP's) having the eyesight of a Bald Eagle, which is 4-5 five times that of less sensitive people. HSP's with traumatic childhoods can develop the eyesight of a Peregrine Falcon, which being 8-10 times more than the less sensitive. And while this example is a simple metaphor, it helps explain how those with trauma-based childhood and high sensitivity see the world through their awareness.

Through this conditioning, Randy became far more aware of surroundings, not just threats but his entire environment. Situations, others would overlook or brush off stood out to him, like beacons in the night. However, threats emanating from his older brother, even when his parents were in the room, created a major influence. The subtle look of hatred for just being alive. The tone of the words spoken, and the realized outcome of those small threats being delivered in the pushes and punches when no one else was around.

The threat was real to Randy, constantly and consistently. His need for adaptation was also real, and yet, there was this deep burning desire not to hide, but rather explore. Each time that part slipped out, it triggered the reaction from his parents who demanded 'Little boys should be seen and not heard.'

But the fire never went out. Even as a very young boy, Randy felt the ache for more, not more stuff, but more meaning, more understanding, more discovery. He wasn't drawn to playgrounds. He was drawn to the abandoned coal mine on the edge of town, a crumbling relic of another time. Most kids stayed far away from it, fearing its old wooden timbers and ghostly impression. Randy on the other hand, felt a deep curiosity, drawn to its mystery and adventure. He would walk into the old mine tunnel, following the old set of rail tracks from long ago. Sitting down, cross legged, surrounded by darkness that lay in front of him, he would let the fear dance around him and through him until it too would sit beside him.

Over the course of several years, Randy would return, going deeper and deeper into the tunnels' darkness until fear would show up. He repeated this ritual over and over, teaching himself to become comfortable with fear, while trusting his sensitivity to detect real risk, not just emotional imbalance.

In those moments, Randy found something he couldn't name yet: sovereignty. In that mine shaft, no one yelled at him. No one shamed him. No one bullied him. It was quiet, yet not empty. For in that mine shaft, he found a friend, one most call fear. This friendship began when Randy was six years old, and to this day they are still friends.

That mine shaft became Randy's first real teacher. A sanctuary made of shadows, where fear wasn't the enemy, it was a guide. He would later call this *self-guided exposure*, the practice of entering discomfort intentionally, to become stronger, braver, more present. But at six years old, all he knew was that being in the dark on his own terms was safer than depending on the light of someone else.

As he grew, so did the pressure to conform. Be a good son. A good student. A good man. And so, Randy did what so many of us do, he became what the world told him to be. He wore a mask. He played the part.

Then at sixteen, he was able to fulfill his dream. He earned his first Scuba Diving Certification. Once again, he found a refuge where few would go. A place where he and his friend, fear, were welcomed. Randy advanced his underwater skills and at age seventeen, he went to San Diego to attend a commercial diving school after he graduated. Returning home, he worked both as a commercial diver and as a scuba diving instructor, guiding other adventurous souls to face their own fear and see a world of beauty and diversity, instead of one full of limiting beliefs. He taught his students at age eighteen that fear was an acronym, which stood for; *Face Every Adversity Realistically*.

For the next eight years, Randy explored the underwater world, logging over 4000 dives, his only real adversary, was the beliefs and behaviors of other people, through his awareness and high sensitivity, he saw more threat in people than any experience he had underwater. Like so many, social expectations demanded he be more responsible, so too did his girlfriend. Marriage. Children. A steady job, twisted Randy into a version of himself that felt like he was caged. His desire to feel, to sense, to test himself was placed in a bottle, only forcing its way out once in a while.

Randy then found solace in the mountains, hiking and climbing higher and higher. Until one day, on November 11th, 1997, he and two of his climbing partners were buried while sound asleep in their tent by four feet of ice and snow. It wasn't because they were in a dangerous spot, it was because nature has a will of its own. It was Randy's training, enhanced by his depth of processing, sensitivity to subtleties, and his friendship with fear, that ultimately saved all of their lives, a story he wrote about in his first book, "Facing Fear through Adventure – An HSP's Story."

This event, however, triggered a profound mental shift in him. His love for his twin sons meant far more than his desire for adventure. This is when Randy locked up his adventurous spirit in a box and hid it away, so he could be the best father he could be. He provided. He performed. But mostly, he complied.

The cost was enormous on his mental and emotional health. Once again, he felt trapped in an ever-shrinking cage. Every time he ignored his own intuition, a part of him dimmed. Every time he chose duty over who he truly was, the ache inside him grew louder.

He wasn't living, he was barely existing. And like the family he grew up in, no one noticed, and no one cared.

And then, one winter night, at a Christmas party he hadn't planned to attend, everything changed.

In the corner of the room sat a 93-year-old man, alone, ignored, like a shadow at the edge of the celebration. While others gossiped and made small talk, Randy was drawn to him. HSPs don't do surface-level. They go straight for the soul. And this man, this quiet elder, was waiting to be seen. They talked. Deeply. Honestly. And then, the old man reached out, placed a weathered hand on Randy's knee, and said through a veil of tears:

"Son, when I die, I want 'I wish I would have' written on my gravestone."

Randy blinked. "What do you mean by that?"

The man's voice cracked. "Because I never did anything I truly wanted. I lived for others. I played it safe. And now… it's too late."

That moment pierced through every mask Randy had ever worn. He walked home that night in the cold, snow biting his skin, and stopped in the middle of a quiet street.

He looked up at the sky and whispered a vow that would change the course of his life:
"I will not be a 'wish I would have' man."

And he meant it.

Within months, Randy walked away from the life that no longer fit. Not recklessly, but radically.
With nothing but two small duffel bags, a journal, and the deep ache to know who he really was, he set off on a journey that would take him through over fifty countries. He wasn't chasing adrenaline. He was seeking truth.

He listened to stories held in jungles under starlit skies. He wept with strangers in dorms and wild camps. He sat in silence with Buddhist monks, finally asking the question that had haunted him since childhood, "What is true wisdom?"

The monk smiled gently and said, "To gather knowledge, live experience, and reflect until the two become one."

That became Randy's compass. Not boldness for the sake of it. Not stillness for retreat. But the fusion of both.

His sensitivity deepened. His courage sharpened. His pain became his teacher. He longed for adventure as a deeply committed High Sensation Seeker does.

He lost things along the way, precious things. There was distance from his children, it wasn't just physical, it was mental and emotional. While his children strongly held onto limited beliefs placed into them, Randy's mindful and emotional connections were evolving. This gap created deep misunderstandings he couldn't control. And so, in Randy's growth to be a better version of himself, he lost his most precious gift, his children's love.

But he found something else. He found himself.

He was able to discard the mask so many expected him to wear. He became the caretaker of his soul, not the people pleaser he once was. He empowered his sensitivity through his desire to seek sensation naturally by truly understanding all of its nuances deeply.

He exposed more than who he is, he discovered, why he is... Whole, weathered, wild and wise.

After fifteen years of exploring, learning, and experiencing, he parked himself on the wild beaches of Mexico's Baja to reflect deeply on this newly aligned life of solitude and understanding, when an unexpected message arrived.

A podcast invitation... From a stranger by the name of Annet.

She wanted to interview him about the paradox of being both Highly Sensitive and High Sensation Seeking, a subject few truly understood.

He almost declined. The pain of relationships had cut him deeply, and although Annet's invitation had nothing to do with beginning a relationship, she was a woman, and he was finally at peace.

But something about her words stirred something ancient. Something familiar. He sensed she would understand more than any other would. Yet he could not explain why he felt this.

With reluctance, He agreed to have a virtual coffee with her, only to allow his developed intuitive High Sensitivity to examine her more carefully, was she a threat like so many others? Or... could she possibly be different.

Being Highly Sensitive isn't just about detecting threats as Randy learned. It's also about detecting what one needs to grow. It's a compass, warning you and yet also guiding you. It took Randy only minutes for his compass to tell him, she held something he missed.

And everything began to change.

When Two Wild Sensitive Compasses Point in the Same Direction
Randy was unaware that Annet had been following his writings for weeks prior to the virtual coffee, struck by the rare clarity and emotional honesty in his words. She found they pulsed with depth, sorrow, fire, and the unmistakable voice of someone who had lived what he taught.

Randy had seen Annet's picture pass by his screen, but quickly kept scrolling, for more information on Highly Sensitive people, not realizing Annet was an expert in the field.

Within minutes of their first on-line meeting, they dropped into the deep waters of shared wounds and wonderings. Their words tumbled out freely, stories they hadn't told, truths they hadn't shared in years with anyone. Not just because the other listened, but because the other understood. They spoke for hours. Then again, the next day. And the next.

It was not flirtation. It was recognition. Two rare souls realizing they were made from the same raw material, sensitive, seeking, starved for something real.

Weeks passed. Walls lowered. Curiosity grew into connection. And then, in true Wild Sensitive fashion, they both agreed to meet in person, Annet flying from the Netherlands and Randy crossing the wilds of Mexico, they met for the first time in the beautiful setting of Playa Del Carmen.

It is here, just as this extraordinary love story begins to blossom, that a dramatic and unexpected twist unfolds.

Despite all of Randy's wisdom, despite the decades he had spent traveling the world, mastering risk, discomfort, and the intricacies of human emotion, his body held a truth even he hadn't fully reckoned with. Beneath the courage, the strength, and the depth of lived experience, something had been silently operating all along: a nervous system trained for survival, not for receiving love.

In the early days of finally meeting Annet face-to-face, after weeks of soulful connection across distance, protected by the wall of a screen, their emotional worlds collided in the most intimate and powerful way. They were no longer voices on a call or words in an inbox. They were human beings, in full sensory proximity, allowing themselves to be seen. And for Randy, that level of closeness triggered something ancient and unprocessed.

Within just days of landing in what should have been a romantic, dreamlike setting, Randy's body began to react, not mildly, but dramatically. He went from the pinnacle of physical health to requiring emergency medical care. His symptoms were serious, even alarming. And yet, when examined through conventional medical lenses, there was no clear diagnosis. No infection. No injury. Nothing "wrong."
Unless, of course, you looked deeper.

What was happening wasn't rooted in his immune system. It was rooted in his nervous system, a system that, like so many men raised in environments where emotional safety was scarce, had learned to equate openness with danger. For Randy, a lifetime of suppressing and managing overwhelming emotion had resulted in a form of biological armoring. His nervous system had become a masterful gatekeeper, carefully modulating emotional exposure to preserve homeostasis, even if that "balance" was based on disconnection, distance, or internalized stoicism.

Many men, especially those wired with high sensitivity, unconsciously develop this kind of embodied defense. It's not a flaw; it's a form of intelligence. When emotional expression is punished, mocked, or ignored, the nervous system takes over. It becomes the vessel through which unspoken needs, untended grief, or unacknowledged joy must move. In Randy's case, his system had survived decades by regulating out vulnerability most saw as weaknesses, by translating emotion into thought or action, but rarely into felt, shared presence.

Now, here he was, fully present with a woman who saw him, all of him, and loved him not despite his depth, but because of it. And his body, confused and unprepared, interpreted that radical exposure as a kind of internal invasion. His nervous system did what it had been conditioned to do: it went into defense mode. Not subtly, but violently. To the body, this kind of emotional shift felt less like a revelation and more like a viral threat. A disruption to its long-held programming. And so, it responded with what it knew, inflammation, collapse, chaos.

From the outside, it looked like a medical mystery. But from the inside, it was a profound moment of reckoning. Randy wasn't breaking down. He was breaking open.

This wasn't weakness. It was a sacred threshold, the body catching up with the heart. A man's system, wired for endurance and protection, now asked to surrender to a kind of love it had never known was safe. And that is one of the most tender truths of the Wild Sensitive: That sometimes, the most dangerous thing we can do... Is finally receive what we've always longed for.

The Road to Becoming The Living Adventurers

In a world conditioned to dismiss vulnerability in men, Randy's past relationships had often left him with deep wounds, not just of heartbreak, but of being unseen, unheard, and used. When he finally had had enough, as many do, and say something, he would be labeled weak for his sensitivity, or too intense for his emotional depth. Yet, Annet saw something different. She saw the fight in him. The quiet, persistent bravery of a man who had spent a lifetime protecting his heart, yet still longed to offer it fully.

When Randy's nervous system began to unravel in those early days of their physical meeting, Annet didn't retreat. She didn't flinch or fix. She simply stayed. Attuned. Grounded. Soft. She knew what was happening wasn't weakness, it was transition. It wasn't fear, it was his body recognizing safety after years of guarding. It was the tenderness of being truly met. And she honored it with the sacred patience only a fellow Wild Sensitive could offer.

After a month together in Mexico, they returned to their respective homes, Annet to the Netherlands, Randy to Baja. But something had shifted. Their bond, far from fading, deepened across the ocean. The connection wasn't fragile. It had weight. Soul. Substance. They both felt it. Knew it. This wasn't a beautiful moment to be remembered. It was a truth to be lived.

For several weeks, Annet listened to the quiet voice within, this calling to live again and do something wild, something deeply sensitive. She bought a one-way ticket back to Mexico.

There was no set plan. No clear roadmap. Only that same soft, steady voice inside that had guided her through every threshold in life: *Go. Explore this. Trust it.*

Their first days of living together were not fiery declarations or sweeping cinematic moments. They were gentle. Careful. Real. Yet, there were no long silences like each had experienced in their previous relationships. Hours passed like minutes as they shared deep meaningful heartfelt talks and the occasional nervous laugh that stretching late into the nights. These talks created moments when each needed to reflect deeply about their past, followed by the need to be held. For the first time in their lives, they both felt truly seen and heard and they learned to honor this intensely for it was something truly special.

They recognized that true love between two Wild Sensitives does not begin with adrenaline. It begins with awareness. With the freedom to exhale fully. With mutual respect for the sacredness of being their true selves. They didn't try to perform or artificially please. They didn't put on masks. They simply tried to meet each other, one breath, one truth, one moment at a time. And they did.

Their love didn't rush to bloom. It unfurled. Petal by petal. Layer by layer. Through deep listening while helping each other see and unlearn past conditionings and limiting beliefs. They lovingly witnessed each other's true fears, holding space instead of trying to fix them.

From their growing sanctuary in Mexico, the desire for shared movement stirred again. So, they set out for Europe together for a month, immersing themselves in the rich landscape of culture, history, and rhythm. Wandering cobbled streets in the Netherlands, Germany, Switzerland, Austria, and Italy. Sharing espresso at tiny Amsterdam cafés tucked into centuries-old stone buildings. Finding their way through the crowds of tourists in Venice with patience and humor. Sitting back in the quiet gardens of secluded villas overlooking the Tuscan hills, sharing a glass of wine, lost in deep, meaningful conversation.

They learned how to be a team not just in connection, but in motion. Not just in magic, but in messiness. Through the busy crowds in ancient cities, something deeper was calling them, and they both could hear it. The kind of call only Wild Sensitives can hear, the pull toward something untamed. Something bold.

So, they returned to the U.S. and did what few couples, even those with decades behind them, would dare to do. They packed up their lives into a single tent, strapped their bags to the back of their beloved motorbike, affectionately named *Music*, and headed deep into the unknown.

Music, named after Willie Nelson's *"A Horse Called Music,"* wasn't just a bike. She was their third companion. A symbol of rhythm, movement, freedom, and the harmony they were building, mile by mile.

They started this new journey in Las Vegas, surrounded by neon and noise, then quickly left it behind. They rode through dusty red canyons, under pine-shadowed mountain roads, into snow-dusted valleys and open highways where sky met land with no interruption. They slept under the stars, washed in freezing rivers, shared meals cooked over one small burner. Some nights were magical. Some were messy. Some were so exhausting they questioned everything. But never each other.

They rode through the shared challenges and the beauty of shared wonder. Through heavy rain, oppressive heat, and mechanical failures. Through awe-struck moments when moose crossed the road at dawn, or when a glacier caught the sun just right and left them both breathless. And through it all, they leaned, into the bike, into the wind, into each other.

The journey stretched 12,000 miles, from the glitz of Nevada to the remote wilds of Fairbanks, Alaska and back. But in truth, the destination was never the point. What they were really building wasn't an itinerary. It was a life. A language. A way of being.

And somewhere along that vast, winding road, a truth rooted in them: This wasn't just a relationship... This was a path, a philosophy, a devotion, a shared invitation to a different kind of living. For they were not just travelers... They were wild, sensitive explorers truly living, *Living Adventurers*.

Not a brand... Not a performance... But a way of saying, Yes, you can feel everything, and still go everywhere. Yes, you can cry at the way a tree leans into the sun… And fix a broken brake line in the middle of nowhere.

Yes, you can be overwhelmed and wise... Tender and tenacious... Soft and strong... Wild and deeply sensitive.

When they returned from Alaska, they didn't unpack just their gear, they unpacked everything they had learned. Everything they had become. And then they made another bold move. They packed up their 'Living Adventurer' trailer, their rolling home of mugs, journals, camera gear, and quiet dreams, and returned to the Baja. Not to escape. But to build.

Nestled in the stillness, on a beautiful white sand beach, surrounded by the gentle waves lapping on the shore, in a new kind of music, they began the next chapter. Not just for themselves, but for all of us.

They wrote... They taught... They recorded.

They opened their hearts to listen to all the Wild Sensitives from around the world, people who had always felt "too much" or "not enough," people who longed for something more.

They held space... They created tools... They gave birth to a map.

To help others, like them, find their own rhythm, their own harmony between depth and drive, softness, and strength.

This book was born there.

Not in theory... In fire and frost... In dirt and devotion... In risk and radical rest... In Randy and Annet.
This is not a book of answers; it's a companion for the journey. A map. A compass and a guide all in one.

You are not too sensitive... You are not too wild... You are not too much.

You are a Wild Sensitive.

And you are not alone... Welcome home!

Why We Need Wild Sensitives

Our goal in writing this book is to help other Wild Sensitives, those of us who feel and crave deeply, and to better understand our unique path. We want to show you that living with both High Sensitivity and High Sensation Seeking is not a contradiction, but a potent combination. When these traits are seen, understood, and embraced, they become the foundation for real, embodied transformation.

It's not just theory, nor about abstract ideas or distant concepts. We're bringing you lived truth, raw, honest stories from our lives, woven with practical tools that helped us navigate emotional turbulence and mental exhaustion. Our hope is that these tools become bridges in your hands, helping you apply knowledge, build skill, and refine technique in ways that are relevant to your experience.

We begin with a true story from 1907, off the rugged west coast of Vancouver Island in British Columbia, Canada. Known today as Barkley Sound, was once feared by sailors who called it the "Graveyard of the Pacific." Many ships mistook this Sound for the Strait of Juan de Fuca, only to meet jagged rocks, merciless tides, and perilous shallows. Some sailors washed ashore onto the wild coastline, injured and freezing with no food, shelter, or direction. Few made it to the small outposts of Bamfield and Port Renfrew. Those that did, told the stories of hardship and survival that were now etched into their bones.

In time, as more lives were lost, a trail was forged through this fierce terrain. It wasn't easy due to the fallen trees, treacherous mud, torrent rivers, and violent storms. Skilled guides began to emerge. Some came from the north, others from the south, with one mission: to help others survive. These guides didn't just walk the trail, they improved it. Clearing debris, building ladders, laying bridges, and installing cable cars over rivers too dangerous to cross. Later, lighthouses and navigation beacons were installed to prevent disaster before it struck.

Today, that trail is known as the West Coast Trail, an 80-kilometer pilgrimage that experienced hikers now trek, not to escape death, but to expand their skills. The trail, once carved from necessity, is now walked with reverence. Trained guides still roam it, offering direction, and support, to modern explorers navigating the unknown.

So, what does this have to do with the Wild Sensitive?
Imagine those sailors as Highly Sensitive Sensation Seekers whose careers, relationships, or identities, have hit the rocks. Those who have been caught in emotional waters they were never taught to navigate. What they need isn't rescue, it's a trail, resources and skills. As Living Adventurers, we've walked that trail, both the literal one and the inner path shaped by our emotional landscapes. We know how disorienting life can be when we feel and crave they way we do. Yet, when we begin to help each other, by sharing how to read the signs, build tools, seek shelter, and most importantly, learn to sail again. We strengthen not only ourselves, but a community of deeply caring people.

This life wasn't meant to keep us anchored, it was meant to be explored. You may not need a guide. But we hope this book becomes your compass. A companion through fog and open sea. A reminder that you are not alone, and that your strength is waiting to be remembered.

With love and quiet courage,
Randy and Annet
The Living Adventurers

Chapter 1

The Highly Sensitive Person

A Deeper Reality Through Lived Experience

"The Wild Sensitive is not fragile, we can be a finely tuned compass, sensing what others miss, feeling what others fear, and holding space for what others rush past. We are not here to shrink in the face of the world, but to meet it with depth, with presence, and with power."

The Living Adventurers

As we begin this amazing journey to explore the Wild Sensitive, we have come to fully understand that there are countless definitions out there trying to capture what it means to be a Highly Sensitive Person (HSP). Some come from science and studies. Others are shaped by stories, shared from one tender heart to another. And then there are the ones floating across social media, fragmented reflections of truth, sometimes diluted, sometimes distorted, but always reaching for belonging.

While each version holds a piece of the puzzle, for us, as Living Adventurers, walking this path with both high sensitivity and high sensation seeking wired into our nervous systems, we've come to understand something deeper: truly knowing what it means to be an HSP isn't found in a single study or a viral quote. It's not something you can memorize. It's something you live.

It takes both research and reality. Both head and heart. Because sensitivity isn't just a trait, it's a way of being. And to understand it fully, we've had to learn to see ourselves clearly in the mirror of science and in the messy, beautiful truth of our lived experience.

Our foundation is firmly rooted in the work of Dr. Elaine Aron, the pioneering researcher who gave the trait its name and form. If you are new to the trait, we strongly encourage you to read her book, *The Highly Sensitive Person*, because it has the theoretical foundation of what it means to be a Highly Sensitive Person. She created the acronym D.O.E.S. which is the model that describes the trait in a clear and understandable way, Depth of Processing, Susceptibility to Overstimulation, Emotional Responsiveness/Empathy, and Sensitivity to Subtle Stimuli, it gives us the language of what being an HSP contains. But language alone doesn't capture the full weight or wonder of this trait.

To truly understand what it means to be highly sensitive, we have to ask: What does it feel like? What does it mean to live with a nervous system that is wired to take in more, to feel more, sense more, reflect more? For us, the question has never been theoretical. It's lived. It pulses through the rhythms of our childhoods, our work, our parenting, our solitude, our doubts, and our wildest leaps. It has shaped the choices we've made, the things we've left behind, and the path we walk now, together.

We didn't grow up knowing we were Highly Sensitive. We only knew we were different. We felt things others didn't seem to feel. We noticed the space between words, the shift in a room when someone walked in, the sorrow behind someone's laughter. These weren't called gifts back then. They were called overreactions, drama, or imagination. So, we questioned our reality. We were even led to believe we were broken. It felt like living in a parallel universe, seeing truth others denied, sensing things we couldn't explain, until one day we discovered there was a name for it: Sensory Processing Sensitivity.

We remember the first time we saw The Highly Sensitive Person by Dr. Elaine Aron. That moment stopped us in our tracks. It was as if someone had seen us, really truly seen us, before we had fully seen ourselves. We devoured it. And yet, even with the comfort of recognition, it stirred deeper questions in us. How do you live like this? How do you thrive, not just survive?

That question followed each of us down very different roads. For one of us, it wove itself through motherhood, years of coaching, and quiet moments of aching self-inquiry. For the other, it curated a life that refused conformity, wandering into old, abandoned coal mines to exploring more than fifty countries in search of meaning and belonging. Neither of us had the words for it back then, but both of us were walking the paradox: deep sensitivity tethered to a relentless hunger for experience, novelty, and intensity.

We don't just feel everything, we craved everything. While this internal contradiction doesn't make sense to others. It doesn't always make sense to us either. For years, we tried to reconcile it, name it, fix it. But what we really needed was a map, a way to hold both truths. Because what the world misread as fragility or recklessness was, in truth, a rare combination of two powerful traits: High Sensitivity and High Sensation Seeking.

The first time we each came across the term "Highly Sensitive High Sensation Seeker," it wasn't just a lightbulb moment, it was a homecoming. It helped us understand why nothing conventional ever fully fit. Why burnout and bore-out danced around us constantly. Why we needed both solitude and edge. We weren't meant to be either/or. We were both. And that understanding became the compass for everything that followed.

This chapter explores the paradox not just through research, but through lived experience, years of falling apart and finding our way back. We're not experts looking in, but two people who've walked this path from within. We're not here with answers, but with resonance. Permission. Possibility. If you've felt like a walking contradiction, you're not alone. You're not broken. You're wired for something rare. Let's walk it together, wild, sensitive, and true.

What Is a Highly Sensitive Person?

A Highly Sensitive Person (HSP) is not a fragile person. Nor are we simply "too emotional" or "overly dramatic." We are individuals born with a biologically different nervous system which causes a completely different lived experience than the majority of the population, this results in us processing sensory input and emotional data at a much deeper level. As Dr. Aron's research, and that of others, shows we make up roughly 20–30% of the population, and this trait appears across over 100 species in the animal kingdom. Why? Because sensitivity is an evolutionary strength. We are the ones who notice first. Feel first. Respond first... Feeling before words.

Have you ever felt it, that subtle tightening in your chest, that quiet tug in your gut that whispers, *"Something's not right here..."*
You may not be able to explain it. There may be no clear facts, no hard evidence. Just a knowing.

Sometimes, it's the sense that a plan will unravel, that someone's words don't quite match their energy, or that a situation is quietly veering off course. You feel the ripple before the wave. You see the fracture before the break. And maybe, just maybe, you speak up.
But more often than not, especially over time, you've learned to stay quiet. Because when you have shared your concerns, you were met with dismissal.

"You're overreacting."

"You're too sensitive."

"You're seeing things that aren't there."

So, you began to doubt your knowing, silencing your insight to protect your place. Still, what you sensed would happen... did. Not because you wanted it to, but because your perception was right, it was the dismissal from others that made you question it.

This is a lived experience for many Highly Sensitive People.
We don't just feel the moment, we read it.
And while others may call it worry or overthinking, let's call it what it truly is:

The trait of the Highly Sensitive Person in action.

This sensitivity, this biologically attuned, finely-wired nervous system, touches every part of how we live. We've felt it in the way stress lingers in the body long after a difficult conversation is over, like a thread still vibrating. We've felt it in moments of beauty that stop us mid-sentence, a shaft of golden light through a window, or the way a child laughs with their whole body.

We can weep from the beauty of a single cello note. We've can be deeply moved by the quiet kindness of a stranger. Even standing in a forest, breath held, can feel sacred. This is the gift of high sensitivity, we're not just touched by life… we're deeply attuned to it.

We notice what others miss. A single cup of coffee doesn't just wake us up, it can heighten everything. Bright lights in a grocery store don't just illuminate, they can overwhelm our finely tuned senses. A slammed door doesn't just startle, it can reverberate through our whole system. Even a room filled with unspoken tension, before a word is said, we know.

But this depth isn't always a burden when met with knowledge, tools, skills, and techniques. When empowered, our sensitivity becomes not just a way of feeling, it becomes a way of navigating. A compass that guides us with clarity, integrity, and presence.

The D.O.E.S. Model: The HSP Experience

Let's look briefly at Dr. Aron's D.O.E.S. model through lived experience perspective:

D – Depth of Processing

We don't just notice, we absorb. We ruminate, deconstruct, and replay conversations long after they've ended. The ripple effect of a single interaction can echo in us for days. This depth gives us the ability to hold space for others with remarkable presence and insight, but it also requires us to guard our own inner world with care. Without intentional boundaries, we risk becoming flooded by our own thoughts.

O – Susceptibility to Overstimulation

Our susceptibility to overstimulation depends on our ability to manage our depth of processing in combination with our sensitivity to stimuli. Without managing it effectively, we find ourselves walking off stages, out of meetings, or away from social gatherings, only to collapse into stillness, trembling not from fear, but from saturation.

E – Emotional Responsiveness / Empathy

We don't just witness others' emotions, we feel them, often as if they were our own. Grief, joy, tension, even anticipation, all move through us like weather patterns we didn't forecast but somehow must navigate. This emotional attunement makes us compassionate friends, partners, and healers. But it also demands discernment. It's important to learn that boundaries aren't barriers, they're membranes: selectively porous, lovingly firm.

S – Sensitivity to Subtle Stimuli

We notice the flicker in someone's tone, the shift in energy when a door opens, the dimming of a lightbulb before it actually fades. We've changed seats in restaurants because the lighting felt off, and while others may laugh, they often end up feeling it too. We're not "too picky." We're perceptive. Our nervous systems catch the whispers others miss.

The Scientific Side: Sensory Processing Sensitivity (SPS)

This trait, also referred to as Sensory Processing Sensitivity (SPS), has been researched for over 25 years and is not a disorder. It is a neutral, innate biological trait that reflects differences in brain function and neural processing. fMRI scans have shown that HSPs have increased activity in areas linked to awareness, empathy, and emotional regulation. Researchers like Michael Pluess, Tracy Cooper, and Bianca Acevedo have added valuable insight to Aron's foundation, reinforcing the science and encouraging further exploration of how sensitivity shows up in various contexts, from relationships to leadership, creativity to burnout.

Sensitivity Is Not the Problem - Misunderstanding Is

The problem is not the trait. The problem is how society interprets it. We live in a culture that celebrates speed, volume, hustle. In that world, sensitivity can feel like a liability. But in truth, sensitivity is a form of intelligence, emotional, intuitive, sensory. It is a skillset, when cultivated, that leads to deep relational insight, creative brilliance, and resilient empathy.

The Lived Experience - Not Just a Definition, But a Life

High sensitivity isn't something we learned in a textbook, it's something we are born with. It shaped how we entered rooms, how we read between the lines of every conversation, and how we sometimes walked away from jobs, relationships, or environments that didn't sit right in our gut, even when logic insists, we stay.

We didn't start out trying to define it. We simply wanted to understand it. Because deep down, we've always been seekers, perpetual learners, not chasing degrees or accolades, but clarity. We followed threads of curiosity wherever they led: a book, a late-night article, a quiet observation in a crowded space. We wanted to know why the world often felt so loud, why we needed more rest, why beauty could move us to tears.

Learning became our way of finding ground in a world that too often felt overwhelming, not to fix ourselves, but to finally live as ourselves. With that, we learned there are both strengths and struggles that come with being a Highly Sensitive person.

The Strength of Deep Empathy and Emotional Insight

We've sat in silence with someone whose heart was breaking, and somehow knew what to say without words. We've walked into rooms and felt the emotional temperature before anyone spoke. It's why friends confide in us. Why strangers open up to us in grocery lines. We don't just sympathize, we feel with. That kind of empathy can't be faked or taught. It's in our bones.

The Strength of Creativity and Rich Imagination

We've written poetry on napkins and dreamed up entire worlds while sitting at the dentist's office. We see metaphors in the rain and feel stories rising from stillness. Whether it's designing a space, writing a piece of music, or simply reimagining a better way to do something ordinary, we live with creative fire flickering just beneath the surface. It keeps life vibrant and meaningful.

The Strength of Detail - Oriented Perception and Intuition

We notice the way someone's eyes flicker when they're not saying what they mean. We catch the faint scent of change in the air before a storm rolls in. We've had moments where we couldn't explain how we knew something, just that we did. And later, we were right. We see the little things that build the big picture. Our intuition doesn't shout, it hums, but we've learned to listen.

The Strength of Ethical Awareness and Social Conscientiousness

We've agonized over choices others brush off. We think about the impact of our words, the ripple effect of our actions. Even as children, many of us were the ones speaking up when something felt unfair, even if our voices trembled. We care, far more than most, about justice, kindness, and doing what's right. But that conscience is one of our greatest gifts in a world that moves too fast. It reminds us to slow down, to notice, to speak with heart. It's not weakness, it's wisdom shaped by empathy, and it's how we help change the world from the inside out.

The Struggle of Burnout and Overwhelm

If we ignore our intuitive signals, we can hit our limit in the middle of a perfectly normal day, heart racing, mind spinning, body begging for stillness. Sometimes it's after a week of too many small yeses. Sometimes it's one loud, crowded event that tips us over. We've left gatherings early to cry in our cars. We've needed days to recover from things others forget by morning. It's not weakness. It's a nervous system asking for relief.

The Struggle of Boundary-Setting

We have said yes when every fiber of us was whispering no. We've held space for others long past our emotional capacity. We've stayed in conversations, relationships, or obligations because we didn't want to hurt anyone, even when it meant hurting ourselves. Setting boundaries doesn't always come easily for us. It feels like building fences with threads. But we can learn. Gently. Bravely.

The Struggle of Heightened Emotional Reactivity

We have cried during commercials. Flinched at criticism that wasn't even harsh. Reacted more strongly than we wanted to in a moment and then replayed it a hundred times afterward. Our emotions don't just show up, they surge. Sometimes, we feel before we can think. And while that can be overwhelming, it also means we're awake to life in a way most aren't.

The Struggle of Social Exhaustion and Overstimulation

We have smiled through conversations while quietly counting the minutes until we can go home. We've left parties early, not because we're shy, but because our minds and bodies were at capacity. We've wandered through malls or offices and felt like every sound, light, and interaction was crashing into us. We love people, deeply. But without space to recharge, even connection can become too much.

The Science Behind the Trait

Science has now caught up with what many of us have always felt: high sensitivity is not in our heads, it's in our nervous system. Through advanced tools like fMRI scans, researchers have discovered that HSPs display increased activation in key areas of the brain. The insula, responsible for self-awareness and emotional tracking, lights up more vividly in HSPs, which helps explain why we can feel subtle emotional shifts in ourselves and others, even before they're named.

We've lived this in everyday moments. Like standing in a queue at a café and suddenly feeling uneasy, not because of what was happening, but because of what was about to. Seconds later, an argument breaks out behind you. Or sitting in a meeting, noticing your colleague's barely perceptible eye twitch and sensing their unspoken frustration, before the group discussion has even begun. It's not magic. It's emotional radar, grounded in biology.

The prefrontal cortex, which helps us reflect, analyze, and make meaning, is also more active in sensitive people. This explains why even a simple comment can spiral into hours of reflection, not because we're fragile, but because we process more data, more deeply. We're the ones who replay that one sentence someone said on Tuesday… in the shower on Friday. The richness of our internal world is constant, which makes us highly creative and perceptive, and sometimes mentally exhausted. This explains why we, as Highly Sensitive people, often get into the challenge with less sensitive people over *"I never said that"* when our prefrontal cortex tells us differently.

We also have a more responsive mirror neuron system, the part of the brain that allows us to emotionally "mirror" others. This is why watching a child cry during a movie can move us to tears, or why we've found ourselves emotionally shaken after listening to a friend describe a breakup, even when we didn't go through it ourselves. We don't just hear the story, we feel it with them. That's mirror neuron resonance in action.

And then there's the amygdala, the brain's emotional warning system. In HSPs, it's more finely attuned. Not in a fearful way, but in a way that notices. We've been in elevators and sensed when someone behind us was holding tension. We've joined a group conversation and immediately felt the unspoken tension, the way two people avoided eye contact, the slight pause before someone laughed. No one said anything was wrong, but we knew. The emotional current was already moving beneath the surface. We don't need drama to detect danger; our system picks up subtle signals others overlook.

Even sensory processing is different. A scratchy sweater tag can ruin our ability to focus. An off-key violin note in an otherwise beautiful orchestra performance can send a jolt of discomfort through us. We've excused ourselves from dinner tables because the lighting was fluorescent, the smell of cologne too strong, or the music just a few decibels too loud. These aren't quirks. They're the result of a highly responsive sensory system that doesn't filter out stimulation like it does with less sensitive people.

This neurobiological sensitivity is a double-edged gift. Without awareness, it can lead to overstimulation, fatigue, or emotional burnout. But with understanding and the right tools, it becomes a superpower, allowing us to pick up on complexity, create deeply, and connect profoundly.

We are not making this up. We are not imagining things. We are simply wired to sense more, feel more, and reflect more. And once we stop resisting that, and start learning to regulate, protect, and honor it, we don't just survive as HSPs. We begin to live vividly, exactly as we were meant to. But for now, let this be your first truth:

You are not here to be less. You are here to live more, with depth, with clarity, with wild-hearted wisdom.

Chapter 2

The High Sensation Seeker
Wired for More

"We don't seek sensation to escape ourselves; we seek it to meet ourselves more fully. The Wild Sensitive craves not chaos, but conscious aliveness: a life rich in meaning, steeped in feeling, and lit by the fire of discovery."
The Living Adventurers

There are those of us who wake with a low hum beneath the surface, a hunger not for food or rest, but for more. More aliveness. More challenge. More discovery. It isn't about drama or danger. It's about intensity, movement, depth and change.

In this chapter we'll explore what defines someone as being a high sensation seeker and what it means to have this fascinating trait. As Wild Sensitives, the sensation seeking trait runs deep within us. It shapes how we move, feel, connect, and grow. And while much has been said about sensitivity on its own, we feel called to share what it's like to live with this trait through the eyes of a sensation seeker, where depth and intensity walk side by side, and where the need for meaning is matched only by the hunger for experience.

So let us be clear: being Highly Sensitive and High Sensation Seeking is not a contradiction. It's not a split. It's not a mistake in wiring. It is integration. It is wholeness. It is a life that doesn't just protect your sensitivity... it channels your fire. It allows your depth to have direction, your empathy to spark action, and your inner wildness to serve something meaningful. This union isn't a flaw, it's a rare and powerful design, one that, when honored, leads to a life of extraordinary creativity, courage, and connection. You were made for more, and both parts of you belong.

This isn't about swinging between extremes, it's about learning to dance with them. We don't have to choose between stillness and motion, solitude and stimulation, tenderness and thrill. We were never meant to. In fact, it is because we hold both that we're capable of navigating life with such nuance. This dual wiring gives us not just a deeper emotional compass, but a wider range of possibilities.

To live as a Highly Sensitive High Sensation Seeker is to live at the intersection of two powerful currents, the inward pull of deep reflection and the outward pull of bold expansion. And while the world often tries to categorize us as either/or, we are here to show what it means to be both/and.

We don't just feel deeply, we move deeply. We don't just seek comfort, we seek sovereignty. And our journey is not about choosing one trait over the other but about learning how to live in harmony with both. That is the heart of The Wild Sensitive.

To fully understand the High Sensation Seeking trait, we begin when it was first named: in the extensive, foundational research of Dr. Marvin Zuckerman starting in the early 1960's, who spent nearly two decades studying why some individuals require more stimulation, variety, and risk to feel truly engaged in life. His model gave us the first language around this intense, expansive way of being, even though in many HSP's it shows up differently.

Many years later, Dr. Elaine Aron, already well known for her pioneering work on High Sensitivity, began to notice a unique group within the HSP population that had distinct differences. These individuals were deeply sensitive and driven toward stimulation, challenge, and novelty. They were the seeming paradoxes. And rather than dismissing them, Aron found the overlap: HSPs who are also High Sensation Seekers.

This crucial insight opened the door for Dr. Tracy Cooper, who would go on to write his second book, *Thrill, The High Sensation Seeking Highly Sensitive Person,* specifically focused on the HSP-HSS individual. His work introduced us to the understanding of how the two traits coexist, conflict, and, when consciously developed, create a unique and powerful way of engaging with the world. Dr. Cooper's book gave many of us our first mirror, and from that reflection, we began to shape our own lived approach.

Zuckerman's defines High Sensation Seeking (HSS) as a temperament trait. Originally, Zuckerman wasn't seeking to define a personality type. He was trying to measure what he called a person's optimal level of stimulation, that invisible threshold of how much excitement, novelty, and arousal a person needs to feel engaged in life. What he discovered instead was an entire class of people whose nervous systems required far more stimulation than the average person to feel truly alive.

In his own words, sensation seeking is "a trait defined by the need for varied, novel, and complex sensations and experiences, and the willingness to take physical and social risks for the sake of such experience." This isn't just a definition, after you apply the HSP lens to it, it becomes a reality we live daily.

Living the Drive for More

If you've ever felt like life becomes flat when it's too predictable, if you've ever found yourself restless on the second day of vacation because the excitement has already settled. If you've walked out of a perfectly fine job simply because your soul felt like it was drying up, you might be one of us. For High Sensation Seekers, a life without novelty or challenge isn't just boring… it can feel unbearable. It's not about being ungrateful or impulsive, it's about needing movement, meaning, and the feeling of aliveness. Without those things, we don't just lose interest, we lose touch with ourselves.

We've felt this restlessness in our bones, staring at a calendar too full of sameness, wondering why our lives look good on paper but feel dull in the soul. We have impulsively booked last-minute trips, enrolled in obscure classes just to learn something new, tried things others found strange or "too much," simply because we needed to feel alive again. We may not have recognized it in the moment, because boredom and needing a change in life seems all too often typical to us.

It isn't about recklessness. It's not about thrill for thrill's sake. It's about engagement, about curiosity, about exploring the edge of what's possible, intellectually, emotionally, creatively, even physically.

Dr. Zuckerman's Four Components of Sensation Seeking

According to Zuckerman's model, the HSS trait is composed of four distinct drives, each representing a different way we seek stimulation. Unlike the D.O.E.S. model from Dr. Elaine Aron, not every High Sensation Seeker may express all four of these, and also not equally, they appear in varying combinations and intensities. In order to understand how the trait shows up differently in HSP's, let's look at how Marvin Zuckerman described them first. Zuckerman emphasized that these four components make up a biologically based personality trait, closely tied to dopamine and arousal systems in the brain. High sensation seekers require more stimulation to reach their ideal level of nervous system arousal, which explains their drive toward intensity, novelty, and challenge.

Boredom Susceptibility (BS)

This is the inability to tolerate repetitive or routine experiences. People high in Boredom Susceptibility quickly become restless, agitated, or even depressed in the face of monotony or predictability. They crave variety, change, and intensity, and will often change jobs, relationships, or environments just to escape boredom-induced discomfort. These people may find themselves saying such things as:

"I can't stand to do something the same way twice."

"I get restless when I spend too much time at home."

Experience Seeking (ES)

This refers to the pursuit of new experiences, not necessarily dangerous ones, but those that are unfamiliar, novel, or emotionally or intellectually stimulating. It can include travel to strange places, trying new foods, psychedelic or spiritual experiences, or exploring new art and music. Experience Seekers often have a strong desire for personal growth, boundary-pushing, and exploration of inner or outer worlds. They uses phrases such as:

"I like to explore strange places."

"I am interested in experiencing altered states of consciousness."

Thrill and Adventure Seeking (TAS)

Dr. Marvin Zuckerman described Thrill and Adventure Seeking as the desire to engage in physically risky and exciting activities that involve speed, danger, or novelty. This dimension reflects an individual's biological urge to test limits and experience the rush of adrenaline that comes from confronting the unknown or the potentially hazardous.

In his view, Thrill and Adventure Seeking was not simply about impulsivity or recklessness, but rather a genetically influenced tendency to seek stimulation through bodily challenges, such as skydiving, scuba diving, motorcycling, fast driving, or mountain climbing. People high in Thrill and Adventurer Seeking aren't merely looking for external excitement, they're wired to feel under-stimulated by ordinary or repetitive experiences, which drives them toward environments that offer high levels of sensory input and unpredictability.

Importantly, Zuckerman distinguished this trait from mere bravado or social influence; for high Thrill and Adventure Seeking individuals, these pursuits are intrinsically rewarding. The behavior is less about proving oneself and more about experiencing a heightened state of arousal, a nervous system "sweet spot" that makes them feel truly alive.

Thrill and Adventure Seekers would be found saying things such as:

"I would like to try parachute jumping."

"I sometimes like to do things that are a little frightening."

"I prefer friends who are excitingly unpredictable."

Disinhibition (DIS)

This dimension is about letting go of social restraints and indulging in behaviors often considered wild or taboo. Disinhibition often shows up as impulsivity, a taste for partying, social drinking, or sexual variety, and an ease with breaking conventional rules. It's not necessarily reckless, but it does reflect a comfort with abandoning control in favor of stimulation. Those with stronger Disinhibition desire may say:

"I like wild parties."

"I enjoy the company of unpredictable people."

From an HSP perspective

From a Highly Sensitive Perspective, the High Sensation Seeking trait shows up differently. One of the basic behaviors of HSP's is risk avoidance. So how can you be an HSP and an HSS? To answer this question, we need to explain a little bit more about what is going on in our brains. It's not a contradiction, but a complex interplay between the Behavioral Inhibition System and the Behavioral Activation System, two powerful forces that shape how we experience stimulation, process risk, and seek out novelty while still needing safety and space to regulate.

Understanding the Two Inner Forces

To understand how Sensation Seeking shows up differently in HSP's than in less sensitive people, we need to explore two powerful systems that shape human behavior: the Behavioral Inhibition System (BIS) and the Behavioral Activation System (BAS). These are not personality traits, but neurobiological systems. More like built-in guidance mechanisms that help us respond to life.

The BAS is like an inner green light. It drives us toward pleasure, novelty, rewards, and excitement. When the BAS is activated, we feel pulled toward possibility: *"That looks fun, let's try it!"*

The BIS, on the other hand, is our inner caution signal. It notices potential risks, conflict, or unfamiliarity and says, *"Wait, something might go wrong here."* When BIS is activated, we pause, reflect, or avoid.

Everyone has both systems. But how strong or reactive they are can drastically shape how we live. Most people lean more heavily on one or the other. But for those of us who are both Highly Sensitive and High Sensation Seeking, we're uniquely wired with a strong Behavioral Inhibition System (BIS) and a strong Behavioral Activation System (BAS), which means we're constantly assessing caution and curiosity, reflection and action.

That means we live in constant negotiation between opposing forces: the urge to leap and the need to look, the craving for intensity and the call for safety. It's not dysfunction, it's dual-function. We aren't broken; we are built for depth and dynamism. But without the right knowledge, tools, techniques and skills, (discussed in chapter 7) this inner tug-of-war can feel like chaos. We may find ourselves paralyzed in decision-making, burning out from too much, or collapsing from too little. Recognizing the influence of BIS and BAS is like discovering the operating system behind our daily experience, and it opens the door to a new kind of self-compassion. We don't have to choose between sensitivity and sensation. Our task is to learn how to dance with both.

For the Less Sensitive Sensation Seekers

For individuals high in Sensation Seeking but low in sensitivity, the BAS tends to run the show. Their nervous systems are wired to chase stimulation, novelty, risk, reward, without the strong internal pause that comes from emotional or sensory depth. The BIS, which helps regulate caution and reflection, is often less active or less sensitive to subtle signals. That means they may leap before they look, choosing action over reflection, thrill over nuance. This isn't inherently wrong, it often leads to bold exploration, but it can increase the likelihood of impulsivity, burnout, or risky behavior. Without the internal depth-scan that sensitivity provides, thrill becomes the compass. They tend to learn by doing, and sometimes by colliding, rather than by contemplating.

Depth of Processing vs. Behavioral Inhibition

According to the research, the Behavioral Inhibition System (BIS) is more active in Highly Sensitive People (HSPs), and while it may look similar to depth of processing, (one of the four components in Dr. Elaine Aron's D.O.E.S. model) it's not the same. BIS is a regulatory system in the brain that controls the impulse to stop, scan, and evaluate, especially in new or uncertain situations. It was originally associated with anxiety, but, as Dr. Aron explained, "now it is understood to have three functions, one of which has nothing to do with sensing danger, but with simply attending to what's going on, including making the best of opportunities." This is a crucial point. HSPs don't freeze because they're fearful, they pause because they are attentive. They take in more detail, more nuance, and more potential outcomes. According to Dr. Aron's own research, "unless HSPs have had many bad experiences, so that they see danger everywhere, they are no more prone to anxiety than those with a less active BIS."

The misunderstanding arises when BIS is mistaken for anxiety in all cases. In truth, BIS fuels attunement, and in HSPs, this manifests as a greater awareness of both external conditions and internal signals. Depth of processing, on the other hand, is not a defensive system. It is the innate tendency to process information more deeply, to analyze, connect, and assign meaning to experiences. Where BIS protects, depth of processing enriches. Together, they explain why HSPs often notice what others miss and feel the need to pause before acting, not because they are scared, but because they are scanning for depth, resonance, and impact. The challenge arises when this attentiveness has been shaped by past pain, leading to over-activation of the protective layer. But at its core, this dual system is a strength, a kind of inward radar that helps us sense, reflect, and respond with clarity and care.

The BIS and BAS In HSP-HSS's

In Highly Sensitive People (HSPs), the Behavioral Inhibition System (BIS) and Behavioral Activation System (BAS) create a nuanced internal dynamic that shapes how they engage with the world. The BIS is typically more active, making HSPs naturally inclined to pause, reflect, and assess before acting, especially in unfamiliar or emotionally charged situations. This heightened BIS isn't rooted in fear, it supports deep attentiveness and thoughtful responsiveness, particularly in safe or nurturing environments. The BAS, by contrast, is generally more moderate in HSPs, they're less driven by novelty for its own sake, and more motivated when the pursuit feels meaningful or aligned with their values.

But in HSPs who are also High Sensation Seekers, the picture shifts dramatically. These individuals are wired with both a strong BIS and a strong BAS, meaning they are deeply tuned in to their environment and simultaneously pulled toward stimulation, novelty, and intensity. Their BAS is more active, making them crave adventure, newness, and expansive experiences, yet due to the strong active BIS, not recklessly, but with depth and purpose.

This creates a powerful internal push-pull: one part of them scans and safeguards, while the other surges forward toward engagement and possibility. When integrated, this dual activation fuels creativity, empathy, and bold, meaningful action. But when unbalanced, it can lead to inner conflict, emotional whiplash, or paralysis, a nervous system caught between protection and pursuit. For the HSP-HSS, life is not just about safety or sensation, it's about learning how to honor both.

The Four Drives of the HSS as seen through the Lens of an HSP
These four drives are all on a spectrum, so they can occur in a person from a little to very intense. In general, males score higher than females, except in experience seeking.

Boredom Susceptibility (BS)
This is often one of the most painful edges for HSPs with HSS. Because they process deeply, routine can feel deadening. Boredom doesn't just feel dull, it feels existentially suffocating. Yet their sensitivity also makes overstimulation costly, leaving them in a near-constant negotiation with themselves.

"We're not just bored by monotony, we're emotionally starved by it."

Experience Seeking (ES)
This is often where Highly Sensitive individual's shine. They hunger for inner and outer exploration, new ideas, cultures, emotional depths, and creative expression. Unlike less sensitive sensation seekers, they're more likely to seek soul-expanding experiences than purely stimulating ones.

"We crave conversations that change us, art that moves us, and places that mirror our longing to belong."

Thrill and Adventure Seeking (TAS)
For HSPs, this shows up less as reckless risk-taking and more as a craving for meaningful challenge. They may be drawn to wilderness treks, motorbike journeys, or public speaking, not for the adrenaline alone, but for the transformation it offers. The risk must feel purposeful. Too much intensity too fast, though, can lead to overwhelm. This drive is the least present drive in general, often surfacing subtly and selectively, emerging only when the environment feels safe enough, or when the desire for growth outweighs the fear of discomfort. For HSP-

HSS individuals, it's about expansion with intention, not stimulation without grounding.

"We don't chase thrills to escape ourselves; we seek them to meet ourselves more fully."

Disinhibition (Dis)

This trait is more muted or conflicted in HSPs. While they may long for freedom, spontaneity, and emotional expression, their strong BIS often creates inner resistance. Some may express this through deep late-night talks, dancing alone, or bursts of creative rebellion, but always in environments that feel secure enough.

"We want to let go… but only where our nervous system feels it won't be punished for opening up."

The Emotional Need for Variety and Aliveness

High Sensation Seeking isn't just about doing more, it's about feeling more. It's a yearning that lives in us, a pulse that craves a rich aliveness in its many forms. A deep inner drive toward vitality, novelty, and emotional intensity. We aren't chasing danger for the thrill of it; we're pursuing depth, meaning, and the feeling of being fully awake. It's the hunger to experience life not at the surface, but from the inside out, to feel music in your skin, to taste adventure in the air, and to discover who we are. We seek moments that make time stand still, whether through movement, conversation, beauty, or insight. We don't want more for its own sake; we want what is real, raw, and unforgettable. High Sensation Seeking is a search for resonance, a desire to feel fully in life, not observing from the sidelines. It's about chasing the spark that reminds us we're alive, and then following where it leads.

A day without stimulation, without some kind of meaningful engagement with the world, can feel oddly hollow, like music played too quietly to move you. But a day filled with purpose, movement, discovery, or unexpected beauty? That's fuel. That's where our systems light up. Where time expands, and we feel ourselves at home in the present.

For us, challenge is energizing, not because it proves anything, but because it activates us. Change doesn't feel threatening; it feels enlivening, like breath after stillness. Risk, when chosen intentionally and aligned with our values, isn't danger, it's growth. It's how we meet the edge of our capacity and stretch into something new. It's not about always doing more. It's about living more, more vividly, more curiously, more wholeheartedly.

And when these needs are unmet, the emotional cost is high. We can grow restless, irritable, even depressed. We may seek out unhealthy stimulation, overworking, overdrinking, scrolling endlessly, or chasing chaos, not because we want destruction, but because we're starving for spark. The truth is, HSS is not a desire for adrenaline. It is a longing for aliveness.

Adventure, novelty, and variety are core needs for the HSP-HSS because they nourish the BAS system (Behavioral Activation System) while also providing the meaning-rich experiences that a highly sensitive nervous system craves.

Unlike less sensitive sensation seekers who may chase stimulation purely for the dopamine rush, HSP-HSS individuals seek experiences that are emotionally and existentially resonant. They don't just want more, they want deeper. Novelty isn't about distraction; it's about expansion. Variety isn't just stimulation, it's opportunity for insight, growth, and connection.

Adventure, in this context, serves a regulatory and integrative role. It offers relief from the existential boredom and psychic constriction that arise when a deeply processing mind is trapped in overly familiar, emotionally flat environments. Without new input, emotional, sensory, or intellectual, the HSP-HSS begins to wither. But with too much stimulation, they burn out. So, they're wired to seek purposeful aliveness, not just activity.

In short: novelty feeds their BAS; depth honors their BIS. Together, these needs reflect their rare inner architecture: not to live chaotically or cautiously, but to live fully and consciously stretched, at the edge where transformation lives.

Final Reflection: A Life That Matches the Fire Within

So, what does balance really look like for us, those of us who feel everything deeply, yet crave the thrill of expansion? How do we nourish both the part of us that longs for safety and the part that hungers for aliveness?

It begins with reclaiming our inner compass, the quiet wisdom that lives beneath the noise of expectation, logic, and fear. Our intuition. That deep, steady knowing that gently tugs us in the right direction, even when the path seems irrational or unclear. The truth is many of us were taught to dismiss it. We were taught to favor logic, to quiet our impulses, to explain everything before we act. But some of our most powerful and beautiful experiences come when we don't wait for reason. When we follow a hunch, a whisper, a pull, and discover, on the other side, that we were right all along.

Again and again, we've watched this unfold, in ourselves and in the sensitive souls we walk alongside. When we dare to trust that inner guidance, life opens. Not always cleanly, not always easily, but meaningfully. Authentically.

And yet, so many HSPs say, *"No one really sees me."* We hear this often. The ache for connection, for recognition. But here's the tender paradox: if you've spent your life hiding parts of yourself, how can anyone truly respond to who you are? People can only react to what they're shown, and if all they see is the mask, the performance, the careful version, they can't connect with your truth.

The moment you begin to share your real self, even if it's awkward, even if it trembles, something starts to shift. You begin to attract the kind of people who can see you. Who resonate with you. Who feel like home. At first, this can feel unfamiliar and risky. Vulnerability always does. But with time, practice, and small brave steps, authenticity becomes less like exposure… and more like coming home to yourself.

As Living Adventurers, we've often heard the same refrain: *"That seems risky."* Whether it's a journey across continents, a vulnerable conversation, or a bold leap into the unknown, others frequently view our way of engaging with life through the lens of danger or even recklessness. But what we've come to understand is this: they are not seeing us clearly. They are seeing themselves, projected outward.

They witness the action, but not the preparation. They notice the leap, but not the years of self-inquiry, skill-building, and quiet recalibration that led to it. Their perception of risk is filtered through their own experiences, their own knowledge, tools, techniques, and capacities. And so, what feels like a cliff's edge to them may, for us, be solid ground.

As Wild Sensitives, we walk with awareness. We know our thresholds, our boundaries, our rhythms. We don't move blindly into intensity; we move with intentionality. Yes, we may dance along the edges. We may even, at times, step beyond them. But we do so while reading the emotional terrain, checking our somatic signals, tracking the match between our inner state and the outer world.

For us, engagement isn't about avoiding risk, it's about being in the right relationship with it. Because we are not only sensitive to subtle stimuli… we are also deeply attuned to ourselves. This is not recklessness. This is refined responsiveness. This is the art of living fully and wisely.

This is exactly what a Wild Sensitive looks like. Not someone caged by fear or driven by impulse, but someone who has learned to honor both the awareness and the spark. Someone who can read the emotional weather, feel the tremors before the storm, and still choose to step forward, not in defiance of their sensitivity, but in devotion to it.

To live this way is not easy. But it is true. And it's the truth we return to, again and again: that our depth is not a limitation, and our hunger for life is not a flaw. They are twin flames and when nurtured in balance, they become our greatest power.

To highlight better what truly an empowered Wild Sensitive experience can look like, allow us to share two of our stories.

Into the Blue - Randy's Offering to the Rite of Passage

We sat at the dining room table one evening, the chill of winter creeping at the windows, a familiar conversation bubbling up between spoonful's of dinner, where should we go for our annual winter vacation?

My twin sons, fifteen and restless, had grown out of the usual beach resorts and amusement parks. Still, someone, I think it was their mother, suggested Disney World. The moment the words hit the air, I felt a full-body cringe. I glanced at the boys. Their faces said it all: the thought of crowds, lines, forced smiles, and character costumes left them as uninspired as I was.

"What if," I said, "we go diving in the Bahamas?"

Their heads snapped up. A pause. Then wide eyes. Something was alive behind them, the thrill of possibility.

Over the next few weeks, I did what I always do when preparing for something sacred: I planned, in detail, every element of the trip. Flights, accommodations, dive charter, gear rentals. Every risk calculated, every detail precise. Not because I feared what could go wrong, but because preparation is what allows freedom to unfold.

A few weeks before the trip, over another dinner, I set down my fork and said, "Okay. We're all set. We're going diving in the Bahamas." The boys smiled, nodding.

"But," I added, "this isn't any ordinary diving trip."

They paused, mid-bite. Eyebrows raised. Curious.

"We're diving with sharks."

Silence.

Then, two chins dropped.

Their eyes darted to each other, then back to me, trying to decode whether I was serious or teasing. I was dead serious.

And I wasn't just throwing them into the deep. I was a Certified Master Diver Trainer, with over 4,000 dives logged in some of the world's most extreme conditions, from under frozen lakes to sunken wrecks, from coral walls to caverns you couldn't see the end of. I'd trained hundreds of people, from open water beginners to advanced wreck and ice divers. And I knew, deeply, that diving with sharks isn't just about knowing them. It's about knowing yourself.

The day of the dive arrived, bright and warm under the Caribbean sun. The boat rocked gently as we geared up, wetsuits clinging to skin, regulators checked and tanks secure. The dive master stood at the front, explaining the protocol for shark diving.

"These are white-tipped reef sharks," he said, pointing into the deep blue. "They're curious, fast, and majestic. But if you're feeling unsure, head to the swim grid and take a look before you jump in."
A father and his teenage son walked to the back, leaned over the edge, and froze. Below them, more than two dozen reef sharks circled slowly, graceful and ghostlike. The water boiled with motion, smooth but powerful.

The boy backed away first, eyes wide. The father soon followed, shaking his head. "That's way too risky," the man muttered, backing out of the dive.

I turned to my sons. They stood at the rail now, silent, watching the movement below. They looked at me. I nodded. Not with bravado, but with confidence. Quiet. Grounded. This wasn't a dare. This was an initiation.

They knew I wasn't leading them into danger. They also knew I wasn't shielding them from life.
They trusted my skills and experience.

We rolled backward into the blue. The ocean swallowed us gently.

Within seconds, we were on the sea floor, a soft landing into white sand.

Before we could even flash the OK sign, they were there, the sharks, swimming through our legs, gliding past with eyes that didn't blink but watched everything. Dozens of them. We were encircled. Immersed. Surrounded not by threat, but by presence.

My sons stayed calm. I could see it in their breathing, their body language. They were alert, but not afraid.

The sharks moved like underwater dogs, curious and engaged. Brushing close. Circling. Coming back. Not once did I see aggression. I saw only grace. That moment, that entire dive, wasn't about adrenaline. It wasn't about proving anything. It was about trust. Trust in the ocean. Trust in their father. And most importantly, trust in themselves.

Few parents would take their children on such an adventure. But this wasn't recklessness. This was a rite of passage. It was memory forged not in fantasy, but in breath, courage, and connection.

As we surfaced, the sun kissed the sea and the saltwater streamed from our masks. They pulled theirs off with huge grins, eyes bright, voices buzzing with energy and awe.

They didn't just survive the dive... They had become shark divers.

And I... I had witnessed a moment I would never forget. Not because it was spectacular, but because it was true.
That's what it means to be a Wild Sensitive.

To take everything you've learned, everything you've trained for, and bring it into the depths of life, not to escape fear, but to meet it with reverence and to share it with those who mean the most to you.

To know the world around you so well... that you can finally trust the world within.

When Annet's Risk Becomes a Return to Self

We don't always recognize the moment our life begins to unravel. Sometimes it starts with a whisper inside, so quiet you almost don't hear it. Other times, it's a storm. For me, it was both. A quiet ache and a growing roar.

From the outsider looking in, everything was perfect. I had a seemingly steady, beautiful life: a loving husband, two incredible daughters on the cusp of adulthood, a house with a garden I cherished, and few financial struggles. It was, in many ways, the "dream" most would cherish." But it wasn't my dream anymore.

As a Highly Sensitive Person with High Sensation Seeking wiring, I had learned to read the emotional undercurrents of life long ago. I could sense energy shifts in a room before anyone else noticed. But the one shift I had ignored for far too long... was within myself.

Little by little, I was losing the thread of who I truly was. It wasn't just that I was unhappy, it was that I was becoming unrecognizable to myself. My marriage, once a source of support, had become a place of stagnation. I craved growth, expansion, and deeper connection. He craved routine, predictability, and security. Our desires weren't just different; they had become incompatible. And the more I tried to stay small for the sake of stability, the more I fractured inside.

It wasn't just the paradox of being both highly sensitive and sensation seeking that was tearing me apart, it was the quiet war between doing what was right for others and finally choosing what was true for me.

My sensitivity longed for soulful intimacy, harmony, and belonging, the kind I had spent years trying to cultivate for everyone around me. But there was another truth rising inside me, one I could no longer silence: the part of me that needed, aliveness, and growth.
And the deeper that truth grew, the clearer it became. I felt I was expanding inside a vessel that was too small, morphing as Wild Sensitives do, no longer fitting into the life I once had. For years, I had been setting my needs aside, trying to hold together a version of peace that no longer aligned with who I was becoming. And the deeper that truth grew, the harder it became to keep sacrificing myself for someone else's version of peace.

So, I decided to take a break, to step away just far enough to find myself again. I wasn't walking away, I was in desperate hope to reconnect with who I truly was, then, maybe I could return (whole again) and still belong to the old life I had. I didn't want to break it, for it was already broken, I wanted to fix it. I believed if I could find my true self again, the emptiness I felt would go away. But first, I had to rediscover who I even was.

With only a small suitcase, I headed away from my quiet familiar city in the Netherlands, to spend three months alone in Barcelona, far from everything familiar, hoping this strange new environment would help me find who I was before all the adaptations, and all the compromises. It wasn't escaping, I was seeking. It was a reconnection with myself.

In the narrow streets of this ancient city, something magical emerged. A woman, both wild and sensitive. The one I had once been so long ago: curious, creative, and deeply passionate. I sat with her, alone, everyday having coffee in a small café, talking. She told me that she had not disappeared, she had only gone quiet. And now... she wanted to live again. I was now faced with one of the hardest choices of my life, allowing her to be free, or keep her caged, silencing her forever and bearing that burden of living an unauthentic life once more.

Returning home, I was faced with a new reality. For I saw the canyon, even more than I had. The veil had been lifted revealing the divide between who I truly was and the life I had built. I tried to bridge it. I truly did. But the gap only grew. I could no longer flatten my spirit to fit into someone else's template of comfort.

So, I made a radical choice, one that felt like both betrayal and rebirth. I left my marriage, and, in what was the greatest heartbreak of all, my daughters, 19 and 20, in the care of their father, where they had stability, safety, and a known future. I didn't leave them emotionally, but I knew that to truly find myself again, I had to let go of being the mother-who-stayed, and become the mother-who-led-by-living.

That choice, to leap into the unknown, wasn't fearless. It was terrifying. It felt like standing at the edge of a cliff and stepping forward into the unknown. Although I was uncertain of what I'd find, I felt this renewed confidence that whatever waited, was meant for me. I could no longer survive the certainty of routine and stagnation, I had to step forward.

And now, two years later, I don't just feel like myself again, I feel more myself than I've ever been. I've built a life of radical authenticity and deep joy. I've found love that sees and celebrates all of me, the quiet depth and the untamed fire, in Randy, a fellow Living Adventurer. I'm no longer just coaching people through transformation. I am living it.

Leaving was the hardest thing I've ever done. It required pain, honesty, and wild courage. But the transformation that came from it was necessary. Looking back, I cannot even imagine the person I once was, lost, abandoned and alone. Because staying would have meant abandoning myself, again.

Sometimes, the greatest risk a Highly Sensitive High Sensation Seeker can take… is to finally follow their truth inside, even when it costs them the life they once built.

Because, sometimes when you jump, you discover you can fly…
Being a High Sensation Seeker means living with a pulse that beats faster than most. It means needing more from life, not because you're insatiable, but because you're designed for expansion. You were never meant to stay in one place, repeat the same loop, or live at half-volume.

And when you give yourself permission to honor this trait, not in rebellion, but in sovereignty and authenticity, your life begins to open. Not wider than others. Just wider than before.

That's the call of the Wild Sensitive within… And it's time to answer.

Chapter 3

Understanding Our Emotional Blueprint
The Roots That Shape Us

"Our sensitivity is not the wound; it's the part that got hurt. But it's also the part that knows how to heal. When we trace our roots with compassion, we stop trying to fix who we are and start reclaiming the truth of who we've always been."
The Living Adventurers

The Early Influences That Shape Us

Before we go deeper into the inner world of the Highly Sensitive High Sensation Seeker, we need to stop and look at something just as important: the early things that shaped us. These are the quiet forces, the ones we may not notice right away. They include our childhood memories, how we were raised, the roles we learned in our families, the rules of our culture, and how our nervous system reacted to all of it.

For many Wild Sensitives, these early layers don't just fade into the background. They shape how we see ourselves, how we deal with problems, and how we connect with people. Some of these patterns started before we even had the words to explain how we felt. Over time, they may have created habits or ideas about ourselves that no longer match who we are. This chapter isn't about blaming anyone or giving ourselves labels. It's about understanding. When we learn where our actions come from, we gain the power to not just make changes, but to heal and take back the parts of us we thought were broken. That's where real alignment begins.

We can't cover every possible influence here, but we'll explore a few that often have the biggest effect. These are the ones that can shape whether we feel strong or overwhelmed, connected or cut off from who we really are.

Sensitivity and the Introvert – Extrovert Mix

A lot of people believe that all Highly Sensitive People (HSPs) are introverts. But that's not true. Research by Dr. Elaine Aron shows that about 70% of HSPs are introverts, and the other 30% are extroverts. Whether your energy flows inward or outward makes a big difference in how you deal with stress, relationships, and rest.

Many extroverted HSPs think they must be introverts because they get overwhelmed in busy places. But staying away from people doesn't always help. Instead of feeling better, they may feel sad or lonely. They try to protect their sensitive side, but forget they also need connection and fun. These are just as important to who they are.

It's easy to see why people get confused. Systems like the Myers-Briggs Type Indicator make it seem like you're either an introvert or an extrovert, with no in-between. But Carl Jung, who came up with these terms, said it best: "There is no such thing as a pure introvert or pure extrovert. Such a person would be in the lunatic asylum."

His idea matters for Wild Sensitives. Many HSP-HSS people look like introverts because they need rest after exciting or intense times. But needing rest doesn't mean they don't want adventure, fun, or connection. These things are part of being extroverted or a High Sensation Seeker. It's not a conflict, it's a dance between quiet and excitement.

Culture and family also affect how we act. Some places, like the U.S., Brazil, or Italy, love big, bold energy. Others, like Japan, Finland, or South Korea, value quiet and calm. Over time, these messages can push us into roles that don't fit. Finding your real rhythm, introverted, extroverted, or both, is a way of coming home to yourself.

Introverted HSPs

Introverted Highly Sensitive People usually take in the world from the inside out. They often like to think before they speak and notice things that others might miss. Loud places, fast-moving environments, or big crowds can feel like too much for them. These HSPs might take longer to feel comfortable and often need time alone to think about what they've experienced.

For introverted HSPs, their sensitivity shows up as deep thinking and quiet reflection. They have rich inner worlds and need alone time like others need air. Even after a fun or loving day, they may feel both happy and worn out. It's not that they didn't enjoy the moment, it's just that their nervous system starts to say, *"That's enough for now."*

They often enjoy one-on-one talks, walks alone in nature, quiet time for creating, or spaces where meaning matters more than speed. Sometimes, they skip social events not because they don't care, but because silence is what they truly need. And many times, they've felt bad for saying no to people they love, simply because their body and mind needed a break.

Core Characteristics:
Energy Source: Recharges through solitude and quiet environments. Social interaction, even when enjoyable, can be draining.

- Internal Focus: Tends to reflect inwardly; they process thoughts and emotions deeply before speaking.

- Preferred Pace: Appreciate slower rhythms, and more intentional experiences.

- Social Style: Prefer one-on-one or small groups over large gatherings. Often seen as calm, observant, or reserved.

- Decision-Making: Takes time to consider options, often preferring to think before acting or speaking.

- Stimulation Level: Sensitive to external stimulation, noise, crowds, fast-paced environments can feel overwhelming.

- Expression: May take time to open up, they may take their time in processing their environment.

Extroverted HSPs

Extroverted Highly Sensitive People (HSPs) face a special kind of challenge. They love being around people, trying new things, and staying active. Social events, exciting places, and creative projects often make them feel happy and alive. But because they are also highly sensitive, their nervous systems take in more detail and feeling than others. This means they can get overwhelmed, even by things they truly enjoy.

We've met many extroverted HSPs who light up in busy cafés, retreats, or group talks. They feel inspired by the energy around them. But later that same day, they may crash, feeling tired, emotional, or foggy. They often describe the feeling like this: "I'm too sensitive for the life I want, and too full of energy for the life that calms me."

This inner struggle can lead to two extremes. Some say yes to everything, every event, every plan, until their bodies make them stop. Others pull back to protect themselves but end up feeling lonely or bored. Neither feels quite right.

But here's the truth: extroverted HSPs aren't "too much." What they need is rhythm and awareness. Their real power comes from knowing how to balance action and rest.

They need time with people, and they need time alone. The key is learning to listen to their energy and move at their own pace.

When they find that balance, extroverted HSPs shine. They grow through deep, meaningful time with others. They learn by being active and involved. They feel alive when they connect, not just with anyone, but in ways that feel real. For them, it's not about chasing every fun moment. It's about choosing what fills their heart, not just their calendar.

Core Characteristics:
- Energy Source: Recharge through social interaction, stimulation, and engagement with the outside world, with the distinction that the engagement needs to be the right kind, it needs to feed their depth of processing.

- External Focus: Tend to think out loud; process ideas through talking or doing.

- Preferred Pace: Comfortable in fast-moving, dynamic settings with variety and activity.

- Social Style: Thrive in group settings, often comfortable with new people and situations. Seen as talkative, energetic, or outgoing.

- Decision-Making: Even though they use their depth of processing they can be more spontaneous, willing to "try and see," and quicker to take action.

- Stimulation Level: Need more external stimulation to feel energized, new experiences, conversations, or environments.

- Expression: Communicate openly and easily.

What They Both Have in Common

Whether they are introverted or extroverted, all Highly Sensitive People (HSPs) have one main thing in common: they take in the world in a deep way. They notice more details, feel more emotions, and pick up more energy from the people and places around them. This happens whether they like calm spaces or busy groups.

Both kinds of HSPs can get overwhelmed by too much noise, too many people, or strong emotions. Extroverted HSPs might seem fine at first, but they still need time to rest afterward. That's how a sensitive nervous system works, it takes in a lot, so it needs more time and space to feel calm again.

For HSP-HSS Individuals

Many Highly Sensitive People (HSPs) are introverts, but not all. When you add the High Sensation Seeking (HSS) trait, things can get more complicated. The line between introvert and extrovert gets blurry. Some people with both traits call themselves ambiverts, people who don't fully fit into one group or the other. Ambiverts need both quiet time and exciting moments. They feel their best when they can move between the two without feeling bad or confused.

Finding that balance can be hard. Society often tells us we have to be one thing. You're either quiet and shy, or outgoing and social. But for Wild Sensitives, it's not that simple. Many of us feel excited by people and tired by too much time with them. We love new experiences but also need space to rest. People might call us "complicated," but we're just listening to two strong parts inside us.

Carl Jung, a well-known psychologist, was the first to talk about introverts and extroverts. He didn't see them as total opposites. He believed both sides live in every person. One is usually stronger, but the other still matters. The part we show less often still helps shape who we are. It can show up in our dreams, our quiet moments, or the way we see the world.

For example, someone who seems outgoing might have a deep, private emotional life. Someone who looks quiet might wish for more adventure or connection. This quiet rhythm makes sense for people with both HSP and HSS traits. We often feel like we are being pulled in two ways, wanting both excitement and quiet time.

As Highly Sensitive High Sensation Seekers, we live in the middle. We want calm, but also adventure. We want meaning, but also action. This doesn't mean we're lost or unsure. It means our brains are built for both deep thought and big experiences. When we give space to both sides, we feel most alive.

Jung's ideas help explain what many of us already feel. They show why we can enjoy a big moment, but still need quiet time afterward. Why we love deep talks, but need rest after them.

This tug-of-war inside can feel strange if we don't understand it. But once we do, it feels easier. We stop thinking our traits clash and start seeing them as a team. Together, they help us build a life that is full, rich, and truly our own.

The Key Distinction

Whether you are an introverted or extroverted Highly Sensitive High Sensation Seeker (HSP-HSS), both are real and important. One might feel pulled toward people and outside energy. The other might love deep and exciting things but need quiet time to think it all through. Neither one is better than the other. Both are special ways of showing what it means to be a Wild Sensitive. And when we understand these differences, we can live in ways that feel honest, strong, and free.

Extroverted HSP-HSSs often feel alive around others and enjoy social adventures. They look for newness through deeper connection. They desire engagement, not for the sake of just being with others, rather for learning, connecting, building.

Introverted HSP-HSSs, on the other hand, often find excitement in learning, nature, or their own thoughts. They enjoy experiences too, but not always the big crowds or loud places.

The Overlap Between Extraversion and High Sensation Seeking

At first, extroversion and high sensation seeking might look the same. People who are outgoing, talk a lot, love adventure, and seem full of energy often get labeled as both. But on the inside, these traits come from very different needs.

Extroversion is about getting energy from being around people. High Sensation Seeking is about wanting strong experiences, through movement, challenge, risk, beauty, or excitement. They can go together, but not always.

Dr. Marvin Zuckerman studied sensation seeking for many years. He found that being a sensation seeker and being an extrovert are only lightly connected. Some high sensation seekers are extroverts, but many are not. And when you add High Sensitivity, the overlap gets even smaller. Dr. Elaine Aron found that only about 30% of Highly Sensitive People are also extroverts. So, extroverted HSP-HSSs are rare, and when they understand their traits, they can be powerful and full of life.

This difference is important. Extroverts often want connection. Sensation seekers, whether introverts or extroverts, want intensity, newness, and rich experience. Some HSPs are pulled toward people. Others want the experience itself, even if it pushes their sensitive system.

Brain science helps explain this too. Extroversion is tied to the brain's reward system for bonding. Sensation seeking is tied to dopamine, the brain's signal for chasing new and exciting things. Even quiet HSPs can have a strong spark inside, a deep urge to speak up, try something bold, or explore the unknown. Carl Jung once said that what we don't show often grows stronger inside. That voice might show up in dreams, art, or strong desires. Ask yourself: Do I want people, or the experience? That small question can guide you toward what fills you up instead of what wears you out.

When HSS Looks Like Extroversion

Sometimes, introverted HSP-HSSs are seen as extroverts. This is because they also love excitement, beauty, and strong experiences. But the real difference is where they get their energy. If doing something exciting brings you joy, but being around people leaves you feeling tired, you're probably introverted, not extroverted. Knowing this can help you avoid getting overwhelmed and help you find a rhythm that feels right for you.

The Impact of Gender Roles

Another big influence on our sensitivity is gender conditioning, the messages we get early in life about who we're "supposed" to be based on our gender. These messages aren't always spoken out loud. Sometimes they come through body language, what we see in media, or the rules we learn at school or home. Over time, they become quiet rules we follow without even knowing it.

For boys and men, sensitivity is often seen as a weakness. From a young age, many hear things like, *"Be strong,"* *"Don't cry,"* or *"Man up."* The natural feelings they have, like sadness, fear, or tenderness, get pushed down or labeled as bad. Instead of learning how to work with these emotions, they learn to hide them. This can lead to shame, confusion, or even anger. Many boys grow into men who feel like they can't be their true selves, and that hurts them and the people around them.

Girls and women often hear a different message. They may be allowed to show more emotion, but they're also told to be polite, quiet, and not "too emotional." Their sensitivity is okay, but only when it looks soft, gentle, or giving. Many sensitive girls grow up learning to care for others before themselves. This can leave them stuck between being true to who they are and being liked by others.

These early lessons stay with us. They shape how we talk, how we set limits, and how we show our feelings. Healing starts when we see these patterns, not as something wrong with us, but as cultural rules we can choose to let go. When we take back our sensitivity, we take back our power. We learn to feel deeply and speak honestly. And that is a strong act of self-love.

Environmental Influences - School, Work, and Culture

For Highly Sensitive High Sensation Seekers, the places we grow up and work in don't just shape us, they help decide how safe, seen, and supported we feel. These spaces affect our identity and what we believe is possible in our lives. In schools where following rules is more valued than asking questions, HSP-HSS kids often learn to hide their depth or hold back their bold ideas. In jobs where speed, competition, or emotional distance are expected, we may feel like we're both "too much" and "not enough." Believing we are too intense, too thoughtful, too curious, too restless, all at the same time.

Culture adds even more pressure. In some countries, being sensitive is seen as a weakness, and the desire for bold experiences is called reckless. In others, blending in is praised, which makes our mix of sensitivity and seeking feel wrong. When we grow up with these ideas, we start to believe them. We adjust. We perform. We shrink. We change ourselves to fit in.

But what others call "being flexible" is often just our nervous system trying to survive in places that weren't made for people like us. Over time, this can lead to deep confusion: Are we being true to ourselves, or just who we had to become?

That's why self-awareness is so powerful. It lets us stop and ask: Are my reactions really mine? Or are they habits from years of adapting? When we ask this with kindness and honesty, we begin to untangle ourselves from old ways of being, and move closer to living in a way that matches who we really are.

The Influence of Social Media and Attention Culture

In today's world, social media plays a big role in how we connect, share, and stay updated. But for Wild Sensitives, it can bring challenges that are hard to see at first. Many platforms reward quick posts, strong emotions, and constant replies. Over time, this can make us feel like we have to share parts of ourselves we don't fully understand yet, just to feel seen, liked, or accepted.

This is called performative vulnerability, when we open up, not from a place of real connection, but to get attention, likes, or praise. It might seem like we're being honest, but it doesn't come from a steady, safe place. Instead of feeling strong, we might end up feeling exposed, unsettled, or more alone.

At the same time, endless scrolling pulls our attention in too many directions. Our minds race, our feelings scatter, and we feel tired. This is known as attention dysregulation, when it's hard to focus on what matters or relax into our own thoughts. For Wild Sensitives, who already notice more than most, this kind of overload can make us lose touch with what really matters inside.

That's why it's so helpful to use social media mindfully. Before we post, we can pause. Before we scroll, we can check in with ourselves. Taking time to protect our focus and asking, "Why am I sharing this?" keeps us true to our values, not caught in the noise. When we use it with care, social media can help us connect in real ways, not pull us away from who we truly are.

When HSP-HSS Combines with Other Influences

High Sensitivity and High Sensation Seeking are each strong traits by themselves. But when they mix with things like our past, trauma, culture, or other ways our brains work, they create a rich and complicated inner world. This world can feel exciting and inspiring, but also overwhelming. High Sensitivity gives us deep feelings, strong empathy, and awareness. But if we grew up in homes or cultures that told us to be quiet, stay small, or hide our feelings, we might have learned to hold everything inside. That can lead to confusion, shame, or emotional overload.

Even if others don't call this trauma, it still affects us deeply. Being pushed to perform instead of feel can disconnect us from who we really are. When sensitivity shows up with things like anxiety, depression, or ADHD, it can be hard to tell what's going on. The signs may look the same, or even make each other worse. Without the right understanding, many HSPs start to wonder if something is wrong with them. But as Dr. Elaine Aron says in her book *Psychotherapy and the Highly Sensitive Person*, sensitivity is not a weakness, it's a strength that needs care, support, and the right words.

High Sensation Seeking brings another layer. It drives our creativity, curiosity, and desire to grow. But without ways to manage emotions, it can spin out of control. Many HSS people are told they're "too much," that their energy is distracting or that their restlessness is a problem. Without a healthy path, their search for excitement can turn into risky choices, burnout, or running from pain. Some move from job to job or relationship to relationship, always chasing something new to feel alive. Others are told their HSS looks like ADHD or autism, where change and excitement are real needs. When misunderstood, HSS can leave someone feeling lost. But with guidance, it becomes a powerful source of energy, strength, and growth.

When both traits live in one person, along with past experiences, mental health layers, and cultural rules, we call it The Mixing Pool. It's not just a symbol; it's something we feel in our minds and bodies. A mix of strong emotions, needs, and choices. Some people long for deep love but get tired in emotional relationships. Others chase dreams or travel the world but secretly want calm. Some push themselves too hard. Others hold back and struggle to act. But deep down, they all ask the same thing: How can I live fully and truly as myself?

These patterns aren't signs of failure. They are normal results of possessing two amazing traits in a world that rarely teaches us how to handle them appropriately. Without proper guidance and support, the Mixing Pool can feel like a storm to survive. But with awareness, care, and reflection, we can begin to understand it and learn how to move through it with skill and technique.

Why Mapping These Layers Matters

If this feels confusing, that's because it is. But it's not random, and you are not broken. There is a way forward. In the next chapters, we'll start to explore that path together. In Chapter 9, we'll share The Six Zones of Life, a tool that helps you notice where you are emotionally and energetically, so you can make better choices. In Chapter 6, we'll look at your values, beliefs, hopes, and goals, the quiet things that shape your life. And in Chapter 11, we'll introduce The Adventure Triskelion, a guide to help you balance your sensitivity, your need for excitement, and your nervous system care in everyday life.

These tools aren't meant to fix you. They're meant to help you understand yourself better. Your complexity isn't the problem, it's part of your path. You don't need to become less. You need to become better at knowing who you are. To learn the language of your inner world. To follow the map that's already inside you.

The Mixing Pool doesn't mean you're broken. It means you're beautifully layered. And the more you learn how you're wired, the more free and fully alive you can be, the way you were always meant to be.

Annet's Story - How Sensitivity Was Shaped

When I was a toddler, I was bright, happy, and full of energy. I loved people and was open to the world around me. But something changed when I was just two years old. That was the year my parents got divorced.

At that age, I didn't understand what was going on. No one could explain it in a way my young mind could grasp. But pain doesn't wait for words. It just arrives quietly and deeply. What I felt was that something was broken, and maybe it was my fault.

When my parents divorced, my mom did her best to comfort me. But I still felt the truth. Someone I loved was gone. From then on, I believed love could disappear without warning. That was when I started feeling rejection sensitivity. I became very aware of people's moods. I looked for signs that I might be pushed away. If someone spoke sharply or seemed distant, I would brace myself for loss.

Like many sensitive kids, I tried to keep the peace. I became a people-pleaser. I moved through life quietly, like a butterfly, pretty but unnoticed. I smiled even when I felt scared. I stayed small to avoid being a burden. I didn't disappear, but I tried not to stand out either.

Then came the bullying. I was teased and left out at school, first in elementary school and again in high school. The message was clear: I was too soft, too weird, too different. I turned inward, unsure how to connect in a safe way. My mom loved me deeply, but I didn't have a model for safe, lasting connection. People felt hard to trust, so I built my own world, one filled with books, stories, and quiet thinking. A place where I could feel alone, but not lonely.

When I turned fifteen, something began to change. I became bolder and more curious. I started to explore. I worked in bars, watched how people acted, and studied their behavior. I became fascinated by human nature. I had a strong need to understand life, others, and myself.

That's when my High Sensation Seeking side showed up, though I didn't have a name for it yet. I hitchhiked across Europe, took big risks, and made brave choices that sometimes scared me. I thought I was an introvert, and I was in many ways, but that word started to feel too small.

I got married. Then divorced. I took jobs that didn't fit, just trying to belong. I married again and became a mother. Everything shifted.

My focus turned to my two daughters. They needed my heart, my strength, and my full presence. Like many sensitive moms, I paused my growth to give them what they needed. That path shaped me. It showed me my strength and the deep love I could give. But under all that love, a quiet voice said, "You're meant for more, too."

That whisper got louder when I started coach training. It didn't just give me tools, it brought me back to myself. It reminded me that my sensitivity wasn't a flaw. It was a strength. I realized I could grow not instead of being a good mom, but because of the mom I wanted to be.

Everything started to shift again. I discovered I love real connection. I feel alive when I guide others and see them grow. I even began to enjoy public speaking, something that once scared me. Little by little, I let go of fear. I stopped hiding. I dropped the need to be perfect or always pleasing. One layer at a time, I came back home to myself.

And now? I'm a proud Wild Sensitive. I don't have to choose between introvert and extrovert, I can be both when I need to. I can go on adventures or rest in quiet. I can lead and hold space for others and myself. I no longer need to hide to feel safe. I belong to me now... And that changed everything.

Randy's Story - Reading the Room to Stay Alive

For as long as I can remember, I felt different. Not in a way I could explain, just in how deeply I felt everything. I grew up in a home where showing emotions wasn't okay. You were expected to stay calm, be quiet, and keep control. My feelings weren't seen as strength, they were treated like a problem. And when you're told your sensitivity is wrong, you don't just get tougher. You start hiding it. You build armor. Thick. Heavy. Always on.

I didn't know it then, but this was when I started using my sensitivity and deep thinking to stay safe. I learned to read a room before I even walked in. I noticed every small change in tone, every look, every tense silence. I changed how I acted depending on who I was with. If someone came home angry, I could feel it before they said anything. If someone seemed upset, I'd try to fix it before they asked. This wasn't about being kind. It was about survival.

After a while, I started to believe that to be loved, I had to be easy. And being easy meant being invisible. So, I stopped being myself. I became whoever people wanted me to be. That's when rejection sensitivity took hold. I didn't just worry about being disliked, I was scared of being hurt. So, I tried to stop anything bad from happening. I kept everyone happy, until I couldn't remember who I really was.

But inside, something else was growing. A part of me that didn't want to stay small. A wild, restless part. The part that needed freedom, excitement, and new experiences. My High Sensation Seeking side had always been there, I just didn't have a name for it. That part of me wanted to take chances, go on adventures, and feel fully alive. But how could I do that when I was still always looking out for danger? I didn't understand how much of this came from past hurt until much later. Until I started asking hard questions. Until I began peeling back the layers. That's when I realized my sensitivity wasn't weakness, it was my shield. It kept me safe when the world didn't. But it also kept me from knowing the real me.

Healing began when I stopped trying to be who everyone else wanted. When I started choosing myself. I found out I'm a deeply feeling man, with a curious mind and a heart that had waited years to be seen. Now, I've learned to hold both parts of me. I can be social and stay grounded. I can connect with others without losing myself. I can look for adventure without running from my pain. I can be soft and strong. Still and wild. I don't need to scan the room for safety anymore, because I've learned how to build that safety inside me, where it's real and lasting.

Chapter 4

Empowered vs. Unempowered

The Turning Point of a Wild Sensitive Life

"We don't heal by becoming someone else. We heal by remembering who we were before fear taught us to perform, shrink, or disappear. The Wild Sensitive doesn't overcome their sensitivity, they learn to trust it, and in doing so, reclaim their power."
The Living Adventurers

Are we living empowered lives or unempowered?

There's a truth we've learned from living life as an adventure. We didn't learn it from books, but from real experiences, through quiet tears shared in hidden moments, the joyful ones that broke us open and the painful ones that helped us heal. We found it in stories spoken with shaky hands and brave hearts, in moments that lifted us up and ones that brought us to our knees. And in the choices we've made, some full of meaning, others that left us broken, but all of them leading us here. The biggest factor that shapes the life of a High Sensation Seeking HSP isn't the trait itself. It's whether we are living in an empowered way or an unempowered one.

The Empowered Wild Sensitive - A Glimpse into Our Everyday

For us, as Living Adventurers, living as empowered Wild Sensitives doesn't mean we've arrived at a perfect, polished version of ourselves. It means we've reclaimed the right to live in rhythm with who we truly are.

Our days are not free of challenge, but they are rooted in awareness. We no longer shrink to fit what's expected, we expand into what's real. There are mornings when we choose rest without guilt, because our nervous systems asked, and we listened. There are moments when we say yes to risk, creativity, or connection, not to prove anything, but because our wildness calls out for it. We've learned the difference between a true no and a fear-based one. Between shrinking out of self-protection and pausing in self-respect.

One of the greatest gifts of this adventure has been the freedom we've cultivated between us, the freedom of honesty and authenticity. We don't have to pretend. We don't have to filter. There is space for our depth, our intensity, and our vulnerability. This space lets us live fully and be open to what life has to offer, knowing we are met with truth, not judgment. That security gives us courage. That trust gives us wings.

We've built lives that honor both our depth and our daring. Sometimes that looks like leading with vulnerability or speaking a truth that shakes the room. Other times, it means retreating for a while to walk with our own thoughts in silence. It's not linear. It's alive. And it's real.

This chapter begins the exploration into the influences that keep us trapped in an unempowered state while guiding us to a path of becoming empowered Wild Sensitives. Before we unpack those layers, we want you to know that living empowered is possible. Not by overriding your sensitivity or chasing stimulation for its own sake, but by letting both work in harmony, as allies rather than enemies. We know how amazing and wonderful life is as empowered Wild Sensitives. We live it every day. Empowerment starts with awareness.

Our personality doesn't change because we are empowered. What changes… is who sits behind the wheel. When we are unempowered, our sensitivity can feel like a sentence. A thing we must survive. We are reacting to a world that is too intense. So we brace, we armor up. We tiptoe through our days trying not to feel too much, say too much, need too much. The traits that could be our fuel feel instead like a cross we have to carry.

We shrink, not because we are small, but because we've been told the world doesn't have space for our fullness. We adapt because we feel unaccepted when we are ourselves. An unempowered HSP often feels like they're always trying to "catch up" and adjust to their surroundings.

We have been there. You may have as well, perhaps you still are? Spiraling after a careless comment. Crying behind the steering wheel after a *"normal"* day of work. Staying silent at dinner parties, not because we have nothing to say, but because we've learned our voice is *"too much"* or *"too different."* We don't speak up when something feels off. We doubt our inner knowing, even when it's spot-on. We stay in friendships that drain us. We take jobs that keep us *"safe,"* even when they slowly erode our joy. And perhaps most painfully, we blame ourselves or our surroundings for not giving us what we want. This is what it feels like to live reactively. To feel like life is happening to us, instead of with us. To treat our sensitivity like a liability, rather than the exquisite internal intelligence it truly is.

But then… something shifts. Sometimes it's a full collapse. Sometimes it's a sentence in a book. Sometimes, it's a quiet voice inside that simply says:

"I can't keep living this way. I need to change something."

That's where empowerment begins. It starts with awareness, that radical, sacred moment of realization that maybe it's not you that's broken. Maybe it's the life you were taught to tolerate. Living as an empowered Wild Sensitive doesn't mean life gets easier. It means we stop abandoning ourselves. We begin choosing from a place of self-trust rather than self-doubt. We learn what calms our system, and we choose it unapologetically.

We start to speak up for our needs without over-explaining. We rest, without guilt. We walk away from the noise, even if it's coming from someone we love. We stop being the emotional sponge for the room and become a sovereign anchor within it. In our empowered state, we don't just feel deeply, we know what to do with what we feel. We set boundaries before we collapse. We create environments that nourish us instead of depleting us.

We no longer drown in other people's waves, we root into our own shoreline. We speak our truth, even when it shakes the room. Not from aggression, but from alignment with our authentic self. This is not about control. This is the power of internal sovereignty.
The shift from *"Why can't I handle the world?"* to *"What kind of world can I create that allows me to thrive?"*

When we begin to seek the answers, everything starts to change. We start choosing relationships that meet our depth with curiosity, not correction or adaptation. We pursue work that honors our unique gifts, whether that's intuition, creativity, presence, or perception. We stop chasing approval and start honoring resonance. We design a life that matches our rhythm, not the one we were taught to survive in. When this begins taking place, so too does something miraculous. Life starts to respond differently.

Because something inside us has changed. We respond to ourselves differently. And that's the shift, the quiet revolution. That's the moment we, as Wild Sensitives, reclaim the wheel of our own life. We know this, because we've lived it. We've canceled plans when our nervous system whispered, *"Not today."*

We've walked away from careers others admired but our souls have quietly outgrown. We've chosen solitude over social performance. And we've stepped out of dynamics that couldn't hold our depth, not with bitterness, but with self-respect. These weren't easy choices. But they were responsible ones. Not responsible in the performative sense, keeping everyone else comfortable, but responsible in the truest sense: accountable to our own well-being, and by extension, more honest in how we show up for others.

Because here's the truth we've come to learn the hard way: Living in an unempowered state is not neutral. It is a form of ill-responsibility, to ourselves, and to those we try to serve. When we abandon our needs, silence our truth, or perform from depletion, we don't just betray our own aliveness, we offer others a distorted version of who we are. One that cannot sustain connection, integrity, or wholeness.

Empowerment, real, rooted empowerment, is the highest form of responsibility. It doesn't mean we become selfish. It means we stop living small for the sake of fitting in. It doesn't mean we feel less. It means we've learned how to feel wisely, with awareness, with reverence, and with boundaries that honor our full humanity.

To be empowered is to lead with self-trust. It's to stop outsourcing our worth. It's to walk our path, not because it's easy, but because it's ours. And when we do that, something profound happens: We no longer serve others from our survival. We serve them from our truth.

Empowerment means we rest when we're weary, without guilt. We rise when our inner fire says, now. We speak when our voice carries truth, not performance. And above all, we return, again and again, to belong to ourselves first. Because Wild Sensitivity, when empowered, is not a flaw to fix or a burden to bear. It is our compass. A sacred, internal guide pointing us not toward comfort for comfort's sake, nor chaos for the thrill of it, but toward a life woven with depth, freedom, and truth. A life that feels lived, not just survived.

Rejection Sensitivity in the HSP-HSS

Rejection Sensitivity (RS), not to be confused with Rejection Sensitivity Dysphoria (RSD), is a learned behavior shaped by relationships, trauma, and personality. It can deeply affect the daily experience of Highly

Sensitive High Sensation Seekers (HSP-HSS). RS influences how we connect with others, express ourselves, create, and take risks. It's not just about being afraid of rejection, it's an emotional reflex often formed by early experiences of being dismissed or misunderstood. For HSPs, who naturally notice small details and feel things deeply, RS can become even stronger. It's important to remember that RS isn't something we're born with, it's a lens we can develop over time through life experiences.

RS is a survival pattern where someone anxiously watches for, expects, and strongly reacts to rejection, whether it's real or imagined. It often starts in childhood, especially in homes where emotional needs were not met or were ignored. For HSPs, this can create a nervous system that is always on alert, searching for signs of being disliked or judged. When mixed with HSS, it creates inner conflict, the desire to express oneself pulls against the fear of being hurt. The result is a complex emotional world where showing up as your true self feels risky, and being open is carefully managed behind layers of protection.

Performance, Perfectionism, and Identity Loss

Another way we learn to cope is through performance. Life can start to feel like a stage play, where every word, action, or facial expression is carefully chosen to avoid being judged. The natural drive of High Sensation Seekers pushes them to be bold, visible, and creative. But when rejection fear takes over, they begin to over-prepare, wear masks, or try to please everyone, hoping to stay safe. Instead of showing up as their real selves, they show up as who they think others want, polished, likable, and easy to accept. On the outside, this might look like confidence or charm. On the inside, it can feel like walking a tightrope, always watching for signs that someone might reject them.

Over time, this creates deep emotional exhaustion and confusion about who they really are. When someone shapes their identity to feel safe, their true self begins to fade. Many HSP-HSS individuals end up in careers, relationships, or roles that seem right from the outside, but feel empty inside. They may be praised or admired, but it doesn't feel real, because they built that success by hiding, not by being honest. And the saddest part? The very traits they hide, sensitivity, passion, depth, are often their greatest strengths. When the fear of rejection silences their truth, they don't just burn out. They lose connection to who they really are. Healing doesn't come from performing better. It starts by being brave enough to be seen, just as you are.

Risk Aversion and Internal Stalling

For the HSP-HSS individual, the need to grow, explore, and try new things isn't just a want, it's a part of who they are. The High Sensation Seeking side loves change, movement, and challenge. But when Rejection Sensitivity (RS) is present, that natural drive gets blocked by fear, fear of failure, judgment, or being "too much." Even things that once felt exciting can begin to feel risky or unsafe. The mind starts thinking about everything that could go wrong. The body tenses. The nervous system sends warning signs. So instead of jumping in, they pause, wait, or slowly step back. This cautiousness may not look obvious on the outside, but it shows up in other ways, like feeling stuck, living small, or feeling burned out from always second-guessing. These people don't lack dreams, they're sitting right next to them, frozen by the fear of messing up. The real fear isn't only failure, it's being seen while failing, being judged, or taking up space in a bold and visible way.

For the Wild Sensitive, this creates a painful inner conflict. One part of them knows they're meant to do more, but another part is scared of what that "more" might cost. This can lead to a quiet sadness, a feeling of lost potential or not living up to who they really are. It can also cause frustration that builds over time. The healing doesn't come from ignoring the fear. It comes from noticing it, learning to manage it, and still choosing to take meaningful steps forward, ones guided by your true self, not by what others might think.

Attachment Wounds and Relationship Patterns

Many HSP-HSS individuals with Rejection Sensitivity carry unhealed emotional wounds from early life, times when their feelings were ignored, judged, or met with mixed responses. These early experiences plant the seed for RS, which grows stronger through the deep feeling and empathy of high sensitivity, and the bold, connection-seeking nature of sensation seeking. In relationships, this can create a rollercoaster of ups and downs, both in behavior and emotions.

The HSP-HSS may want deep connection and jump into closeness quickly, craving the honesty and intensity they long for. But as soon as things feel too emotionally risky, when a partner seems distant, a friend doesn't reply, or a group feels "off", they may suddenly feel overwhelmed with anxiety. What often follows is a pullback, a shutdown, sometimes without warning. This pattern of reaching out and then withdrawing can confuse loved ones and leave the HSP-HSS feeling ashamed or misunderstood. In groups, they might swing between being full of life and disappearing without notice. Their nervous system picks up on tiny changes in tone, mood, or attention, and these subtle shifts can trigger strong emotional reactions that others don't even notice. This often leads to a painful cycle of craving closeness but fearing rejection, which results in mixed signals in relationships. Healing this pattern takes more than just noticing it. It takes nervous system care, clear communication, and slowly building trust with people who can meet them with understanding, kindness, and depth.

Creativity, Visibility, and Vulnerability

For many Highly Sensitive High Sensation Seekers, creativity is more than a hobby, it's a source of life. Whether it's through art, writing, performing, leading, or creating ideas, these individuals often feel driven to express and imagine. They naturally notice what others miss and sense what others don't say. But for those with Rejection Sensitivity (RS), sharing their creativity with the world can feel scary. They often swing between wanting to be seen and fearing being judged, misunderstood, or ignored. Every creative effort feels personal, like a part of themselves.

So, when their work is met with silence or criticism, it can hurt deeply. Many HSP-HSS creatives end up holding back. They edit too much, stay quiet, or hide their best ideas in journals or files, never shared. They may begin exciting projects but stop just before finishing, not because they aren't capable, but because putting their work out there feels too risky.

Their HSS side craves being seen, but that same visibility can feel dangerous. It offers both the joy of impact and the fear of being exposed. And yet, the only way their gifts can reach others is by allowing that risk, by facing the fear and choosing to share anyway. The real challenge isn't whether they have something valuable, they do. The deeper work is learning to express themselves without needing control over how others respond. Their worth doesn't depend on likes, praise, or approval. It lives in the bravery it takes to be true and to be seen.

Overcompensation and the Loss of Self

When Rejection Sensitivity starts early in life, it can change how a Highly Sensitive High Sensation Seeker sees themselves. To feel safe from judgment or emotional pain, many try to overcompensate. They build bold, confident, or successful identities that look strong on the outside but often feel empty inside. These masks might earn praise or attention, but they come more from the need to survive than from being real.

Others go in the opposite direction. They pull back, hiding their wild energy and deep emotions so they won't stand out. They quiet their voice, hold back their needs, and let go of their dreams to avoid being criticized. Both paths, overdoing or disappearing, can lead to confusion about who they really are.

The question *"Who am I, really?"* becomes hard to answer when so many actions come from fear instead of truth. For HSP-HSS people, this is especially painful. They are built for depth, growth, and honest expression. But when they hide who they are to stay safe, they lose more than their voice, they lose the ability to follow their inner wisdom. Healing starts with seeing where fear shaped their personality. It's about slowly uncovering what's real beneath the masks. This isn't about changing into someone else. It's about remembering the person they were before fear told them to stay small.

Self-Responsibility and the Healing Journey

Healing Rejection Sensitivity as a Highly Sensitive High Sensation Seeker isn't about making the fear go away. It's about learning how to move forward even when fear is present. The first step is building self-compassion and learning to comfort yourself, offering the care you may not have received as a child. When old voices of shame or fear show up, your voice today must become stronger. Along with this, body awareness and calming your nervous system are important. RS isn't just in your thoughts, it's also felt in your body through tightness, shutting down, or panic. Learning to notice where rejection shows up physically, and how to calm those feelings, helps bring you back to your center.

Over time, practicing rejection resilience through safe, small steps, what we call Self-Guided Exposure, helps you grow your ability to express, connect, and be seen without feeling overwhelmed. It's not about pushing yourself too far; it's about building trust and strength from the inside. Emotional awareness is also key: learning to tell the difference between real and imagined rejection helps you respond thoughtfully instead of reacting fast. Was that silence truly personal? Or just a small moment of distance? Was their comment hurtful, or did it just touch an old wound? When you meet rejection with understanding instead of fear, you gain the power to live with both boldness and sensitivity, without one shutting down the other.

RS as a Compass, Not a Curse

Rejection Sensitivity is often seen as a weakness, something to fix, hide, or get rid of. But for the Highly Sensitive High Sensation Seeker, RS isn't a broken part of you. It's a mark left by caring deeply in a world that didn't always know how to meet that depth. It's the effect of needing connection and being told, in clear or quiet ways, that some parts of you were *"too much."* But when we look at it with compassion, RS becomes more than just a wound, it becomes a guide. It shows where healing is still needed, where your voice still wants to speak without fear.

For HSP-HSS individuals, the goal isn't to stop feeling sensitive to rejection. The goal is to understand it, work with it, and build the tools, awareness, and inner strength to keep choosing life, love, and bold self-expression anyway. This isn't about becoming fearless, it's about becoming free. Free to be sensitive. Free to be bold. Free to belong to yourself, even if the world doesn't always get it. When RS is met with skill instead of shame, it stops running your life and starts pointing you home.

Push-Pull Dynamics and Nervous System Conflict

Many HSP-HSS individuals often feel a strong inner struggle between wanting and fearing. The HSS part of them wants to be seen, take risks, and keep moving forward. But the HSP part, shaped by Rejection Sensitivity, is afraid of judgment, being left out, or failing. This creates a painful trap. *"I want to put myself out there,"* they think, *"but I'm scared of how people will react."* This doesn't mean they lack motivation. The stuck feeling comes from a battle inside. Understanding this helps take away the shame. We're not weak or unreliable, it's our sensitive nervous system caught between the need to express and the need to protect, between wanting to be seen and fearing what that might bring. When we learn to see this clearly, we can calm the fear, respect the desire, and take steps forward with confidence.

Emotional Regulation and Mental Adaptability

Many people, especially men, were never taught how to manage their emotions. Instead of learning how to name, express, and work through feelings, they were taught to push them down, avoid them, or act like they didn't matter. From a young age, we're often told that showing emotions means being weak. As adults, this can show up as anger hiding sadness, numbing through work, addiction, or constant distraction, or shutting down when emotions feel too big. What may seem like calm or control is often just hidden stress. For HSP-HSS men especially, this emotional build-up can feel like a quiet storm, craving excitement but lacking tools to handle the emotional waves, which can lead to burnout, sudden outbursts, or loneliness disguised as strength.

For HSP-HSS individuals, emotional regulation isn't just about staying cool, it's about learning to ride intense emotional waves that come faster and stronger than most people feel. Our depth means we don't just feel emotions, we think about them, replay them, and react to them in layers. Without good tools, this can lead to emotional overload, big reactions, or complete shutdowns. But emotional regulation is a skill, and like all skills, it can be learned and strengthened. It starts with awareness: noticing our feelings before they explode. Tools like body check-ins, deep breathing, and the PERRR Method (Pause, Evaluate, Recognize, Regulate, Respond), which we explain in Chapter 10, can help us pause before reacting. We start to learn that feeling something strongly doesn't mean we have to act on it right away.

This kind of emotional strength isn't about ignoring feelings, it's about working with them. And when combined with mental adaptability, the ability to shift how we think, change viewpoints, and stay flexible during hard times, we stop being driven by emotion and become more grounded. Emotional regulation gives our sensitivity support. Mental adaptability gives our restless energy direction. Together, they help turn emotional chaos into clarity, and daily survival into confident, empowered living.

Somatic Echoes and Trauma Triggers

For the HSP-HSS, trauma isn't just a memory, it's a feeling in the body. The body remembers rejection through small signs: a certain tone of voice, a delayed reply, or a gesture that feels off. These "somatic echoes" can shake our confidence and cloud our choices. HSS traits push us toward new and exciting things, but those same experiences can reawaken old pain. Empowerment, in this case, means rebuilding trust in our body's sense of safety and confidence. As Gabor Maté explains, healing happens when the body, not just the mind, feels in control again.

When that inner control is restored, we shift from reacting on impulse to responding with calm. We move from feeling fragile to feeling steady and strong.

From Reaction to Sovereignty

Shifting into self-responsibility is a turning point on the HSP-HSS journey. It's when we stop hoping others will fully understand us, fix things, or make it easier to be who we are. This isn't about blame or judging ourselves, it's about taking back our power. When we stay in reaction mode, reacting to the past, our surroundings, or how people treat us, we stay stuck in survival. But self-responsibility asks us to pause and reflect: *What do I need right now? What can I control? What's mine to shift?* It means learning how our nervous system works, caring for our emotions, and gaining the tools we never learned before. This is where true empowerment begins, not by waiting for the world to change, but by becoming the steady, caring presence we've always needed. For Wild Sensitives, self-responsibility isn't about becoming tough, it's about showing respect for who we are. It's how we stop just coping and start creating a life on purpose.

Burnout, Bore-out & the Identity Fog – The Push-Pull World of the Wild Sensitive

While we can't cover every influence that shapes a person's personality, we'll look at a few key ones, those that often decide whether we feel strong or stuck, connected or confused.

For many of us, the real struggle isn't just being too sensitive or too intense. It's being both. It's waking up one day totally burned out, your body drained, your mind overloaded, your feelings stretched thin. Then waking up the next day feeling bored and desperate for something different, your spirit begging for adventure or change.

This is the push-pull life of the unempowered Highly Sensitive High Sensation Seeker. We burn out when there's too much going on. We bore out when there's not enough. Somehow, we keep swinging between the two, wondering if we're losing it. This is the confusing, in-between space where many Wild Sensitives live, thinking something is wrong with them, because no one ever showed them how to explain what's really going on inside.

The Burnout of Too Much

Burnout usually means emotional, mental, and physical exhaustion from too much stress or doing too much for too long. But for the HSP-HSS, it feels different. For the HSP, burnout is like the nervous system shutting down. It happens from feeling too much, too often, without enough time to rest. It's pushed by perfectionism, deep care for others, and trying to do everything. It's not just being tired, it's feeling drained to the core. Now add in High Sensation Seeking. For HSP-HSS people, burnout comes not just from taking in too much, but also from our strong drive to chase experiences. We crave intensity, excitement, and challenge. But our sensitive systems take in the world like it's in high definition. So, we dive in deep and fast, and then sometimes crash.

Even things that matter to us can lead to burnout if we don't take time to rest. Deep talks, travel, creative projects, they lift us up, but can also wear us out. Our systems don't just feel more, they get overwhelmed more. And since we often say yes to what excites us, we forget to save space for recovery. Burnout feels like crying for no reason, being tired even after sleep, and hearing that quiet voice that says, *"Why can't I handle this?"* But it's not that we're weak. It's that we've taken on too much, too quickly, for too long.

The Bore-out of Not Enough

Then there's the other side, the quiet, dull pain of not enough. Bore-out happens when our HSS side is ignored for too long. When we keep saying no, play it too safe, and build a life so steady that it becomes stuck. It also happens when we give in too much to people who don't have the HSS trait, putting their needs ahead of our own. This isn't laziness. It's a lack of engagement. Life feels flat. The soul drifts.

We might think we just need more rest. And sometimes, we do. But often, what we really need is movement, not stillness. Adventure, not escape. We confuse restlessness with being tired. We mistake feeling numb for burnout when we're actually hungry for meaningful excitement.

Bore-out can lead to depression, not from doing too much, but from feeling cut off. A soul shrinking slowly. Not because something is wrong, but because it isn't being fed.

The HSP in us needs meaning. The HSS in us needs motion. When both are missing, we shrink. And when we lose that balance, we start to feel separate from life around us.

Over- and Underfunctioning - Two Sides of the Same Strain

HSP-HSS individuals often end up in one of two extremes: over-functioning or under-functioning. In over-functioning mode, we try to manage everything. We anticipate others' needs, control every little detail, and take on roles like fixer, planner, or caretaker. We push for perfection, not to impress, but to avoid judgment and make sure no one sees us struggle. Being busy becomes a way to protect ourselves, to feel needed, and to avoid the shame of messing up.

The other extreme is under-functioning, where we pull away. We start saying no to opportunities, avoid taking risks, and emotionally shut down. Instead of staying involved, we disappear. We don't just rest, we vanish. A part of us still wants to leap, to live fully, but our nervous system says, *"Too much. Too risky. Stay small."* We ache for more, but hold back, and then blame ourselves for feeling stuck.

False Fire vs. True Fire

Not all stimulation is the same. False fire is when our drive for excitement is controlled by pain. It shows up as working too much, taking on too much, acting out, or getting caught in drama. It's not true aliveness, it's a nervous system trying to distract itself from hurt. This kind of fire leads to burnout. True fire, on the other hand, is steady and grounded. It still wants adventure and challenge, but comes from purpose, not pain. It's the difference between reacting and choosing. Between running away and moving forward with meaning. Learning to tell the difference is a key part of being truly empowered.

What fuels these fires often starts with what we believe. In Chapter 8, we talk more about limiting beliefs, the deep thoughts we've picked up over time, like *"I'm too much," "I'm not enough,"* or *"I'm only loved when I perform."* These beliefs feed the false fire. They push us to chase excitement to prove we matter, to fill empty spaces, or to avoid hard feelings. This fire burns fast, but it doesn't last. True fire comes from affirmed beliefs, truths we've questioned, tested, and made our own, like *"My sensitivity is a strength"* or *"I belong just as I am."* These beliefs lead us toward things that fill us up instead of drain us. When we change the stories we tell ourselves, the reasons we seek excitement shift too. We stop running away from who we are, and start walking in step with our true self.

The Freeze–Perform–Flight–Fight Cycle

When we don't feel safe inside, survival takes over. For many Highly Sensitive High Sensation Seekers (HSP-HSS), this isn't something we plan. It's a response we've learned over time by trying to survive in a world that often misunderstands or overwhelms us. Our sensitive systems pick up on even the smallest signs of danger. It's not just the obvious threats, we sense it in a look, a tone, or a moment of distance. These small things can feel like danger. And when that happens, our nervous system kicks into a familiar cycle of defense.

The first step is often freeze. Before we speak or act, we pause. We scan the space, read body language, pick up energy. This isn't about being unsure, it's how our brains process deeply. Our system is asking: *"Am I safe?"* Freeze is not weakness, it's awareness. It's the first defense for someone who has learned to be alert to the world.

If we still feel unsafe, we may shift into a protective behavior we call perform. This isn't acting for attention, it's about survival. We adjust ourselves to fit in, to keep the peace, or to stop conflict before it starts. We become helpful, cheerful, and capable, doing what others expect, even if it means hiding parts of ourselves. We overwork, avoid conflict, and lose touch with what we need. It works for a while. People praise us. But inside, we start to feel empty.

As Wild Sensitives, we know this well. We call it the *Chameleon Effect*, a habit of changing our energy, voice, or personality to match the room. It's not lying, it's what happens when sensitivity meets survival. We speak softer in some places, louder in others, and hide our truth to avoid problems. But doing this all the time wears us down. We get tired. We forget what we truly feel. We lose our sense of self. But when we notice this pattern, we can make a change. We can ask ourselves, *"Am I shifting to connect or to stay invisible?"* That question brings back our power. We can still adapt, but now with awareness. We check in with ourselves first. We honor our truth and pace. This is how we move from performance to presence, from surviving out there to feeling whole inside.

When performing becomes too much, we often shift into flight. We cancel plans. We don't reply. We pull away. Not because we don't care, but because we're running low. We need space to recharge. This isn't rejection, it's self-protection. We disappear not to hurt others, but to heal ourselves.

If nothing else works, and we feel trapped, we may finally move into fight. For Wild Sensitives, fighting doesn't come easily. It's the last step. We're not trying to hurt, we're trying to be heard. We've held it in too long. So, the boundary we didn't set earlier comes out now, sometimes loud and raw. We're not fighting to win. We're fighting to be seen.

We don't choose this cycle, it lives in us. It's our way of staying safe. But if we stay stuck in it, we feel tired and disconnected. Healing starts when we see the wisdom in these reactions. We stop blaming ourselves and start guiding our responses. We learn to pause with presence, perform only when it feels right, retreat only when needed, and speak up before we break. That's when survival becomes sovereignty. That's when we stop living just to protect ourselves, and start living with purpose.

From Surviving to Thriving

This is the journey of the Wild Sensitive, not to get rid of contradictions, but to hold them with courage and curiosity. Being both highly sensitive and high sensation seeking isn't a problem to fix or a puzzle to solve. It's a unique way of being that doesn't need resolution, it needs understanding. For those of us living with this dual nature, the goal isn't to be less sensitive or to hide our craving for excitement. The goal is to fully live in both truths without tearing ourselves apart in the process.

Many of us have spent years swinging between extremes. From burnout to bore-out. From doing too much to shutting down. From wanting deep connection to needing time alone. But real growth, the kind that empowers us, begins when we stop swinging and start blending. When we understand, we don't have to choose sides. The part of us that needs safety and the part that longs for adventure aren't enemies. They need to work together. We stop trying to fix ourselves and begin truly understanding who we are.

Burnout and bore-out aren't opposites. They're two signals from the same cause: living out of sync with our true nature. It happens when we follow someone else's speed, values, or timeline. When we ignore our own signals, by pushing too far or pulling away too often, our body and mind respond. The symptoms may look different, but the root is the same: we're out of alignment.

So, the answer isn't to choose stillness over action, or endless activity instead of peace. The answer is to build a life that honors both. A life that moves with the rhythm of our inner world, a rhythm that shifts with time, growth, and self-knowledge. Balance can feel stiff, like a scale that tips too easily. Rhythm, however, flows. It makes space for both effort and ease, movement and stillness. It helps us act from awareness, not fear.

And it all starts with permission. Permission to be complex. Permission to stop twisting ourselves to fit into neat boxes. Permission to stop being easy to label, and start being fully alive. Because Wild Sensitives weren't made to shrink. We were made to be fully seen, deeply felt, and truly free.

Retreat, Isolation, and Self-Sabotage

When we haven't yet learned how to handle the tension between our sensitivity and our need for excitement, we often fall into habits like retreating, isolating, or self-sabotaging. These behaviors may start out looking like self-care, taking a break, setting boundaries, or turning inward. But slowly, they can shift from healthy choices into avoidant patterns. We begin dodging anything that might feel too intense or expose us emotionally. What once felt like rest becomes hiding. We stop sharing our thoughts, pull back from connections, and avoid new chances, telling ourselves it's safer to stay small.

Then comes the sabotage: the unanswered texts, the dropped projects, the exciting invitations we turn down even though we want to say yes. Why? Because as we get closer to the things we truly want, our fear grows stronger. Our nervous system sends a warning: *"What if it's too much? What if you fail? What if they reject you again?"* These fears don't always speak loudly, but they quietly guide us away from progress and back toward shrinking ourselves. The tricky part is that these behaviors can look like self-care, making them harder to spot. But the signs are clear. Real self-care helps us feel stronger and more present. These patterns drain us. When thinking turns into overthinking, and comfort becomes a cage, we're no longer caring for ourselves, we're avoiding life.

Relational Tension and Emotional Load

Relationships can feel like walking a tightrope for the HSP-HSS. We crave deep, real connection, but we also need space and emotional safety. We may connect fully with someone, then suddenly pull away, not because we don't care, but because our nervous system feels overloaded. In friendships and family life, we often absorb others' emotions, becoming the helper or peacekeeper until we're too drained to stay. We may hold back our truth, afraid we're *"too much"* or hard to be around.

In work, similar patterns show up. We're often praised for our insight and energy, yet behind the scenes we struggle with overstimulation, emotional fatigue, and shallow or high-pressure environments. Even small changes, a different tone, a late reply, can shake us. On the outside, we may look calm, but inside we're riding emotional waves. Without good tools to handle this, all relationships, personal, social, or work-related, can feel like too much. Without clear boundaries, we can end up feeling alone in the very connections we want the most.

In the next chapter, we look at one of the most misunderstood parts of being a Wild Sensitive: the difference between being naturally sensitive and being hyperaware because of trauma. For people who aren't highly sensitive, hypervigilance is usually caused by trauma. It develops as a way to stay safe in environments that feel uncertain or unsafe. It's something they learned, not something they were born with.

But for Wild Sensitives, it's not the same. We're born with this awareness. Our nervous systems are made to notice small shifts, tones, looks, moods, that others miss. This sensitivity isn't caused by pain; it's part of who we are. It helps us feel deeply, notice quietly, and respond with care.

Still, if we've had trauma in childhood, that natural sensitivity can become even stronger. The system that's made to notice and feel becomes louder and more reactive. That can look like hypervigilance, even to ourselves. But the truth is more layered. Trauma didn't cause our sensitivity, it just turned up the volume on something that was already there.

In the next chapter, we'll unpack this difference. We'll explore how the Wild Sensitive nervous system works, how trauma shapes it, and why understanding the gap between true sensitivity and trauma-based alertness matters. Because when we see our sensitivity as strength, not damage, we begin to trust our intuition, not fear it.

Chapter 5

How Trauma Distorts Self-Perception

Sensitive, Not Shattered: The Wild Sensitive's Journey Back to Belonging

"Not all awareness is born from fear. Some of us were never scanning to survive, we were sensing to connect. The difference isn't just semantics, it's the soul of how we walk the world. As Wild Sensitives, we don't just notice more, we feel more, with purpose, presence, and a compass rooted in truth."

The Living Adventurers

What Is Trauma, and it's Influence on the Highly Sensitive?

Trauma doesn't always arrive as one catastrophic event. Much more often, it's quieter than that. It can be the absence of the feeling of safety just as much as the presence of harm. It's the moments when our nervous system couldn't cope, and no one helped us come back to calm. Put simply, trauma is what happens inside us when we experience something too overwhelming, too fast, too confusing, or too painful, without enough support. For some, that might be a car accident or loss. For others, it's years of emotional neglect or physical abuse. Sometimes, it's just growing up in a world that never felt safe to be who you are.

Now layer this understanding onto the nervous system of a Highly Sensitive Person, which is already wired to process everything more deeply. And so, when trauma meets sensitivity, something unique happens. For many Highly Sensitive People, trauma doesn't just leave a mark, it rewires our inner compass. It replaces responsive awareness with reactive protection. What was once intuitive sensitivity becomes cloaked in what many believe to be hypervigilance, not because we are broken, but because our nervous systems learned to survive a world that didn't understand us. We stopped trusting our emotions. We learned to anticipate danger even in secure places. We mistake nervousness for intuition. We confuse peace with boredom, and chaos with love.

Trauma Teaches Us to Cope, Not to Belong

Most unhealed trauma for HSPs leads to one of two patterns:

Over-functioning: Becoming perfectionists, people-pleasers, or emotional fixers. We stay ahead of every possible threat by scanning, soothing, performing.

Under-functioning: Withdrawing from life, avoiding stimulation, staying small and silent to protect our nervous system from further harm.

And in both cases, we lose touch with our original sensitivity, the one that was alive, intuitive, open, and beautifully attuned. But here's the most important truth. Sensitivity is not the trauma. Sensitivity is the part that got hurt. It's also the part that can help us heal. Because HSPs are also more resilient than we're given credit for. We process deeply, yes, but that means we can integrate deeply too. We can turn pain into wisdom, disconnection into discernment, and fear into self-trust, when we have the right tools, support, and understanding.

This is where the science of differential susceptibility offers hope. It tells us that the same sensitivity that makes us vulnerable to harm also makes us more responsive to healing. We're not just more affected by negative environments, we're also more deeply transformed by positive ones. When we're learn the tools, develop the skills and techniques, we begin to trust the connections built into our nervous systems, not just to cope, but to recalibrate. Sensitivity isn't the wound. It's the fertile ground where resilience, adaptability, growth, and self-trust can take root, if nurtured wisely.

When Trauma Meets Sensitivity

For many of us, trauma wasn't a single moment, it was a pattern. A slow erosion of our feeling of safety. A thousand tiny breaches in trust. It came through being ignored, misunderstood, criticized, or left to navigate overwhelming experiences alone. And when you're a Highly Sensitive Person, those moments hit harder, sink deeper, and stay longer. Because we process so much, so deeply, our nervous systems don't just remember what happened, they remember how it felt. And when that feeling was too much for us to handle, and no one helped us hold it, it didn't just pass. It became part of our wiring. This is where trauma lives for many HSPs, not always as clear memories, but as reactions:

- The flinch when someone raises their voice.
- The exhaustion after seemingly normal interactions.
- The shutdown when too many things happen at once.
- The voice in our head that says, *"Don't trust what you feel."*

Trauma doesn't mean we're broken. But it does mean parts of us were overwhelmed before we had the tools or support to process what was happening. And so, our sensitivity, meant to be a compass, gets tangled with fear. We stop trusting our instincts. We live in a state of readiness, always scanning for the next breach, the next demand, the next moment where we'll be *"too much"* again. That's not sensitivity. That's what sensitivity looks like when it's been wounded.

The Shift into Self-Responsibility

But once we begin to understand our sensitivity, not as a flaw, but as an essential part of who we are, something powerful begins to shift. We stop fighting ourselves. We stop blaming the world for not making space and instead start making that space for ourselves. This is the moment we begin to step out of the victim mindset, not by denying what hurt us, but by refusing to stay powerless in the face of it. We start asking new questions: What do I need? What nourishes me? What boundaries support my well-being? And most importantly: What can I choose, even in small ways, that honors my sensitivity instead of betraying it? This is where empowerment begins, not with perfection, but with presence. With noticing our patterns, owning our reactions, and learning to respond differently. Taking responsibility as a Highly Sensitive Person doesn't mean pushing through or toughening up. It means learning to listen to ourselves more honestly and then caring for what we hear.

The Nervous System Conflict: BAS vs. BIS

To understand the conflict that this creates in us we have to understand what our internal drives are and how they function. As mentioned in chapter 2, The Behavioral Activation System (BAS) is the system that drives us toward novelty, movement, and reward, it fuels the HSS hunger for aliveness. The Behavioral Inhibition System (BIS), on the other hand, governs caution and withdrawal, and in a healthy nervous system, it helps regulate sense of safety. But when trauma is present, the BIS becomes extremely active, often interpreting even small risks as threats.

For the HSP-HSS with trauma, the natural tension between the BAS and the BIS becomes more than just a functional push-pull, it becomes a source of chronic internal conflict. This doesn't just slow down action, it can completely shut it down. The result is a painful loop: the person feels an inner urge to leap into something new, a project, a relationship, an opportunity, but as soon as they get close, the overactive BIS kicks in, flooding the system with anxiety, shame, or fear. They might start something and then abandon it, chase intimacy and then emotionally withdraw, or seek adventure only to crash emotionally afterwards. It's not inconsistency, it's the nervous system in a constant tug-of-war between expansion and self-protection.

Recognizing this conflict as a trauma-informed pattern, not a personality flaw, is the first step toward healing. By learning to track these internal shifts based on *"When I leap, I feel..."*, the HSP-HSS can begin to build awareness, soothe the inhibition system, and gradually create space where sense of boldness and our sense of safety can coexist.

Empowered Paths Toward Integration
True empowerment for the HSP-HSS with trauma is not about choosing between sensitivity and sensation seeking but about learning how to integrate both in a way that feels safe, embodied, and empowering. This process often requires the support of a skilled, trauma-informed therapist, especially when past experiences have deeply shaped the nervous system's sense of safety. Somatic therapy can be especially powerful, helping the body release stored tension and reprocess the physical imprints of emotional pain.

Working at the level of the nervous system, not just the mind, allows healing to reach the places where trauma first disrupted regulation. Alongside this, attachment repair through safe, secure relationships creates the space to relearn trust, emotional consistency, and being fully seen without fear. For many Wild Sensitives, empowerment happens not in isolation but through connection. Integration also requires reprogramming how the nervous system responds to stimulation, learning how to stretch into boldness without tipping into overwhelm.

This is where Self-Guided Exposure becomes a vital tool: choosing small, intentional experiences that invite growth while respecting your system's capacity. We talk about this extensively in chapter 9 – The 6 Zones of Life. These practices are not quick fixes, they are gradual, compassionate pathways to reclaiming your original vitality. Integration means you no longer have to abandon one part of yourself to protect another. Instead, you begin to move through the world with both your depth and daring, alive and aligned.

Identity Repair and Reclamation

For the Highly Sensitive High Sensation Seeker, trauma doesn't just leave emotional wounds, it often fractures identity. Sensitive, deep-processing individuals tend to internalize painful experiences more fully, and over time, many begin to doubt their instincts, suppress their desires, and distance themselves from the parts of them that once felt vibrant, curious, and alive. They may abandon creative impulses, bold ideas, or dreams of adventure, not because those things no longer matter, but because somewhere along the way, they learned that being fully themselves was unsafe.

The world told them they were too much, too intense, too emotional, too inconsistent. And they believed it. Identity repair is the slow, intentional work of unlearning those distortions and reclaiming the original self, the self that existed before the fear, before the masking, before the world taught them to shrink. It's about returning to the version of who they were before they were hurt. The one who felt called toward something meaningful, even if they didn't yet have the words for it. This reclamation is not about becoming someone new, it's about remembering who you are, and finally giving yourself permission to live from that place, fully and unapologetically.

"Who were you before the world taught you to be afraid of your own fire?"

Hypervigilance vs an HSP's Sensitivity to Subtitles

As Living Adventurers and empowered Wild Sensitives, we've spent our entire lives immersed in the lived, layered reality of what it means to sense deeply and seek boldly. During the last two years, we have been intensely researching, conducting countless interviews, holding deep meaningful conversations with therapists, educators, and fellow Wild Sensitives, and we have come to recognize a vital distinction that is often overlooked: the difference between hypervigilance and sensitivity to subtleties. While these two experiences may look similar on the surface, their origins, functions, and emotional consequences are profoundly different.

What we offer here is not a clinical diagnosis or absolute truth, but a meaningful lens shaped by both science and soul, by our training and our tears. We acknowledge there is still much to explore in the unfolding understanding of human behavior, especially within the complexity of Highly Sensitive Sensation Seekers. But this next section reflects our ongoing commitment to truth-telling, through the eyes, hearts, and lived experiences of two Wild Sensitives learning to walk this world with both discernment and compassion.

Unpacking Hypervigilance vs. Sensitivity to Subtleties

The word hypervigilance is often used broadly, sometimes carelessly, to describe anyone who seems *"too aware," "too sensitive,"* or *"too reactive."* But for those of us walking the Wild Sensitive path, clarity matters. Especially when that word begins to blur the line between a trauma-trained survival response and an innate perceptual strength.

According to Dr. Elaine Aron, Highly Sensitive People (HSPs) are born with a unique trait that includes sensitivity to subtleties, the natural ability to pick up on minor shifts in tone, energy, environment, or emotion. This sensitivity is not created by trauma, though trauma can intensify it. It is not a flaw to fix, but a trait to understand. It's not about being on high alert, it's about being deeply attuned.

By contrast, hypervigilance is not an inborn trait. It is a nervous system adaptation, often developed by those who were not naturally sensitive, but became watchful and alert in order to survive inconsistent, chaotic, or unsafe environments. Where HSPs feel to connect, the hypervigilant scans to protect. Both forms of awareness can look similar on the surface, but their roots, purpose, and impact are vastly different.

This distinction matters, because when we mislabel an HSP as hypervigilant, we pathologize something sacred. And when we overlook true hypervigilance in someone who needs healing, we miss a chance to offer intervention.

Let's look at two children, one a less-sensitive child, the other a Highly Sensitive Child, both living through the same trauma-based experience.

Both children grow up in a home with unpredictable emotional volatility. One or both caregivers are loving at times, but also reactive, withdrawn, or overwhelmed. The environment is not abusive in the obvious sense, but it is emotionally inconsistent. The children never know what version of their parent they'll get when they walk into the room. Laughter one moment, silence the next. A calm hug today, a slammed door tomorrow. This is the soil they both grow up in. But their roots run differently.

Child A: The Trauma-Trained Protector (Less sensitive)

This child was born with a naturally less sensitive temperament. They tend to be less reactive to subtle shifts in tone, energy, or environment and often process external stimuli in a more straightforward or outwardly expressed way. They are not emotionally numb, they simply move through the world with a baseline nervous system that is less finely tuned to the undercurrents of feeling or atmosphere.

However, when a child like this is raised in an emotionally unpredictable or chaotic environment, something profound begins to happen. They start to watch carefully, not because they're intuitively attuned, but because they must be. Their nervous system, not wired for deep sensitivity, is instead trained into hyper-awareness out of necessity.

Over time, this child begins noticing things they wouldn't naturally focus on, the sound of footsteps in the hall, the way keys are tossed on the table, the tension in their parent's body language. These are not curiosities; they are survival cues. Internally, the child begins to live in a near-constant state of bracing, asking themselves over and over *"What's coming next?"*

From this emotional terrain, hypervigilance takes root. The child becomes mentally quick and externally sharp, but emotionally distant. Their radar isn't calibrated for connection; it's tuned for threat. The nervous system adapts not to feel more, but to predict danger and avoid harm. Their awareness becomes a shield. Their scanning becomes instinct. As they grow into adulthood, these children often become exceptionally observant, able to read rooms, assess dynamics, and anticipate reactions with uncanny speed. But often, behind this perceptive front deep exhaustion can arise. Many struggle to trust their own feelings, because their responses were always shaped by what was necessary, not what was natural. For them, control feels like safety, and anything unknown feels dangerous. Their sharpness, while impressive, is often a mask for burnout, a nervous system that never learned how to rest.

Child B: The Innate Sensitive (HSP)

This child was born Highly Sensitive, it's not something they become, it's who they are from the beginning. Their nervous systems are wired to process experience more deeply, making them exquisitely attuned to tone, energy, and mood. While others may need overt signs to notice a shift in the environment, these children feel subtle changes in their environment, as vividly as others see color or hear sound. A sigh, a glance, the slight tightening of a parent's shoulders, all register, often before any words are spoken. When they grow up in emotionally inconsistent or unpredictable homes, the environment doesn't create this awareness; it amplifies it.

Unlike the trauma-trained child who learns to scan for safety, this child isn't scanning, they are feeling everything, all the time. And because the emotional weight arrives before they have words to understand it, their internal world can feel confusing and overwhelming. They sense disappointment, tension, or sadness long before it is named, and often begin to assume responsibility for it. A thought quietly forms: *"Maybe if I just behave better, everything will stay calm."* Their sensitivity, meant for connection and depth, begins to bend toward emotional absorption.

Over time, this child becomes incredibly attuned to others but often disconnected from their own inner needs. They're expressive, intuitive, emotionally intelligent, but their gift comes with the cost of carrying more than is theirs. They often believe, unconsciously, *"If I can feel it all, maybe I can stop the hurt."* And so, they merge with others' emotions, often blurring boundaries between their own pain and someone else's.

In adulthood, these individuals often step into roles as guides, healers, artists, using their depth to help others make meaning of life. Without the support to understand their trait, they may become emotionally enmeshed, over-responsible, or energetically drained. With guidance, their sensitivity becomes wisdom in motion, a balanced, embodied knowing, where emotional depth is honored and boundaries are held with grace. It's not just a trait. It's a compass for meaningful living.

The Key Difference

	Child A: Hypervigilant *(Less sensitive)*	Child B: Sensitive to Subtleties *(HSP)*
Why they became aware	Need to protect themselves	Were already aware due to inborn trait
How they processed the home	Through cognitive scanning	Through emotional and sensory merging
Primary fear	"If I don't stay alert, I'll get hurt."	"If I don't absorb this, I'll lose connection."
Long-term emotional pattern	Control, withdrawal, mistrust	Over-empathy, overwhelm, self-blame
Awareness is...	Trauma-trained and reactive	Innate and receptive
Healing focus	Learning to feel, rest, and trust again	Learning to differentiate what's theirs from what's not

Why This Matters

Two children. One home. One becomes alert out necessity. The other becomes attuned because they were always attuned and the chaos sharpened the signal. This difference matters deeply, because it changes how we understand ourselves and each other. The hypervigilant child does not need to become more sensitive, they need to feel safe enough to stop scanning. The highly sensitive child does not need to toughen up, they need help owning their depth without drowning in it.

Hypervigilance is trauma-created, fast, and defensive. High sensitivity is inborn, deep, and relational. One is reactive, the other receptive. Though they may look alike externally, their motivations, and most importantly, their healing paths, are entirely different.

With this understanding in place, we're now going to take a closer look at the many ways trauma impacts us in adulthood, whether we are highly sensitive or not, empowered or still unempowered. Trauma doesn't just shape how we respond to stress; it weaves itself into our relationships, self-perception, ambitions, and sense of safety. By exploring these nuanced effects, we'll begin to map the difference between surviving and truly living, and how Wild Sensitives can move from bracing for life to fully embracing it.

Trauma-Trained Un-empowered Less sensitive: Hypervigilant Adult

The unhealed, less-sensitive hypervigilant adult is someone who didn't enter the world with heightened emotional sensitivity, but whose nervous system was reshaped by repeated early experiences of unpredictability, neglect, or emotional threat. As a child, they learned that safety came through control, not connection. Their emotional radar wasn't built-in, it was constructed out of necessity, sharpened by a need to detect danger before it arrived. They didn't feel everything, they watched everything. And they never stopped.

Now, as adults, they carry that vigilance into every corner of their lives, but instead of recognizing it as a trauma adaptation, they see the world itself as unsafe, and themselves as a perpetual target of harm or betrayal. They may speak from a place of deep resentment: *"People always let me down," "I have to do everything myself,"* or *"You just can't trust anyone."* These beliefs, rooted in early protection, have calcified into worldview. They often feel misunderstood, underappreciated, or emotionally distant, not because they lack the capacity to connect, but because they no longer feel safe enough to try.

Emotionally, they are fast but fragile. Quick to react, quick to defend, and slow to trust. Rest feels impossible. Intimacy feels dangerous. They may over-function in relationships or work roles to feel in control, while beneath the surface, they're exhausted, disconnected, and often angry. Their life becomes a series of tightly managed circumstances meant to avoid vulnerability, which they equate with powerlessness.

But the tragedy is this: their sharpness is not who they are, it's who they became to survive. They are not broken. They are over-armored. And the cost of that armor is peace. Without healing, their awareness remains a burden they cannot set down, and life becomes something to defend against, rather than engage with. Yet even here, there is hope. The moment they begin to question whether safety might come through trust, not just control, is the moment their path to freedom begins.

Trauma-Trained Empowered Less sensitive: Hypervigilant Adult

The trauma-trained, empowered less sensitive adult is someone who may not have been born with a naturally sensitive nervous system, but whose early life was shaped by emotional chaos, inconsistency, or relational instability. To survive, they developed hypervigilance, a deeply intelligent adaptation that taught them to read micro-expressions, shifts in tone, and unspoken emotional cues with razor-sharp precision. Unlike intuition, their awareness wasn't innate, it was constructed under pressure. It was built to protect. And for a long time, it did.

But what sets the empowered version apart is this: they've come to recognize that survival mode is not the only mode available. They've begun the work of separating who they became out of necessity from who they truly are. Rather than clinging to control through constant scanning, they've started to explore the possibility of safety without hyper-awareness. They still notice details others miss, but now, they question whether everything must be a threat. Their nervous system may still spark at times, but they've learned to pause, breathe, and choose instead of react.

In relationships and at work, they no longer over-function by default. They've developed the courage to let others carry some of the weight. They may still feel the tug to manage everything, but they're learning that vulnerability isn't a weakness, it's growth. This shift doesn't happen overnight. It comes through therapy, deep self-inquiry, mentorship such as life coaching and guiding, and moments of quiet bravery. Slowly, they trade vigilance for presence, and tension for trust.

Empowerment for the trauma-trained less sensitive isn't about erasing their hypervigilance, it's about reclaiming agency over it. Their insight remains sharp, but now it's grounded. Their boundaries are clear, but not rigid. They learn to rest, to exhale, to feel safe in stillness, not because the world has changed, but because they have. They are no longer ruled by what happened to them. They are led by what is possible for them.

The Traumatized Un-empowered HSP

The traumatized, unempowered HSP is someone who entered the world with a nervous system biologically wired for depth, depth of perception, depth of emotion, depth of processing. From the beginning, they noticed what others missed: tone shifts, emotional undercurrents, subtleties that lived between the lines. But instead of being nurtured in this depth, they were met with confusion, criticism, or neglect. Their emotional responsiveness wasn't guided, it was dismissed. And slowly, they internalized a dangerous message: *"Something is wrong with me."*

As children, they were often overwhelmed by environments that were too loud, too chaotic, or too emotionally inconsistent. When their tears were ignored, when their insights were brushed off, when their intensity was labeled *"too much,"* their sensitivity began to feel like a liability. Rather than being taught how to work with their nervous system, they were forced to hide it, suppress it, or armor it. This didn't erase the sensitivity, it froze it in place, raw and unprocessed.

Now, as adults, these unempowered HSPs often live at the mercy of their sensitivity, not in relationship with it. They may see themselves as broken or weak. Everyday life feels like an emotional minefield, and they rarely feel grounded or resourced enough to cope. A critical comment can unravel them. A missed cue can lead to hours of rumination. Their language may sound like: *"I can't handle conflict," "Everything is too much," "I wish I wasn't like this."* These aren't dramatics. They are pain, speaking through the mouth of someone who never learned how to hold their trait with strength.

Instead of leaning into their deep intuition and perception, they default to emotional avoidance, over-accommodation, or self-erasure to survive. They are hyper-attuned to others but often disconnected from themselves. They shut down at the first sign of tension or stretch. Their inner world, once full of beauty and insight, becomes a space of emotional overwhelm and isolation.

But this HSP is not broken. They are unsupported, and unempowered. Their nervous system is not the enemy, it is a powerful tool waiting for a steady hand. With the right guidance, boundaries, and emotional education, their fragility can become flexibility. Their deep perception can become a gift, not just to others, but to themselves. The shift from unempowered to empowered doesn't mean feeling less. It means feeling with clarity, capacity, and choice.

The moment they stop trying to suppress their trait, and begin learning how to co-regulate with it, they move from victimhood to self-belonging. Sensitivity, once seen as a wound, becomes the compass it was always meant to be. And the path to sovereignty begins not in changing who they are, but in remembering who they were before the world taught them to be ashamed of it.

The Traumatized Empowered HSP

The empowered HSP who has known trauma as a child carries a nervous system that was never built for defense, but for depth. From the very beginning, they experienced the world through rich emotional landscapes and subtle energetic shifts, feeling what others missed, sensing what others dismissed. Their trauma didn't create this capacity, it simply amplified it, sharpening what was already profoundly alive inside them. Unlike hypervigilance, which is built from fear, their sensitivity was magnified by pain, not formed by it. And in that pain, they began the long journey of learning how to carry something powerful with care.

As they enter adulthood, what sets them apart is not just what they feel, but how they've learned to relate to what they feel. They are no longer at the mercy of their sensitivity. They've learned its patterns, mapped its emotional weather, and built the tools to navigate it wisely. They no longer absorb by default, they discern. They still sense the unspoken, still read energy before words, still notice shifts others don't, but now, they do it with boundaries, clarity, and choice.

They are driven by the desire to live in alignment, to bridge their inner emotional world with the outer experience of life. They show up not to fix or absorb others' pain, but to walk alongside it, offering presence without losing themselves. They know what it feels like to be flooded, to be pulled into others' emotional storms, while anchoring themselves. Their sensitivity, once overwhelming, is now a refined internal compass, one that guides them toward truth, integrity, and deep connection.

Empowerment, for the traumatized HSP, doesn't mean becoming less sensitive. It means becoming fiercely self-aware, learning to meet their trait with compassion, to hold space for others without carrying their weight, and to trust their own emotional reality. They are often the ones others turn to for guidance, for resonance, for meaning, because their insight is not intellectual, it's embodied. Their presence carries a quiet power, rooted not just in what they know, but in what they have survived, transformed, and integrated.

In this empowered state, their sensitivity is no longer a wound, it is wisdom in motion. A source of healing, leadership, and soulful depth that doesn't overwhelm, but uplifts. Their nervous system isn't a burden, it's a gift that's been earned, refined, and reclaimed.

The Traumatized Un-empowered Wild Sensitive

The unempowered HSP-HSS who experienced trauma in childhood is often caught in a life-long inner contradiction they were never taught how to navigate. Born with two powerful temperamental traits, deep sensitivity and a drive for stimulation, novelty, and expansion, this individual was hardwired to live fully, but also to feel deeply. When their early environment was unstable, emotionally neglectful, or even mildly traumatic, their already intense inner world became a battlefield of unmet needs, misinterpreted messages, and unprocessed pain.

As children, they craved exploration and freedom, movement, adventure, and rich sensory input. But they also needed emotional safety, attunement, and gentle guidance to manage the flood of sensation and emotion that followed every new experience. If caregivers ignored, misunderstood, or punished either side of their temperament, telling them they were *"too much," "too dramatic," "too sensitive,"* or *"never satisfied"*, these messages imprinted deeply. They learned not to trust their internal compass. Their need for stimulation was labeled reckless, while their emotional depth was pathologized.

Now as adults, unempowered HSP-HSS individuals, often live in a state of fragmentation. They swing between extremes, one moment chasing stimulation to avoid the heaviness they feel inside, and the next withdrawing in overwhelm when they've taken in too much. This push-pull creates chronic identity confusion: *"Who am I really? The wild one or the gentle one? The dreamer or the doubter?"* They may struggle to commit to careers, relationships, or goals, not because they lack ambition or care, but because their nervous system is constantly overloaded or underfed.

Without healing, their sensation-seeking becomes impulsive, not intentional. They leap into experiences hoping to feel alive, only to crash into emotional dysregulation or shutdown. Likewise, their sensitivity, when unsupported, becomes a source of shame and self-protection rather than wisdom and connection. They may appear spontaneous or adventurous on the outside, but inside, they are often exhausted, disoriented, and emotionally raw. Relationships can feel like traps or threats. Solitude can feel both safe and suffocating. They crave deep connection but fear the vulnerability it requires.

This internal war often leads to patterns of burnout, bore-out, over-functioning, and emotional collapse. They may numb with distraction, overwork, over-helping, or constant stimulation, anything to outrun the inner dissonance. Without the right tools, their traits work against each other: sensitivity overwhelms the thrill, and thrill bypasses the sensitivity. They may describe themselves as lost, misunderstood, or broken. But they are none of those things.

They are untrained in their duality, not incapable of balance. Their power lies not in suppressing one side of their nature, but in learning how to integrate both, to build nervous system capacity, emotional clarity, and values-based decision-making. With support, they can learn to create experiences that stretch them just enough and soothe them just right. They can learn the language of their discomfort and the difference between emotional truth and inherited belief. And most importantly, they can rewrite the story that told them they had to choose between being wild or wise.

Because the empowered HSP-HSS doesn't swing between opposites, they bridge them. And this version, still buried beneath the unhealed noise, is already there, waiting to rise.

The Traumatized Empowered Wild Sensitive

The Empowered Wild Sensitive is a HSP-HSS who has experienced childhood trauma and made the radical, courageous choice to heal, integrate, and own their dual nature. Their sensitivity was never absent, it was always present, alive, attuned, and deeply affected by their early environment. And their drive to explore, expand, and experience the fullness of life was also always intact, even if it was misunderstood, stifled, or redirected in unsafe ways.

As a child, this individual felt the full weight of contradiction. They were deeply impacted by rejection, inconsistency, or emotional abandonment, but also pulled by a hunger to leap, to taste freedom, to discover what lay beyond the walls of safety. They may have been the child who cried themselves to sleep at night, yet climbed trees too high the next day just to feel the wind. They may have tiptoed around unstable caregivers and still been the first to wander beyond the edges of the familiar. Their nervous system was shaped by both caution and courage. Trauma didn't erase either, it magnified the distance between them, stretching their sense of self across opposing needs, making safety and stimulation feel like rivals.

But the empowered Wild Sensitive didn't stay fragmented. Somewhere along the way, through therapy, mentorship, community, or their own fierce devotion to truth, they began to reclaim the parts of themselves that were split. They stopped pathologizing their sensitivity. They stopped apologizing for their intensity. They stopped chasing sensation just to prove they were strong or shrinking their depth just to be accepted. They began to see that their trauma had not stolen their power, it had hidden it beneath survival patterns, waiting to be unearthed, re-integrated, and finally lived.

This person has faced the pain of their past, not to dwell in it, but to understand how it shaped their beliefs, their behaviors, and their nervous system. They know their triggers, and they've built tools to regulate their body before those triggers spiral into shutdown or shame.

They no longer confuse overstimulation with excitement or emotional absorption with connection. They have learned to name what they need, space and stretch, grounding and growth, solitude and stimulation.

In adulthood, the empowered Wild Sensitive is often magnetic. Not because they perform, but because they embody a rare integration. They are present. Curious. Deeply intuitive. When they enter a room, they notice the energy, but they also know which energy belongs to them. They no longer carry everyone else's pain by default. They can feel deeply with others, without losing themselves in others. And when life calls them to leap, to take a risk, to go on an adventure, to follow a wild desire, they know how to prepare, center, and recalibrate.

They still get overwhelmed. They still need rest. But they know how to build rituals, boundaries, and practices that make expansion sustainable. They are often coaches, guides, leaders, creatives, or quiet revolutionaries. They don't seek attention, but they do command presence. Their story isn't perfect, it's textured with pain, beauty, and the truth of becoming. What makes them powerful is not that they escaped trauma, but that they walked back through it, with compassion and curiosity, and came out whole.

The Empowered Wild Sensitive doesn't live to please or prove. They live to align. Their nervous system no longer dictates their destiny, it guides it. Their high sensitivity is no longer their weakness, it's their compass. And their high sensation seeking isn't recklessness, it's their call to aliveness. Together, these traits form a nervous system that is both alert and awake, one that moves not from fear or fantasy, but from integrated truth.

They are not empowered because they are wild... They are wild because they empowered. And their life is not about fitting in, it's about belonging to themselves fully, freely, and without apology.

The Empowered Wild Sensitive Wayfinder

The Empowered Wild Sensitive Wayfinder is a rare and luminous expression of what's possible when a HSP-HSS not only survives childhood trauma, but alchemizes it into clarity, capacity, and courageous purpose.

This person did not have an easy beginning. Their early years were marked by multiple traumatic experiences, emotional abandonment, instability, loss, or even subtle but repeated invalidation of their emotional world. These traumas didn't just leave scars, they etched patterns of protection into their nervous system. But the Wayfinder didn't stop there. Rather than remain trapped in cycles of survival, they chose the slow, often painful work of healing and integration.

They didn't just read books on growth, they lived it. They studied their own nervous system with the same care an explorer studies a map. They examined their beliefs, tracked their patterns, and sat with emotions many people spend lifetimes avoiding. They pursued education, not only academic, but somatic, relational, and experiential. And most importantly, they didn't seek healing to become "normal." They sought it to become whole.

At some point in their adulthood, the Wayfinder intentionally entered the world, not to prove strength, but to cultivate it. They placed themselves in challenging environments: wilderness treks, deep relational work, creative risks, leadership roles, cultural immersions, anything that required their full presence, their resilience, and their ability to regulate and respond. These weren't impulsive leaps for stimulation; they were initiations, designed to sharpen wisdom, test integration, and stretch the very edges of what it means to live well with both depth and daring.

Through these intentional challenges, they built resilience, not the kind that hardens, but the kind that bends and returns stronger. They cultivated adaptability, the ability to stay centered in unfamiliar or intense environments. And they honed endurance, mental, emotional, and somatic strength that lets them sustain growth without collapse. Where once they may have been easily overwhelmed by too much input, too much emotion, too much noise, now, they know how to manage intensity without being consumed by it. Their heightened sensitivity remains, but it no longer rules them. It guides them.

The Wayfinder's depth of processing becomes their secret power. They reflect before responding. They integrate before moving on. They feel deeply, but not destructively. Their extreme sensitivity to subtleties gives them a perceptive edge: they notice shifts in group dynamics, unspoken truths, and subtle opportunities others miss. Their emotional attunement is rooted not in enmeshment, but in a profound connection to self, body, and environment.

The result? They are grounded, clear, and unshakably aligned.
These individuals do not live without pain. But they no longer flee it. They meet it with tools. With skills. With techniques. Their relationship to discomfort has matured; it is no longer a threat, but a teacher. They've transformed their nervous system from a battlefield into a compass.

And while the empowered Wild Sensitive Wayfinder is rare, they are not unreachable. This path is open to any Highly Sensitive Sensation Seeking Person willing to commit to healing, learning, exploring, and stretching, bit by bit, with reverence for both the wild and the wounded parts within. It's a path of layered strength, sacred truth, and embodied leadership.

They are not simply survivors... They are the ones that show the way. They live not just from intuition, but from embodied wisdom. And they carry the message:

"You can live fully, love fiercely, and stretch wide, without abandoning your depth. You were not made to shrink or split. You were made to find the way. And then light it for others."

Chapter 6

Beliefs, Values, Desires, and Goals

Building a Life That Belongs to You: The Power of Examined Beliefs and Chosen Direction

"We were never meant to just follow the map we were given. We were born to build our own compass, to walk toward the pulse of our purpose, and to chart a destination that makes our soul come alive. As Wild Sensitives, we don't just seek the path, we shape it. One belief examined, one value honored, one desire awakened, one goal chosen... at a time."

The Living Adventurers

The Map... The Compass... The Purpose and the Destination

There comes a moment on every inner journey when life no longer feels quite the same, not because the world around us has changed, but because something within us has. A subtle stirring begins to rise, a quiet yet insistent tension between the version of ourselves that the world has reflected back, and the version that has been whispering from within all along. That inner voice, often ignored or misunderstood, gently urges us to remember who we truly are. But the world around us is loud. It yells who we should be. And over time, many of us learn to follow the noise instead of trying to listen to that whisper.

For many Highly Sensitive people, that whisper is barely audible. It gets buried beneath the voices that promise certainty: teachers, parents, systems, traditions and Mandalorians that all say, *"This is the way."* We're handed maps disguised as beliefs. Beliefs passed down from others and told to follow them. And so, we do. Not because they show us the way, but because we're afraid we don't, we will get lost. Over time, as Highly Sensitives, that whisper fades into the background of our minds as all of our focus is paced on expectations to follow that map we were handed.

Yet, as Wild Sensitives, that whisper never really quiets. It's steady, alive, even demanding in its gentleness. It doesn't scold; it beckons. It knows something more is needed to make us empowered. While we too were handed maps and told to follow, the whisper ask's; *"Where is our compass?"*

Those around us warned: *"Out there, beyond the path we have set, it's dangerous. Stay where it's safe. Trust the map, you do not need a compass."* So, we continued to cling to beliefs that they gave us. The ones that never quite felt right. We stayed in these lives that felt familiar and settled for its illusion of safety. The truth is it was really just survival.

We are here to tell you, your beliefs are just that, a map. A map that we often inherited. We didn't choose it, and we have never questioned it, we simply follow those that gave it to us along the same trail.

But a map, no matter how detailed, is useless without a compass. If beliefs are the map, what then is this compass? That compass is one's core values, the deep truths they hold about what matters most to them. They do not always speak the language of logic or point us in the right direction. Why? Because something is interfering with our compass.

Imagine you hold a compass in one hand, and it is pointing North. In the other hand you hold a powerful magnet. The closer you bring the two together, the less accurate that compass becomes. Bring that magnet close enough, and the compass no longer points North, it only points at the magnet.

The magnet represents fear, the more fear we hold, the more distorted our compass becomes.

So we must ask, those we are trusting to lead us, the ones that gave us this map they are following, do they have a compass? Even more important, how close is their magnet to that compass? While we all have a magnet, not all of us have our own compass.

This moves us to ask, what is this pull we've always felt, the ache, the fire, the craving that won't go away. The one that invites us to leave the path. That's not restlessness. That's one of our most important calls, purpose. It is held within our desires. It's our soul's way of telling us what we are here for, not just what we want, but what we're wired to live for. All too often, as we follow this path others have set for us, wondering, why are we here? What's the purpose of just following along? For us Wild Sensitives, our deep emotional connection screams out a feeling of emptiness, unfulfillment for we lack real purpose.

This brings us to the next question as we trod along this path we now follow. *"Where are we going?"*

The ones that follow as we do, suddenly look up with sad faces. *"Retirement"* is the reply before lowering their heads again to stare at the bleak and dusty trail. This is the destination to which they have come to accept. This is their goal.

For us, Living Adventurers, our wild sensitive nature needed something far more than to follow this mindless and emotionless path. We wanted a different destination, our own goals, not just to 'retire,' but to truly live an amazing life filled with meaning, connection, and wonder. We realized to do this, we must step off the path and let all those behind us carry on. We needed to carefully examine the map we had, build our own compass while reducing the magnet given to us by culture, family, or fear. Then we reached deep into our souls and found our purpose by listening to our desires, not the loud ones shaped by ego, but the quiet ones shaped by truth. Next, we carefully constructed small steps that would take us through the jungle of unexplored territory to reach our new destination. That wonderful, fulfilling life, the one that feels like home in both body and spirit.

Sure, we could safely follow the herd of people, or we could create our own map, compass, purpose and destination. In true Wild Sensitive style, we would not do this recklessly as so many believe. For us, we are constantly gaining knowledge, building the tools, and practicing every day to develop better skills and techniques so we can make our way through that jungle with confidence, courage and pride. We confidently face challenges and celebrate our successes. We have learned to set up camps to pause, enquire and reflect, before moving forward.

So, if you feel like you've been walking a path that no longer makes sense…

If the ground beneath your feet feels as if it lacks purpose…

It's not because you're lost... It's because you're simply following blindly...

In this chapter, we invite you to take a step off the path, let others pass you by while we take a look at your map, your compass, your purpose and destination.

The Map we Call Beliefs

Beliefs are not just thoughts; they are internal maps, formed through experience, emotion, repetition, and the meanings we assign to those moments, especially in childhood. For Highly Sensitive Sensation Seekers, these beliefs don't live only in the mind; they are etched into the nervous system. They shape how we interpret the world, what we reach for, and how confident we feel doing so. Many of the beliefs we carry into adulthood were never consciously chosen. We inherited them from caregivers, teachers, culture, and systems that often had good intentions but lacked emotional attunement. Phrases like *"Be careful," "Stop crying,"* or *"Calm down"* may seem minor on the surface, but when repeated without explanation or softness, they imprint deeply. They don't just say no to a behavior, they say no to who we are. Over time, we internalize these messages: *My desires are dangerous. My curiosity causes problems. Wanting something leads to punishment.*

This is how limiting beliefs are born. They come from shutdown without clarity, correction without connection, and boundaries delivered without love. These beliefs convince us that our instincts can't be trusted, that being ourselves puts connection at risk. They lead to shame, perfectionism, self-suppression, and people-pleasing, especially for HSP-HSS individuals who feel everything more intensely and seek meaning in every experience.

In contrast, affirmed beliefs are grounded in a solid foundation of clarity, and attunement. When a child is told, *"No, sweetheart, I can't let you do that because it could harm you."* they don't hear rejection, they feel protected. They learn that boundaries can be loving, that mistakes don't equal disconnection, and that curiosity isn't wrong, it's something to be guided. These beliefs form the foundation for inner trust, resilience, and authentic exploration.

Unfortunately, most of us didn't grow up in environments that helped us create these affirmed beliefs. We were handed maps, fixed rules, rigid identities, inherited fears, we call magnets. Yet we were never taught to build a compass, let alone how to use it. We weren't shown how to align beliefs with our values, or how to check if what we believed was even ours to begin with.

As children move into school and society, these maps get even more confusing. Teasing, exclusion, labels, and unspoken rules reinforce early beliefs. The sensitive, curious child begins collecting "evidence" that they're too much, not enough, or somehow different. And without emotional guidance, those messages solidify.

By adulthood, we may find ourselves stuck, not because we're broken, but because we're living according to beliefs we never choose. Beliefs built on survival, not sovereignty. So we walk the path laid out by others, instead of our own.

Here's your turning point: beliefs can be rewritten. They are not fixed truths. They are agreements, and agreements can change. We don't just throw the old map away and look for a new one. We realize we are the map makers. In order to re-write your map, we need to fully understand the difference between Limiting and affirming beliefs.

A limiting belief says, *"If I express myself, I'll lose love."*

An affirmed belief says, *"I can be fully myself and still be loved."*

A limiting belief says, *"My needs are too much."*

An affirmed belief says, *"My needs are valid, and I have a right to honor them."*

Beliefs become powerful not because they're true, rather because we never question them. Yet, the moment we become curious, as true Wild Sensitives are, we begin to ask what we believe and why? It is in that moment those old beliefs begin to lose their grip.

You don't need anyone's permission to rewrite your map. You're not here to live by other people's limits, or expectations, you're here to make your own map that fits your own journey.

How to Examine a Belief: The 3 Red Flag Questions

Now that you understand how beliefs are formed, and how deeply they can shape our emotional landscape, it's time to learn how to examine them. Because not all beliefs are worth keeping.

Think of your mind as a map room, full of maps. Some ancient and dusty, others freshly printed. Some were useful once but are now outdated. And we believe them as useful only because you've never given yourself permission to question them. So how do you know which beliefs are accurate, and which are leading us astray?

You look for red flags. These are the quiet indicators that a belief may not be grounded in your truth, your growth, or aligned with your values. They are the whispers that say: *"This might not belong to me anymore."*

1. Where did I get this belief?
This question uncovers origin. Was the belief taught to you? Inherited? Formed during a specific experience? Or does it feel like it's always just... been there?

If your answer is, *"I don't know, I've just always believed this,"* that's your first red flag.

This suggests the belief may have slipped in unconsciously, through repetition, conditioning, fear, or survival. That doesn't make it "bad," but it does mean it deserves a closer look.

If your answer is clear and grounded, *"I learned this from experience,"* or *"It came from a moment of clarity,"* that's a good sign. But you still need to ask the next two questions.

2. Can I explain why I hold this belief?
This question reveals intention. Is the belief rooted in logic, values, or lived experience, or is it driven by fear, shame, or avoidance?

If your answer is, *"I'm not sure"* or *"It just feels safer that way,"* That's your second red flag.

This may indicate the belief is rooted in emotional protection, not conscious choice. Often, limiting beliefs stay in place not because they're true, but because they keep us "safe" from discomfort, vulnerability, or risk.

If your answer includes real examples, thoughtful reflection, or emotional clarity, you're likely moving toward an affirmed belief, but there's one more question.

3. Why is this belief of value to me?

This is the heart question. Why does this belief matter to you? What role does it play in your life? Does it move you toward expansion, or keep you locked in protection?

If your answer is vague, *"I guess it helps me avoid getting hurt"* or *"I don't know"*, that's your third red flag this is often the clearest sign of a limiting belief, a belief that is not aligned with your current values or goals, but one you continue to carry out of habit, fear, or inherited expectation and you should work at replacing it with an affirmed belief. If your answer is aligned with your growth, *"It helps me stay connected to what matters,"* or *"It reflects who I'm becoming,"* That's a strong indication of an affirmed belief, congratulations.

Here are two examples, one limiting and one affirmed, that we run through the 3-question framework:

Limiting Belief Example: *"I'm not the kind of person who can lead."*

1. Where did you get this belief? *"I don't know… I've always felt that way."*

Red flag: No origin points or conscious memory. The belief was likely absorbed through a negative experience, not chosen.

2. Can you explain why you hold that belief? *"I get nervous in groups and worry I'll mess up."*

Red flag: Based in fear, not principle or value.

3. Why is this belief of value to you? *"I guess it protects me from embarrassing myself…"*

Red flag: The belief serves avoidance, not growth.

Conclusion: This belief is limiting. It's vague, fear-based, and self-protective. It keeps the person from stepping into possibility or being seen fully.

Affirmed Belief Example: *"Honest conversations create deeper relationships."*

1. Where did you get this belief? *"I learned it through years of coaching training and personal growth work. The moments I've had the most connection have always come after honest dialogue."*

Clear origin, rooted in lived experience.

2. Can you explain why you hold that belief? *"Because every time I've opened up honestly, even when it was hard, it led to more trust, clarity, or healing. Even if the result wasn't perfect, the connection deepened."*

Grounded in reflection and emotional truth.

3. Why is this belief of value to you? *"Because connection is one of my core values. I'd rather have real relationships than superficial ones, even if it's harder. This belief helps me show up authentically."*

Anchored in values and personal vision.

Conclusion: This is an affirmed belief, it is clear, intentional, and supportive of the person's deeper purpose.

Beliefs are not just thoughts you think. They are agreements you've made, sometimes unknowingly, with your past, your pain, or the world around you. But here's the good news: All agreements can be reviewed, rewritten, and reclaimed.

Even if a belief once served you, it might no longer fit who you are becoming. And as a Wild Sensitive, someone with deep emotional intuition and a craving for growth, you have every right to re-evaluate and evolve your beliefs.

Your Compass and Magnet

For us, as Wild Sensitives, those who live with both the depth of high sensitivity and the craving of high sensation seeking, values are not just ideals or aspirations. They are our internal compass, the steady instrument that helps us navigate a world that often feels overwhelming, overstimulating, or misaligned.

Our values help us discern not just what to do, but how to live. They guide our relationships, shape our priorities, and offer direction when life gets messy. Values tell us what matters, not in theory, but in practice. They help us know when to say yes, when to say no, and when to walk away. For the Wild Sensitive, whose nervous system is constantly processing layers of meaning, emotion, and potential, having clear values is not optional, it's essential.

Imagine your values as a compass, beautifully crafted, calibrated to your truth. This compass doesn't point north in a geographical sense; it points toward alignment. Toward what feels right in your bones. But like any compass, it can be distorted. And the biggest distortion for Highly Sensitive individuals is fear.

Fear is the magnet.

It doesn't destroy the compass; it simply throws it off course.
Fear tells us:

- *Follow the map you were given.*
- *Stay on the path others tell us to stay on, it's safer.*
- *Listen to what you're told, we know better.*
- *If you follow your own path, you'll be alone.*

When fear gets too close, our compass doesn't stop working, it just points us toward false safety instead of authentic direction. And over time, if we keep making decisions based on avoidance or approval, we end up far from ourselves. As Living Adventurers, we have come to know fear as an acronym, Face Every Adversity Realistically. While there are somethings we should fear, most of our fears are based on unrealistic beliefs.

Our job as Wild Sensitives is to keep the magnet of fear small, and as far from our compass as possible. We all carry fear, that's human. But we don't have to let it sit on top of our navigation system. We must learn to recognize when fear is influencing our choices, and gently set it aside, returning instead to what our values tell us is true.

Not All Compasses Are Built the Same

Some of us were handed compasses that never really worked. Our values were shaped not by reflection, but by survival. We internalized values that were handed down, not chosen. This is why some people spend their lives chasing status, certainty, or approval, not because these are bad things, but because they were told these are the things that matter most. In the past, many years ago, survival took on a much different meaning. Back then our paths were limited. Today we have far more choices and the freedom to follow our own path if we desire.

Over time, these unconscious or poorly constructed values begin to crack. They lead to burnout, identity confusion, or chronic dissatisfaction, especially for Wild Sensitives who are wired to seek meaning, not just motion.

Examples of Poorly Constructed Personal Values:

"I must always be liked."
Leads to people-pleasing, burnout, and self-erasure.

"Be the best at everything."
Fuels perfectionism, constant comparison, and anxiety.

"Never upset anyone."
Prevents boundary-setting and emotional honesty.

"Keep the peace at all costs."
Encourages conflict avoidance and emotional suppression.

"Winning means worthiness."
Disconnects self-worth from inner truth and overemphasizes external validation.

These are not evil values. Many are protective. But they're not sustainable. They don't nourish our deeper needs as Wild Sensitive individuals. They keep us stuck in the Safe Zone, never truly feeling either comfort or growth.

Examples of Healthy, Aligned Personal Values:

"Authenticity over approval."
Encourages self-expression and fosters real connection.

"Growth over perfection."
Invites curiosity, learning, and emotional resilience.

"Honest communication, even when it's hard."
Builds trust and prevents resentment.

"Freedom with responsibility."
Honors the Sensation Seekers craving for expansion, while staying grounded.

"Rest is sacred."
Validates the sensitive system's need for recovery and balance.

These values don't just sound nice, they feel right. They support the unique rhythm of the Wild Sensitive. They allow us to move through life not as a reaction, but with intention.

Returning to Your True North

When you begin to consciously name and live by your values, something profound shifts. Decision-making gets clearer. Self-respect deepens. And the emotional confusion so common to the true wild sensitive life begins to untangle. Your compass becomes reliable, not because life gets easier, but because your direction becomes clearly yours. Ultimately, having sound core values saves energy, mentally, physically and emotionally.

The more you check in with your values, the more easily you can recognize when fear has crept in and distorted your path. And the more you live in alignment, the more access you gain to the Goldilocks Zone, where life feels 'Just-Right'.

You don't need to build a perfect compass. You just need a compass built for you, then you need to start listening to it.

Your Purpose

Our desires are not just luxuries that get lost under our needs and wants in life. For the Wild Sensitive, desire is our purpose in motion. It is the inner spark that lights the path forward, not just telling us what we want, they remind us why we're here. Desires are not shallow wants; they are soul-level signals. They are how our deeper self-communicates with us about what makes life worth living. Whether it's the desire to create, to connect, to understand, to explore, or to be seen, these longings are what make our experience rich, meaningful, and alive.

Desire, for all its beauty, must be handled with care. Especially for those of us who feel everything intensely and crave more from life, it's easy to dream in sweeping, expansive visions only to feel paralyzed when those visions feel impossibly far away. When a desire remains out of reach for too long, our nervous system begins to lose trust. We can become emotionally fatigued, disconnected, or discouraged, not because we've lost our purpose, but because the path to it feels ungraspable.

This is why achievable desires matter so deeply. They give us momentum. They restore faith. They become fuel we can actually use. Big dreams, like living on Mars, writing a bestselling book, or becoming a world-changing leader, are not wrong or unrealistic. But they require scaffolding. We need smaller, grounded desires to pave the way. A longing like, *"Someday I want to live on Mars,"* becomes reachable through desires like, *"I desire to learn to fly a plane,"* or *"I desire to study science,"* or *"I desire to explore what it feels like to look at the stars from the desert."* These stepping-stone desires move us closer to the dream without overwhelming us. They offer us access. They offer us a purpose we can act on now.

Without desires we can't actually move forward; thus, losing connection to our purpose. The fire dims. We may still crave, but we stop reaching. We protect ourselves from hope because hope, when unmet, starts to feel like uncomfortable pain. But when we shape our desires into forms that are achievable, even if small, even if slow, something profound happens. We begin to believe again. We begin to move. And in that motion, we feel alive.

For Wild Sensitives, this alignment is essential. Because when we are without purpose, without desire we can pursue, we can fall into apathy, bore-out, depression and victimization. But when our desires are clear and within reach, we become anchored. Motivated. Energized. We remember why we exist. Not to perform. Not to please. But to experience, fully and freely.

Healthy desires sound like: *"I desire to feel strong in my body." "I desire to speak my truth without fear." "I desire to travel somewhere that awakens something in me."* These aren't shallow goals, they are rooted calls toward aliveness. And every time we move toward one of them, we are reaffirming our purpose. We are saying, *I am here. I am becoming. I am listening to what life is calling me toward.*

Desires are not distractions. They are the directions in which you need to travel. They are not selfish. They are sacred. They are how your sensitive sensation seeking soul reminds you that there is more and that you are allowed to move toward it.

Your Destination

In the journey as a Wild Sensitive, we too need goals to achieve. Yet, our goals are not mere checkboxes or finish lines, they are the very thing that give shape and structure to our growth. Just as our values guide us like a compass and our desires give us purpose, our personal goals become the destinations that mark our success. When we learn to set the destinations of our life, tangibly, measurable, and realistic, we truly become empowered.

But here's what many forget: our destinations must also be reachable in order to remain motivating. If they're too far, too vague, or too grand without structure, it can overwhelm our nervous system and that's especially true for HSP's. A desire without an attainable goal becomes a weight rather than a wind. That's why our destinations, just like our desires, must be both achievable and measurable.

This doesn't mean we cannot desire big. It means we learn how to build toward our big desires in parts, with each step intentionally designed to support our emotional, mental, and physical needs. We call those parts milestones.

Milestones are not just progress markers, they are moments of meaning. Each one exists for a different reason. Some are practical. Some are celebratory. And some are deeply personal. For the Wild Sensitive, who processes life with greater depth and complexity, these milestones are not optional, they are essential for maintaining emotional momentum and avoiding overwhelm.

Here are the core types of milestones we as Wild sensitives need:

Celebration Milestones: These are joy points. A chance to Pause, Enquire, Reflect, Recognize and Respond (PERRR) how far you've come. These help reinforce beliefs, build confidence, and create space for gratitude.

"I launched my first podcast episode, I'm proud of this step, let's go celebrate at our favorite restaurant."

Knowledge Milestones: These are moments to gather knowledge and information that will equip you for the next leg of the journey.

"Before I pitch my idea, I want to understand my audience better."

Tool Development Milestones: These are training grounds, opportunities to build skills, practice new techniques, or try new tools before moving forward.

"I want to practice public speaking before applying for that leadership position. I think I will sign up to a Toastmaster Class"

Rest & Recuperation Milestones: These are sacred pauses for renewal. They honor the Wild Sensitive truth: we cannot sustainably charge ahead. We must stop to breathe, recover, and reconnect to our inner rhythm.

"After completing this phase, I'll take a solo retreat to decompress."

Each of these milestones is a mini-destination, and each one holds just as much value as the final destination. The story of our journey isn't just found at the end, it evolves in every one of these meaningful steps along the way.

Why Measurable Goals Matter

A goal, to be effective, must be clear. That means we must be able to define it in real terms. Not *"I want to feel better,"* but *"I want to reduce my daily anxiety levels by learning breathwork and using it 3 times a week."* Not *"I want to be successful,"* but *"I want to start and sustain my first creative business within the next 12 months."*

Measurable goals help the Wild Sensitive track progress without becoming lost in abstraction. They offer grounded reassurance, proof that we are, indeed, moving forward. They allow us to calibrate, reflect, and pivot with purpose.

The Journey Matters as Much as the Destination

As Wild Sensitives, we know the danger of linear living, the constant trudging toward retirement or recognition, without ever stopping to live. We've seen what happens to those who grind toward a goal while forgetting to savor the sunrises, the conversations, the personal awakenings along the way.

We are not here to merely arrive. We are here to become. One milestone at a time. Planning your goals with intention doesn't just ensure you reach the end, it ensures you gather meaningful stories, rich self-understanding, and emotional sovereignty as you go. That's what makes a Wild Sensitive life so powerful, the understanding that the journey is not just preparation for the destination; the journey is the destination, unfolding in stages.

So, when you sit down to name your goals, don't ask only, "Where do I want to go?" Ask also, "Who do I want to be while getting there?" And "What parts of this journey deserve to be celebrated, studied, practiced, or accepted?" The destination you're heading toward will be all the richer for it.

Chapter 7

The Four Pillars of Transformation
Knowledge, Tools, Skill, and Technique

"Knowledge lights the path, but without tools we stumble. Tools shape us, but without skill we misuse them. Skill gives us strength, but without technique, we freeze in the storm. True transformation begins not when we collect these pieces, but when we learn to carry them, wisely, wildly, and well."
The Living Adventurers

When navigating emotional or mental barriers as Wild Sensitives, whether rooted in trauma, belief systems, nervous system dysregulation, or relational dynamics, we have found that healing and mastery of one's understanding is not always clear. Many offering guidance cast out terms such as Knowledge, Tools, Skills and Techniques, without truly explaining the difference or how they intertwine with one another.

We understand, as Wild Sensitive's, we need much more detail than just words, we need explanation to truly connect the dots. We also understand, these are not just abstract concepts; they are the scaffolding that holds us up as we shift from reactive survival to responsive sovereignty. From internal fragmentation to external mastery. This, in itself is part of the journey.

While knowledge, tools, skills and techniques are all separate, yet they are also layered. To move through these layers with intention, we must understand each of their foundational components that empower any true transformation.

Knowledge, the Awareness That Sparks the Journey

Knowledge is where transformation begins, and it always starts with awareness. Awareness is the moment you notice a pattern, a struggle, or a repeated emotional response. Those that wish to remain unempowered will react with avoidance, rejection or defensiveness upon becoming aware. While those that have opened the door to empowerment think, "There must be more to this."

This begins your journey, a path we as Living Adventurers have traveled many times and have guided others through. Yet, to continue this journey, one must begin to develop an interest or curiosity, not wondering, where does this path lead, but believing it leads to where they need to go. Next, they must find the courage to take just one step forward. Those that attempt this journey on their own may succeed, yet we have seen time and time again, they reach a certain point before giving up. They typically reach a point on the path that challenges them too much or have gotten lost along the way. They get frustrated, even afraid to keep trying.

Many, begin the journey with only awareness, blindly feeling their way through. Just by reading this book, you are proving to yourself, you are seeking knowledge, before venturing to the deep, which is exactly what you need to do.

After the courage to take that first step comes the curiosity to obtain more information. While some may read one book, those that have read a hundred books would be far more knowledgeable. But knowledge alone is not wisdom. This we learned from a Buddhist monk, while traveling through the jungles of Laos. The monk explained that true wisdom is the acquisition of knowledge intertwined with practical experience and understanding how the two connect with one another.

As Wild Sensitives, this is our calling, our mission in life, to acquire as much wisdom as we can so we can live meaningful, fulfilling lives. Read the books, take the training, watch the videos, and learn as much knowledge as you can, while not letting that stop you from experiencing life.

As part of our acquisition of knowledge, we must learn to incrementally step forward. As we do, we observe, we feel, and we process. In other words, we PERRR (Explained in Chapter 10). All of this knowledge acquisition should take place either in our 'Goldilocks' Zone or our 'Comfort' Zone (Explained in Chapter 9).

As we discussed in chapter 6, we need to learn what beliefs we hold and why. What our core values and why. What desires we have and why. Then what our key personal goals in life are. In learning this, we discover our direction, then develop our map and compass with purpose for heading there. Without this knowledge, we can easily become lost.

Knowledge also helps us gain insight, not just facts, but a better understanding as we move through the path. We learn psychological aspects such as fear responses, attachment theory, cognitive distortions. We learn emotional fluency and are better able to name and track our own emotions and the emotions of others. We open the door to self-inquiry, exploring personal histories as related to our belief systems and value mapping.

Knowledge has the power to either reinforce what we already believe, or to gently challenge and expand it. Sometimes, it affirms our existing constructs, even the limiting ones, leading us to say, *"See, I was right to stay small."* That's an unempowered lens, one that keeps us circling the familiar. But other times, knowledge cracks something open: *"Maybe I'm not broken. Maybe I'm just untrained."* That's an empowered shift, one that makes room for growth.

Knowledge can either liberate or limit, depending on the questions we're willing to ask, and the values that shape our desire to learn. Insight alone doesn't free us, it's how we relate to it that determines whether we stay confined or begin to expand.

The wonderful thing about acquiring knowledge, is our minds hold an unlimited capacity to store it. But here's the important thing to remember, make sure the knowledge you are storing is accurate, reliable and constantly being updated. Because, outdated knowledge means, outdated beliefs.

What Are Personal Development Tools?

Turning knowledge into lived transformation, one choice at a time. Personal development is often talked about like a mindset, a lifestyle, or a philosophy. But if we strip it back to its essence, personal development is about growth, and growth doesn't happen through awareness alone. Growth requires application. That's where tools come in.

If knowledge is awareness, then tools are what help us implement that awareness into our everyday lives. They are the bridge between what we know and how we live. Tools give structure to change, rhythm to regulation, and traction to transformation. Without tools, we are left with ideas, beautiful, inspiring ideas, but no real way to embody them.

As Wild Sensitives, we often see deeply. We read emotional subtext. We reflect. We learn. But knowing how to change, how to show up differently, or how to support our nervous system when it begins to fray, that requires something more tactile, repeatable, and specific. That requires tools.

What Makes Something a "Tool"?

A personal development tool is any intentional method, structure, or intention that helps you:
- Regulate your nervous system
- Make aligned decisions

- Build emotional resilience
- Process experiences
- Maintain your sovereignty
- Deepen your connection with yourself and others
- Translate inner shifts into outer action

Tools can be mental, emotional, somatic, behavioral, or environmental. They can be physical objects or repeatable efforts. What defines a tool is not how complex it is, it's how skillfully it supports your growth.

Just like a skilled artisan selects the right tool for shaping wood, clay, or stone, a Wild Sensitive must learn which tools shape their inner landscape best. The hammer has its place. But if you're working with glass, you need a brush. The same is true in personal development: every situation, every emotional state, every stage of growth requires a different kind of support.

Why Tools Matter for Wild Sensitives

As Wild Sensitives, we live with what we call the "paradox of the Wild Sensitive," we crave stimulation but can burn out quickly. We love meaning but drown in superficial engagement. We long to expand but are easily dysregulated. Our wiring is rich, complex, and deeply alive, but it also means that mainstream self-help advice rarely fits.

That's why personal development tools matter even more for us. They give us the custom support structure needed to hold our growth, not force it. They help us regulate in real-time, choose intentionally, and stretch at a pace that honors both our sensitivity and our desire for bold living.

Some Examples from This Backpack

Let's look at a few of the tools you're going to learn more about in this book, each one crafted to support a specific kind of growth for Wild Sensitives like you. All of these we discuss in more detail in chapter 10.

The 7-P Rule
Proper **P**rior **P**lanning **P**revents **P**iss **P**oor **P**erformance
This foundational tool is more than a mantra; it's essential in preparing for transformation. It reminds us that change begins with understanding ourselves, our needs, and the terrain ahead, not with rushing into action. Without this tool, even the best practices may feel like misfires. With it, we build the right mindset for sustainable growth.

The 3-R Rule
Recognize – **R**egulate – **R**eclaim
A real-time nervous system tool for interrupting emotional reactivity. You Recognize the trigger, Regulate your body, and Reclaim your voice. Perfect for emotionally charged interactions where old habits or beliefs threaten to hijack your clarity.

The P.E.R.R.R. Method
Pause – **E**nquire – **R**eflect – **R**ecognize – **R**espond
A decision-making framework for moments of overwhelm or confusion. It helps you slow down and sort through inner noise before taking action. For Wild Sensitives, whose minds and hearts often flood quickly, this tool provides a calm, step-by-step path to clarity.

The L.I.G.H.T. Method
Listen – **I**nquire – **G**row – **H**old Values – **T**ransform
A communication tool designed to maintain connection while protecting emotional sovereignty. This tool is especially powerful in hard conversations or moments where you risk losing yourself in relational dynamics.

Emotional Landscape Mapping
A visual/emotional framework that helps you identify which of the six internal "zones" you're in from Safe to Risk. This tool empowers Wild Sensitives to respond to their emotional state with care, instead of reacting from disconnection or confusion.

Somatic Grounding & Breathwork

Tools that bring you back to your body when emotion or sensation begins to overwhelm. These techniques regulate the nervous system without needing cognitive processing, essential for moments when thinking feels impossible.

Curiosity Over Conformity

A micro-tool for social environments, encouraging you to stay inquisitive before adapting. This protects Wild Sensitives from over-blending or losing themselves in group dynamics, allowing them to remain present and authentic.

Anchor Objects & Sensory Tools

These are tangible, tactile items that serve as gentle reminders of safety, comfort, or presence, especially when the nervous system feels overwhelmed. Whether it's a grounding stone you hold in your palm, a familiar scent that evokes calm, or a soft texture you run your fingers across, these tools offer non-verbal pathways to regulation. In moments when talking feels too much or practices feel out of reach, anchor objects act as quiet allies. They speak the language of the body, helping to reorient your awareness, slow your breath, and remind you: you are here, you are safe, and you are held.

Reflective Debriefing

A post-experience tool for integrating emotional events, conversations, or overstimulating environments. Reflective prompts help the Wild Sensitive clear emotional residue, preventing rumination or internalized shame.

Tools Are Not the Goal - Skillfulness Is

It's important to remember: having tools doesn't mean you know how to use them. Just like someone can buy a full set of woodworking gear and still ruin their first project, personal development tools require guidance, practice, reflection, and patience.

You might try a grounding method and feel nothing. That doesn't mean it failed. It means you're learning. You might use a decision filter and still feel uncertain. That doesn't mean you're broken. It means you're growing.

And no tool, no matter how good, replaces the need for context. Not every breathwork technique works for every trauma survivor. Not every journaling prompt lands in every emotional state. That's why we encourage you to return again and again to the 7-P Rule: prepare, personalize, and pace yourself.

The Inner Craftsman

Ultimately, tools don't change your life. You do! However, tools can support that change. They give us something tangible to work with, helping us become more aligned. You are the craftsman of your own becoming. Your tools? They are your customized trusted set, chosen not because someone said they'd work, but because you tried them, shaped them, and found what fits.

So don't be in a rush to "master" them. Let them live with you. Let them teach you how to work with yourself, not against yourself. That's what makes them powerful. Not their novelty, but their fit.

What Do We Mean by Skill?

The more we practice, the more we belong to ourselves. If tools are the means, skill is the mastery of use. In the context of personal development, skill is the practiced ability to apply a tool effectively and appropriately, again and again, in real time, and in ever more nuanced situations. A tool alone doesn't create change. It's how you use it, when you use it, and how consistently you use it that makes the difference. More importantly, it's what you use it on. Going back to we wouldn't use a hammer on glass, in most cases, yet there are the rare few we would, depending on the situation.

This is what turns theory into transformation. Skill is what lets a breath regulate your body. It's what helps a boundary land without guilt. It's what makes a micro-novelty practice wake up your curiosity instead of overwhelm your nervous system. Skill is the difference between knowing a method and living it.

Skill Is Developed Through Practice

Like any meaningful craft, skill doesn't arrive, it is built. You wouldn't expect to play a song beautifully the first time you touch a piano. Nor would you expect to hike a mountain without training your muscles. The same is true with emotional tools, boundary setting, regulation, and self-reflection. You practice. You refine. You return.

The more you practice using a specific tool, like a grounding breath, a somatic check-in, or a decision framework, the more natural and effective it becomes. The response time gets shorter. The nervous system learns the rhythm. The muscles of emotional agility grow stronger. Eventually, you don't just know the tool, it becomes part of your way of being.

But What If I Struggle to Build Skill?

Many people, especially Wild Sensitives, find that building skills take time, compassion, and patience. Some people develop skills quickly, especially if the tool is aligned with how they naturally learn or engage with the world. Others need more repetition, more regulation, or more trust in their own process. Some, need a guide to assist them. This doesn't mean something is wrong. In fact, the greatest obstacles to developing skill are rarely about ability, they are about belief.

Limiting Beliefs That Can Block Skill Development:
- *"I should already know how to do this."*
- *"I'm too sensitive to manage this kind of discomfort."*
- *"If I was stronger, I wouldn't need this tool."*
- *"If I can't get it right the first time, I must be failing."*
- *"Other people don't need this, so maybe I'm broken."*

These thoughts don't reflect your truth. They reflect your conditioning, old messages passed down by family systems, school structures, cultural norms, or trauma imprints. They are learned limits. And like any belief, they can be unlearned.

Skill Can Be Rewritten, If You Choose To

This is one of the most hopeful truths in personal development. Skills are not fixed traits. They are trainable capacities. And beliefs are not permanent truths. They are stories you can revise. If you've struggled with consistency, confidence, or integration, pause before shaming yourself.

Ask Yourself:
- *"Is this really about my ability… or about my belief in my ability?"*
- *"Who taught me what success should look like?"*
- *"What would change if I gave myself permission to learn slowly?"*

You don't have to believe every voice in your head. You get to become the voice of encouragement and curiosity inside you. You get to return to the tool. You get to practice. And every time you do, you become more skilled at becoming yourself.

So remember, you're not just collecting tools, you're building a life. One skillful choice at a time. You don't have to rush mastery, you just have to stay in relationship with the tools long enough to let them shape you. That's how skill is born, not from perfection, but from practice.

What Do We Mean by Technique?

Where skill becomes flexible, responsive, and wise. If knowledge is awareness, and tools are what help you apply that awareness, and skill is the practiced ability to use that tool well, then technique is the art of adapting that skill to different conditions.

It's one thing to know how to use a tool. It's another to be able to use that tool effectively across varied environments, challenges, and emotional terrain. That's where technique lives, in the dynamic, applied wisdom of practice under pressure, variation, and real-life unpredictability.

Technique Is Adapted Skill
- **Knowledge**: Being able to choose which tools apply to which situations
- **Tool**: What you use (e.g., breathwork, boundary script, reflection framework)
- **Skill**: How well you've practiced using that tool in one or two familiar ways
- **Technique:** How skillfully can you use that tool across multiple settings, conditions, and emotional states

Skill makes the tool effective. Technique makes the skill transferable. This matters deeply for Wild Sensitives, because our inner and outer environments change rapidly. One moment we're calm and connected. The next, overstimulated, emotionally flooded, or sensing tension in someone else's tone before they've spoken a word. If we've only practiced a tool in stillness, it may not hold under stress. But when we've built technique, that same tool becomes a trusted ally anywhere.

The Adventure Analogy: Las Vegas to Alaska on a Motorbike
Let's say you want to ride from Las Vegas to Alaska and back on a motorcycle. That's over 10,000 miles. A stunning, rugged journey. High temperatures, remote towns, unpredictable weather, and a whole spectrum of terrain.

You start with:
- **Knowledge**: You study the route. You learn about elevation changes, border crossings, wildlife, fuel stops, weather patterns. And which would be the best motorbike for such a journey.

- **Tool:** You get the bike. It's well-built, capable, powerful, the perfect match for the terrain.

- **Skill**: You learn to ride the bike on smooth pavement. Learning how to shift gears, twist the throttle and apply the brakes. You become skilled... in that setting.

But let's go further. Let's strap your gear on. Then ride in the wind. Then in the rain. What happens when the road turns to gravel? When the fog rolls in and you can't see? When your partner's on the back and the balance shifts?

It's not just skill you need, it's technique, and it only develops through variation, repetition, and resilience.

Applying This to Personal Growth

Let's translate the analogy into emotional practice.

Say your tool is the 3-R Rule, Recognize – Regulate – Reclaim, (We will define this tool better in chapter 10). You first practice it in a calm setting, maybe after a journaling prompt or with your coach. That's where skill begins.

To build technique, you do this:
- Practice the 3-R Rule when triggered by a family member
- Use it during a live conflict with a partner
- Apply it while overwhelmed in a social setting
- Try it after receiving critical feedback at work
- Adapt it to your child's meltdown
- Use it mid-exposure during a creative risk
- Practice in low-energy states, high-energy states, and unexpected disruptions

Now the technique becomes yours, not just in thought, but in nervous system memory. You don't need to search for the tool, your body starts to reach for it because it's been trained across varied terrains.

Why Technique Matters for Wild Sensitives

We are multi-layered beings. Our needs shift moment to moment. Our nervous systems respond to tone, texture, light, emotion, energy, and unspoken expectations. Which means: no two situations feel exactly the same, even if they look similar on the surface.

If we only develop skill in controlled or ideal circumstances, we may freeze, collapse, or disconnect when the terrain gets rough. But with technique, we become adaptive and responsive, not just reactive. In developing techniques, we are better able to:

- Set boundaries not just in writing, but in real-time
- Regulate breath not just on a yoga mat, but in a crowded room
- Reflect not just when journaling, but while standing in a triggered state
- Navigate conflict not with a script, but with flexible integrity

Technique lets you stay sovereign in more situations, because you're not relying on ideal conditions to show up as yourself.

You don't need to become a master overnight. But you do get to become a practitioner, someone who uses what they know in the real world, not just in safe containers. And the more you apply your skills in new settings, the more confidence grows, not because everything goes smoothly, but because you've learned how to adapt, recover, and recalibrate. Technique is not about performance. It's about readiness. It's about trust.

It's about becoming the kind of person who, no matter what terrain they walk into, has the inner resources to walk through it wisely. That's the art of personal development in motion. That's the Wild Sensitive way.

Chapter 8

The Four Intelligences of the Wild Sensitive

IQ, EQ, PQ, SQ: The Hidden Languages of the Empowered Sensitive

"When your mind, heart, resilience, and intuition align, you stop breaking yourself into parts just to fit in. You begin to move through the world as whole, wise, and wildly alive. This is the power of a Wild Sensitive fully integrated."
The Living Adventurers

When we looked across the vast landscape of material being produced that helps us understand the Highly Sensitive and the High Sensation Seeker, we hardly ever hear of the measurable intelligences we can actually apply. So much of the discussion centers around coping, calming down, or managing "triggers." Rarely does it point toward what's possible when we understand our inner wiring as intelligent, powerful, and ready to lead.

As Wild Sensitives, we've spent years swimming in a sea of labels that miss the mark. Introvert. Overthinker. People pleaser. Too intense. Too sensitive. Too much. Too emotional. Too inconsistent. For many of us, language became a kind of prison, reflecting only fragments of who we are. We were called dramatic when we were emotionally honest. Dismissed as detached when we were simply overwhelmed. Praised for our adventurous spirit one day and judged for needing solitude the next. Not because we were inconsistent, but because the world lacks language for nuance.

The danger of these labels isn't just that they're incomplete, they're misleading. They start to shape how we see ourselves. We begin filtering our choices through them, mistaking the box for the truth. When someone tells us we're too sensitive, we begin to question our natural boundaries. When we're praised for being energetic, we override the need to rest. When we're told we're introverted, we avoid the very adventures that might light us up.

Bit by bit, we lose connection with our own rhythm. We stop trusting our preferences. We silence the internal voice that actually knows what we're ready for. The answer isn't better boxes, it's better language. One that honors our complexity. One that says: *you're not broken. You've just never been spoken to in a language that reflects your truth.*

That language begins here, with a framework we call the Four Intelligences of the Wild Sensitive. In this chapter, we'll explore the four well-known intelligences as related to us, the Wild Sensitive. IQ (Intellectual Quotient), the capacity for logic, analysis, and problem-solving. EQ (Emotional Intelligence), our ability to understand, express, and manage emotional dynamics. PQ (Positive Intelligence®), the strength of our mental fitness, resilience, and mindset. And we will also discuss something we, have come to recognize through years of lived experience and guiding others on this path as SQ (Sensory Intelligence®), a deep attunement to subtlety, to the body's signals, to unspoken energies and emotional landscapes. This is the intelligence of nervous system fluency, of knowing without needing proof.

For Wild Sensitives, these four intelligences are not abstract concepts. They're alive within us, often in heightened form. But without understanding, without guidance, they can feel like burdens instead of gifts. IQ becomes overthinking. EQ becomes emotional flooding. PQ is replaced by inner sabotage. And SQ gets mistaken for anxiety when it's actually intuitive wisdom.

This chapter isn't about self-improvement for performance. It's about self-activation for alignment. These intelligences are vital parts of you. When understood and integrated, they help you lead, not just others, but yourself, through complexity with clarity.

IQ – The Architect of Clarity

At its core, IQ, or Intelligence Quotient, refers to our capacity for logical reasoning, abstract thinking, pattern recognition, memory, and problem-solving. It is the engine of cognitive clarity, the part of us that organizes the chaos, makes sense of systems, and builds mental frameworks that allow us to navigate complexity. HSPs, particularly those who are also HSS, IQ takes on a deeper dimension.

One of the defining characteristics of high sensitivity, as described by Dr. Elaine Aron, is Depth of Processing, the natural tendency to reflect, analyze, and integrate information more deeply than the average person. This trait isn't just emotional; it is profoundly cognitive. HSPs often notice subtleties others miss, then spend more time mentally and emotionally evaluating their meaning. This slow, rich engagement with ideas and experiences is like a form of neurological composting, it produces more intricate mental models, richer connections, and deeper insights over time. In short, it naturally cultivates the very capacities that IQ is designed to measure.

For the Wild Sensitive, a high IQ doesn't simply mean being "smart." It's not about test scores or memorizing facts. Instead, it often manifests as deep pattern recognition, philosophical inquiry, an ability to hold paradox, and a hunger for intellectual exploration. These are the HSPs who spiral into existential wonder at age ten, who read ancient myths and ask what they reveal about human nature, who see how seemingly unrelated threads in the world, politics, weather, music, emotion, are subtly interwoven.

But this gift, like all gifts, has its shadows. Depth of Processing, when unregulated or unbalanced, can lead to analysis paralysis, where decision-making becomes exhausting because the mind won't stop running scenarios. It can lead to existential overwhelm, where the search for meaning turns into a burden instead of a guide. The sensitive nervous system, when paired with high cognitive output, can burn itself out if emotional regulation and somatic awareness are not also cultivated.

Many Wild Sensitives can often find themselves mentally overstimulated when they begin to juggle too many tasks or conversations, especially if the content is emotionally charged or lacks depth. You may notice yourself ruminating, mentally replaying past dialogues or rehearsing future ones, because your brain is wired not to skip over details, rather it is naturally wired for depth. You crave intellectual substance and complexity, yet feel depleted when it isn't paired with emotional management or downtime. These are signs of a strong cognitive engine in need of rhythm and refinement.

To strengthen and support your IQ as a Wild Sensitive, consider engaging in practices that both honor your mental hunger and protect your cognitive bandwidth. Choose one complex system, like psychology, ecosystems, mythology, or human design, and study it not just as theory, but as a mirror. Ask how it applies to your own life story. Journal recurring thought loops, not to fix them, but to see them more clearly. Give your mind intentional space to work, followed by intentional rest to recover. You are not a machine. Your brilliance thrives in cycles, not in nonstop output.

IQ for the Wild Sensitive is not about how much you know, it's about how you know. It is the part of you that seeks clarity amidst chaos, that finds shape in complexity. When integrated with your emotional, sensory, and positive intelligences, IQ becomes a tool of navigation, not just understanding. It helps you name the landscape of your inner and outer worlds so that you can move through them with purpose. For the

Wild Sensitive, a cultivated IQ is not just a sign of intelligence, it is a compass, pointing toward a life of meaning, insight, and mindful direction.

Understanding your IQ begins with curiosity, not comparison. These aren't measurements of your worth, they are insights into your wiring. Many unempowered Wild Sensitives shy away from conversations of a deep intellectual level, either because we've felt misunderstood by traditional systems or because their intelligence doesn't always show up in the ways society celebrates. But IQ is only one part of the story, and it deserves to be reclaimed as a piece of your self-awareness, not a judgment.

When you understand how you think, feel, sense, and respond, you begin to lead from wholeness. You begin to trust that your depth, your brilliance, and your intuition were never separate. They were always speaking in four different voices. Let's begin listening to each of them.

EQ – The Guardian of Empathy

Emotional Intelligence, or EQ, is the inner capacity to recognize, understand, regulate, and express emotions, both your own and those of others. Often described through five foundational pillars, self-awareness, self-regulation, motivation, empathy, and social skills, EQ is the intelligence of relationship. Not just with other people, but with ourselves. For many, it's a skill developed through practice and intention. But for Wild Sensitives, EQ begins as something much deeper. It starts as a felt experience, long before it's ever named or measured. It lives in our bones, our breath, our earliest memories.

Wild Sensitives are born with heightened emotional receptivity. We don't just observe emotions, we absorb them. We pick up on micro-shifts in tone, posture, energy, or silence before a single word is spoken. Our empathy isn't conceptual, it's cellular. We walk into rooms and feel sorrow that isn't ours. We anticipate tension, joy, grief, and need before it's verbalized. We sense when someone is hurting behind a smile, or retreating behind a raised voice. This is not over-sensitivity, it's refined attunement. Yet many of us were told we were *"too emotional," "too intense,"* or *"too much,"* when in truth, we were simply more perceptive.

This depth of emotional tracking is the foundation of emotional intelligence. Dr. Elaine Aron's research confirms that emotional responsiveness is a core feature of high sensitivity. But the real transformation happens when that natural responsiveness is paired with skillful regulation. Because while many HSPs feel deeply, not all know how to work with what they feel, or even identify whether it belongs to them. This is where EQ evolves from being a raw trait into a tool of wise emotional leadership.

For Wild Sensitives, emotional intelligence isn't just about managing emotions. It's about forming a partnership with them. Emotions aren't enemies to control or weaknesses to mask, they are the key to our inner selves. They are messengers, each one carrying information about our needs, boundaries, values, or alignment. Sadness may signal something unexpressed or unmet. Anger can alert us to a boundary that's been violated. Joy might point toward what nourishes us most. When we ask, *"What is this feeling trying to tell me?",* we begin shifting from overwhelm to insight. Emotions stop being something we drown in, and start becoming something we learn from.

Yet for many HSP-HSS individuals, emotional imbalance is common. The inner volume is turned up so high that the emotional body becomes flooded. Without strong EQ tools, our internal world becomes chaotic, crying unexpectedly, over-apologizing, avoiding conflict, or feeling shame for simply having emotions. We often hold space for others without remembering to hold space for ourselves. And the emotional overwhelm doesn't just stay inside, it lives in the body. We might feel tightness in the chest, constriction in the throat, pressure in the stomach, or a constant sense of being "full to the brim" with unsaid words or absorbed energy.

To deepen your emotional intelligence, start by developing an intentional relationship with your feelings. Begin each day or pause throughout it to check in with yourself: *"What am I feeling right now?"* And follow it with: *"What is this emotion asking of me?"* Let your inner landscape be a space of curiosity rather than judgment. Journal. Meditate. Move. Cry. Laugh. Express. Emotions want movement, not control.

Learn to distinguish between what you feel and what you've picked up from others. Ask: *"Is this mine to carry?"* When you feel overwhelmed by someone else's emotions, pause and gently return to your own center. Empathy is a gift, but when untethered, it can lead to enmeshment. Emotional intelligence allows you to remain compassionate without becoming consumed.

Your body can also become a teacher. Notice what happens in your chest when someone interrupts you. Notice what contracts in your gut when you say yes but mean no. Emotional intelligence is not just emotional knowledge, it's embodied awareness. Every time you breathe into discomfort instead of avoiding it, every time you name a feeling rather than suppressing it, you grow your EQ. Each of these small choices creates inner spaciousness where once there was only tension.

In the integrated life of a Wild Sensitive, EQ becomes your emotional compass. It helps you lead with compassion but stay anchored in self. It allows you to feel fully without losing yourself in the process. It's the quiet inner whisper that says: *"This matters,"* and the bold outer voice that declares: *"And I matter too."* It helps you navigate connection with clarity and protection, empathy and boundary, tenderness and truth.

When paired with IQ, PQ, and SQ, your EQ becomes more than a trait, it becomes a gateway to transformation. Because a well-developed emotional intelligence doesn't just help you survive your sensitivity, it helps you translate it into courage, leadership, and relational wisdom.

Cultivating your emotional intelligence isn't about becoming someone new, it's about becoming fluent in the language your heart already speaks. With practice, your EQ will become the calm center in the storm, the inner compass that keeps you aligned with your truth. And from that place, you don't just navigate the world more skillfully, you change it.

PQ – The Sage Within

Positive Intelligence®, or PQ, is the capacity to recognize and shift the mental patterns that either sabotage or support us. Coined by Shirzad Chamine, PQ is often described as the ratio of time your mind works for you versus the time it works against you. For Wild Sensitives, those of us who feel deeply, process rapidly, and seek meaning like oxygen, this is more than a mental fitness model. It's a lifeline. A survival strategy refined into a sacred art. It's how we make peace with the very mind that once made us feel unsafe.

Most Highly Sensitive People know what it feels like to be hijacked by their inner critic. That critical voice, the Judge, shows up not as a fleeting thought, but as a loop: relentless, familiar, embedded. It partners with other internal saboteurs like the Pleaser, the Avoider, the Hyper-Achiever, or the Controller. These voices may have helped us survive emotionally volatile homes, social rejection, or environments that punished sensitivity. They were adaptive once. They helped us stay small enough to avoid harm, helpful enough to be needed, perfect enough to escape criticism. But over time, what once protected us begins to limit us. These mental reflexes become bars in an invisible cage.

This is where PQ becomes transformative. It reframes mental fitness as something beyond forced positivity or false confidence. PQ is about reclaiming your inner landscape, turning your mind into a place that supports rather than sabotages your wellbeing. It's the daily practice of observing your thoughts, recognizing the patterns driven by fear or judgment, and shifting toward what Chamine calls the Sage perspective, centered, clear, curious, and compassionate.

For Wild Sensitives, PQ is the essential bridge between raw awareness and empowered action. Most of us already notice everything. We feel the mood in a room change before anyone speaks. We sense subtle power dynamics, hear what goes unsaid, and pick up emotional tones like frequencies. But without strong PQ, this perceptive gift can turn against us. We become flooded, frozen, or reactive. We doubt ourselves, spiral in shame, or seek external validation to soothe our inner unrest. But with practiced PQ, we develop what is called mental fitness: the capacity to pause, decode the pattern, and choose a new response.

The somatic experience of low PQ is often tension and contraction. It's a racing mind that won't settle. A knot in the stomach after social interaction. Sleepless nights replaying what you could have said better. It's the loop of over-apologizing, the dread of being misunderstood, the shame of feeling like you're "too much" again. Even joyful moments can be clouded by self-doubt or anticipatory anxiety. But with consistent PQ practice, these patterns soften. You begin to notice the saboteur as a part of you, not the truth of you. You build space between the thought and the reaction, the judgment and the identity.

PQ invites a new kind of intimacy with your inner world. It's not about perfection; it's about pattern recognition. When you feel a trigger arise, practice what Chamine calls a Sage rep: drop into the body. Touch a surface and notice the texture. Listen for a distant sound. Feel your breath in your nostrils. Let the moment be enough. These micro-moments of presence bring you out of narrative and into now. Over time, they retrain your brain toward calm, clarity, and choice.

When challenges arise, and they always will, PQ empowers us to ask different questions: *"What is the gift here?" "How can this grow me?" "What would my Sage say?"* These questions don't erase pain, but they transmute it. Journaling can become a powerful tool here. Try this practice: Write down a difficult situation. Identify which saboteur was triggered and how it reacted. Then write a second version from your Sage's voice, what would it say about what just happened? This isn't fantasy; it's mental rewiring. It shifts your mindset from fear to insight, from reaction to response.

In the life of a Wild Sensitive, PQ is what allows your IQ, EQ, and SQ to flourish. It keeps you from being swept away by emotional waves, mental loops, or sensory overload. Without PQ, our gifts can become burdens. But with it, those same gifts become tools for impact, leadership, and inner peace. Sensitivity becomes strategy.

PQ is the inner lighthouse, a steady flame that reminds you: you are not your saboteurs. You are the one who sees them. You are the one who chooses again. You are the one who can transform old mental habits into new neural pathways, into self-trust, into peace. The waves may still crash, but now, you have an anchor.

Engaging with this practice doesn't mean changing who you are. It means reclaiming your sensitivity as a gift, not something to manage, but something to master. When PQ aligns with your EQ, IQ, and SQ, your inner world shifts from chaos to coherence. You stop surviving your thoughts, and begin guiding them. And that's the real alchemy. With Positive Intelligence, you stop trying to escape your complexity, and start honoring it. You become the calm in your own storm. The lighthouse within. The quiet, unwavering center in a noisy, demanding world. That is the gift of PQ. That is the way of the Wild Sensitive.

SQ – The Inner Guide

Sensory Intelligence, or SQ, is the embodied awareness that arises from a finely attuned nervous system. For Highly Sensitive People, and especially for those who are also High Sensation Seekers, SQ is not just the ability to detect subtle stimuli; it's the deep, instinctive wisdom of the body. It's how we know before we know, how we feel what others miss, how we register energy, truth, or misalignment before language even enters the room.

Dr. Elaine Aron describes this trait as "sensitivity to subtle stimuli," and she's right, but we believe it goes deeper. SQ is not only about receiving more input; it's about how we process, interpret, and respond to that input. It lives in the spaces between logic and emotion. It's breath shifts, goosebumps, intuitive chills, stomach knots, and cellular knowing. It's the moment when something in you whispers, *"Pay attention,"* even when everything looks fine on the surface. It's the chill of truth, the buzz of a moment that matters, the quiet alarm of something that just doesn't feel safe.

In the life of a Wild Sensitive, a developed SQ shows up as powerful intuitive orientation. You can walk into a room and immediately feel the emotional temperature. You can sense fatigue before it becomes burnout. You might notice how light shifts your mood, how certain fabrics agitate or soothe your system, how crowded places make your skin buzz. Nature might recalibrate you instantly, the rustle of leaves, the scent of rain, the warmth of sunlight on your face grounding you more deeply than words ever could. This is not fragility. This is a form of intelligence. It's nervous system literacy.

But, as with all forms of intelligence, imbalance invites challenge. Without regulation and conscious awareness, SQ can feel overwhelming. You may become overstimulated by noise, clutter, crowds, or even joy. You may live in a low-grade state of alertness, never quite feeling safe in your own skin. You might find yourself needing more recovery time than others after a seemingly ordinary day. Some Wild Sensitives attempt to manage this by numbing, zoning out, avoiding sensation, disconnecting from the body. Others become hyper-aware, scanning their environment so vigilantly they never rest. In both cases, what began as a gift turns into overload.

The physical signs of low SQ regulation are recognizable: shallow breathing, chronic jaw tension, digestive issues, racing thoughts, adrenal fatigue, or that classic "wired and tired" feeling that leaves you both restless and drained. You may feel disconnected from your body, like you're floating above your life, observing instead of participating. But these symptoms aren't signs of weakness or failure. They're messages. The body is speaking. It's saying: *I'm overloaded. I need care. I need you to listen.*

Cultivating SQ begins with building a two-way relationship with your body. Instead of reacting to your body or ignoring it, you learn to partner with it. Slow down. Practice body scans, not to fix, but to listen. Close your eyes and check in from head to toe: What's tight? What's open? What's calling for attention? This simple act of noticing brings you back into your body, into the moment. We recommend using the *6 Zones Model* we share in Chapter 9 of this book. Naming the zone you're in can instantly help you orient. Awareness creates space. And space creates choice.

Anchoring practices are essential tools for regulation. Ground through your feet. Place a hand over your heart. Gently sway. Breathe deeply into your belly. Use sound, scent, or texture to root yourself. Learn your personal cues for sensory overwhelm. Don't wait until you crash. Watch for your yellow lights before they turn red. Ask yourself regularly: *What does my body need right now? Is it rest? Hydration? Movement? Stillness? Connection?*

In the fully integrated Wild Sensitive, SQ is no longer a burden, it becomes a trusted navigation system. It tells you when a *"yes"* is real and embodied, and when a *"no"* is not only okay but necessary. It helps you make decisions not just with your head or heart, but with your whole system. You begin to respond to life in real time, with your entire being, not just emotionally or intellectually, but somatically.

SQ is the intelligence of the wild body, the body that knows how to listen, how to signal, how to guide. It is ancestral. It is intuitive. It is sacred. It's the part of you that remembers what your mind may forget. It doesn't ask, *"What should I do?"* It asks the deeper question: *What does aliveness feel like here?*

This intelligence can't be found in textbooks. It's cultivated through presence, practice, and patience. Through learning to interpret your body's messages not as threats, but as guidance. As Wild Sensitives, we often carry shame about how deeply we feel the world. But what if that depth was never something to hide? What if your body's way of sensing was always meant to lead you?

Remember: cultivating SQ is not about becoming less sensitive. It's about becoming more sovereign. It's about tuning in, not turning off. It's about learning the language of your body, your most ancient guide, and allowing it to lead you home to yourself. When your SQ works in harmony with your IQ, EQ, and PQ, you don't just survive stimulation. You choose which signals to follow, which to release, and how to root into your own embodied truth. Because this is not just about managing your sensitivity. This is about mastering your aliveness.

As we come to the close of this chapter on the Four Intelligences of the Wild Sensitive, it's important to reflect on what this framework offers us, not just insight, but transformation. In a world eager to define us by our deficiencies, it is an act of quiet rebellion to claim our intelligences. Society rarely highlights the exceptional potential that Wild Sensitives hold across IQ, EQ, PQ, and SQ. Instead, we're often reduced to oversimplified labels, overthinker, people pleaser, too emotional, too intense. These labels distort the truth, framing our complexity as dysfunction. But when we peel back those imposed definitions, something else emerges, power, clarity, and coherence.

Each intelligence we've explored, Intellectual (IQ), Emotional (EQ), Positive (PQ), and Sensory (SQ), is more than a category. Each one offers a vital waypoint in the Wild Sensitive's inner map. On their own, they guide. Together, they integrate. When we cultivate them in harmony, something profound shifts: we stop fragmenting. We stop fighting ourselves. We begin navigating life with clarity, steadiness, and self-trust.

These four intelligences are not isolated skills to master. They are interconnected systems, threads of awareness, perception, and response, that together weave a more coherent, empowered version of us. They help us stay steady in storms, curious in confusion, and grounded in complexity. They don't erase our sensitivity; they anchor it. They don't fix our contradiction; they help us live it with grace.

Imagine facing a moment of internal overwhelm. In the past, it might have spun you into anxiety or retreat. But now, something has shifted. Your Positive Intelligence (PQ) reminds you to pause and be curious. Your Sensory Intelligence (SQ) tunes you into your body's subtle signals. Your Emotional Intelligence (EQ) identifies the real feeling beneath the surface. And your Intellectual Intelligence (IQ) steps in to help you structure your next move. Within moments, you've shifted from chaos to coherence. From survival mode to self-leadership. This is not just emotional regulation, it's nervous system mastery.

If you're curious to explore where your current levels of IQ, EQ, PQ, and SQ stand, not to measure your worth, but to deepen your self-awareness, we invite you to visit wildsensitive.com. There, you'll find assessments, tools, and supportive practices to help you develop each of these intelligences in a way that aligns with your unique rhythm and sensitivity.

To better understand your Intellectual Intelligence, explore strategies to work with your cognitive strengths and challenges. Reflect on how your mind processes, solves, and synthesizes.

To deepen your Emotional Intelligence, access guided self-reflection tools, emotional mapping resources, and somatic practices to help you feel without drowning.

To strengthen your Positive Intelligence, discover how to identify your dominant saboteurs, interrupt self-sabotaging patterns, and shift into Sage perspective.

To build your Sensory Intelligence, explore your sensory thresholds and the practices that regulate, ground, and empower your body's innate wisdom.

When all four intelligences, IQ, EQ, PQ, and SQ, are not just accessed but truly lived, something extraordinary happens: you stop surviving your sensitivity. You begin leading with it.

You step into the world no longer fragmented, no longer apologizing for your depth. You become a truly empowered Wild Sensitive, not by escaping who you are, but by turning your depth into direction. Not by choosing one trait over another, but by living the full, integrated range of your complexity with quiet courage and bold clarity.

Because when you live in harmony with all four intelligences, you don't just manage your sensitivity, you elevate it. You don't just cope, you navigate. And in doing so, you evolve into something truly rare. Something luminous. Something the world deeply needs now more than ever: *The Wild Sensitive Wayfinder.*

Chapter 9

The Living Adventurers Guide to the 6 Zones of Life

A map for the Wild Sensitive, where safety and growth no longer need to be at odds.

'Society taught us there are only two zones: safety or risk. Stay small or leap big. Hide or hustle. But we are Wild Sensitives, we live in the space between. In nuance, rhythm, and sensation. Life is not a binary, it's a terrain. And when we learn to map where we truly are, we stop being ruled by fear and start moving with choice, truth, and aliveness.'

The Living Adventurers

For most of us, especially those wired with high sensitivity and a hunger for depth, the world has handed us a very limited map. One that says: You are either safe… or at risk. You are either tucked into the familiar or thrown into the fire. You are either playing small in the Safe Zone, or braving discomfort in the Risk Zone.

But this binary lens is not only incomplete, it's very misleading. It teaches us to fear growth and romanticize security. It flattens the emotional landscape of life into a tug-of-war between hiding and hustling, shrinking, and leaping. And for Wild Sensitives, those of us who feel deeply, think richly, and move between caution and craving, this model simply doesn't work. That's why we, as Living Adventurers, created the 6 Zones of Life.

This guide offers a more nuanced, compassionate, and empowering framework, one that reflects the real psychological terrain we walk as Highly Sensitive High Sensation Seekers. It reveals that there are not two zones, but six distinct states we move through as we stretch, regulate, pause, and grow. Some invite us to rest and restore. Others challenge us to expand. Some offer just the right amount of stretch, and one, the Floating Zone, asks us to listen inward before we move at all.

Each zone holds value. Each teaches something different. And most importantly, each zone is valid. You are not broken for craving comfort. You are not weak for needing safety. Nor are you reckless for wanting to stretch. But until we name and normalize these spaces, we stay trapped in the myth that growth must hurt and that stillness means stagnation.

As Living Adventurers, we hear it constantly... *"Be safe."*

And our answer?... Safe is an illusion. Not because we seek danger, but because we seek aliveness. Safety is essential, but when it becomes a cage, it keeps us from discovering who we really are. We're not here to live small just to avoid pain. We're here to feel fully, move intentionally, and expand wisely, on our own terms.

This map is for you if you've felt stuck in comfort but feared the chaos of change. If you've tried to "push through" only to burn out and needed to retreat and if you've wondered why the world praises risk but doesn't honor rest.

As Wild Sensitives, we need to know not only where we are emotionally and energetically, but also what that zone is asking of us, and what tools we need to support ourselves there. That's what this guide offers, a practical, compassionate way to decode your inner landscape. Once you learn this map and begin to listen to your body's signals through each zone, you'll gain the power to move not from pressure or fear, but from attunement and choice. It's about reclaiming agency, building self-trust, and making aligned decisions that honor your rhythm rather than override it.

The 6 Zones are not rules. They are reflections. They are not rigid boxes. They are dynamic invitations and when you understand them, you unlock the ability to live in a way that is richer, truer, and far more fulfilling. Let's step out of the social conditioning and let's explore the full emotional terrain of life. Let's find the zone that fits you now and walk together toward what's next.

The Safe Zone — Protection and Isolation

Where stillness meets sovereignty, and the only real sanctuary is the one you build inside.

Have you ever heard the words, *"This is a safe space?"*

Maybe it was spoken by a therapist, a coach, a teacher, a group leader, or in an online forum. Maybe you were in a circle of sharing, a healing retreat, a classroom, or even a social media comment section. The words are meant to offer comfort, to create a sense of ease and welcome. And often, they are said with genuine care.

But here's the truth that many of us come to learn, sometimes painfully. True safety can't be guaranteed by anyone else. No matter how many guidelines, ground rules, policies, or ethics are in place, the presence of even one other person introduces complexity. Another person brings their own beliefs, reactions, projections, and wounds. Even the most well-intentioned moderator cannot prevent someone from saying something that lands as hurtful or triggering. Even the most loving guide can unintentionally cross a boundary. Even the most "safe space" can suddenly feel anything but. And that's because safety, real, felt, embodied safety, isn't an external structure. It's an internal state.

It's the zone you create within yourself, where you can exhale without defense, sit with your truth without performance, and rest in your own presence without fear of emotional attack or collapse. That's what we as Living Adventurers call the Safe Zone.

It's not found in a room. It's not granted by a title. It's not a promise someone else can make. It's something you slowly build, breath by breath, decision by decision, inside your own emotional landscape.

Why the Safe Zone Matters for Wild Sensitives

For us Wild Sensitives, safety has always been a complex experience. We long for it, yet we often struggle to find it. We can be triggered by subtle shifts in tone, nuance, or facial expression. We carry deep emotional memory, and we notice the tiniest breaches of authenticity. We are hardwired to sense unsafety, even when no one else does. That's what keeps us safe.

That's also why we must stop chasing safety in other people or places and start cultivating it inside ourselves. Because here's what we've learned as Living Adventurers, a therapist's office can feel secure, but if we don't feel safe in our own body, healing won't happen. An online group can feel validating, but one comment can still unravel us if we haven't built internal regulation. A friend's house can feel like a haven, but if our nervous system is stuck in hyper awareness, peace won't land.

We're not saying these environments aren't valuable, they are. Some are Secure. Some even help us access the Goldilocks Zone of optimal stretch. But none of them can promise true safety. Because safety is not something that happens to us, it's something we learn to create from within.

What Is the Safe Zone, Really?

The Safe Zone is not about comfort. It's about containment. It's the place where your nervous system is regulated, your mind is steady, and your emotions are held gently, not ignored, or suppressed, but witnessed without overwhelm. It's where you feel sovereign in your own space, free to feel fully without needing to explain or justify anything to anyone. And here's what may surprise you, the Safe Zone is always and reliably found when you are alone.

Why? Because aloneness strips away the external performance. There's no one to manage. No energy to read. No social script to follow. No subtle pressure to be "okay." You get to just be. Fully. Quietly. Truthfully. On your terms.

This doesn't mean you must isolate to feel safe. In fact, we're big believers in connection. But it does mean that until you know how to feel safe with yourself, you will be constantly scanning your environment for safety breaches in the words you or others use, the look they give, and the rules that need to be followed to keep it a 'Safe Place'.

When we enter the Safe Zone, we step into something sacred, a space where even our own self-judgment is not allowed to follow. Negative self-talk, internal criticism, shame spirals, performance anxiety, these are not welcome here. And if they are present, if that critical inner voice is still speaking… you are not in your Safe Zone. You are in your Risk Zone, even if you're physically alone.

The Safe Zone, for us as Wild Sensitives, is more than quiet. It's a sanctuary.

It's the log by the gentle, flowing river where the noise of the world fades into the background. It's the cabin in the woods that only you now about, curated and cozy, where every object says, *"you belong here"*. It's the song through our headphones that melts the tension in our chest and says, *you don't have to try right now"*.

It is the only place where the armor comes off. Where the masks drop. Where no roles are required. And where we get to simply be…. Raw, honest, unfiltered, without fear of judgment, not even from ourselves.

Here, we are not fixing. We are not proving. We are not adjusting to anyone else's expectations. We are simply resting, with our breath, our body, and our truth. And it is from this internal refuge that all other zones become more navigable.

When we know how to return here, fully and without condition, we carry the foundation that allows us to stretch, to explore, to rest, and to rise. This is your Safe Zone. Claim it. Build it. Return to it when needed and let it remind you who you are, when the rest of the world forgets.

How to Begin Cultivating Your Safe Zone

First, find physical solitude, even for a few minutes. Let your body feel what it's like to exist without outside input. Close your eyes and breathe slowly. No fixing. No trying. Just being.

Place your hand on your heart or chest. Remind yourself: *"Right now, I am safe with me."* Listen... What does your body say when no one else is watching? What truth arises in stillness? Let this become a ritual. Your Safe Zone becomes stronger with repetition. It becomes easier to access over time. This isn't about avoiding the world. It's about learning to trust that when the world becomes overwhelming, you know where to go.

Another extremely important understanding regarding the Safe Zone is that it must be visited with intention and not become a permanent residence. This is why the constant push to 'Be Safe' by society can actually be very crippling to many. While the Safe Zone is sacred, calming, and necessary for our nervous systems to reset, it's important to understand that the Safe Zone is a refuge, not a retreat from life.

Potential Downside for the Safe Zone

If misunderstood, the Safe Zone can become a seductive trap. What begins as rest quietly morphs into withdrawal. What starts as protection can harden into isolation. And over time, what once helped us feel whole can begin to shrink us.

Staying too long in the Safe Zone, without reengaging, exploring, or stretching can lead to a growing discomfort with novelty or challenge, even when it's aligned and needed. This is where the belief that anything outside of the Safe Zone becomes risk and even danger. This is often driven by limiting beliefs and past conditioning creating a fear-based worldview where the unknown is reflexively labeled unsafe.

This leads to a diminished curiosity and dulls motivation, leading to emotional stagnation. It increases avoidance behaviors that reinforce fragility rather than building resilience. It raises feelings of loneliness, disconnection, or unexplained anxiety.

We say this not to pressure you to leave your Safe Zone, but to remind you, safety is momentary. It is where you pause and gather your breath, not where you give up on the wind. While we all need to feel safe now and then, we also need to feel alive.

Let's return, for a moment, to the image of the cabin in the woods. Picture the hike you took to get there, steep, rugged, and demanding. Your body aches, your breath is shallow, but finally, you arrive. Inside, you light a fire in the stone hearth to warm your cold tired muscles. You reach into your backpack and prepare a nourishing meal sitting quietly at the table gathering your thoughts. Then, you pull out your sleeping bag and lay it on the soft bed that invites your tired limbs to rest. It's beautiful. It's earned. And it's exactly what you need.

But eventually, the food in your pack will run out. The stacked firewood will burn to ash. The bed will need washing, and silence will settle in too deeply. With no one to talk to, no challenge to meet, and no new path to follow, the comfort begins to erode into isolation. What once restored you now begins to shrink you. This is why the cabin, like the Safe Zone, must be used wisely. It is meant to restore, not contain. To hold you for a while, not harbor you forever. It will always be there to welcome you back, again and again, but only as a resting place between the stretches that shape your becoming.

You will enter many spaces in your life that give you the illusion of safety. Some can offer more levels of comfort, while others can be very misleading. But when you begin to carry your Safe Zone within you, you don't have to fear the unknown. You stop needing external validation. You stop outsourcing your emotional stability. You start trusting that you, your presence, your breath, your awareness, are your first and most reliable sanctuary.

So, the next time someone says, *"You're safe here,"* smile inwardly and remember: *"That may be true… but my real safety begins with me."* Welcome to your Safe Zone. Let it hold you. Let it steady you. And when you're ready, your floating zone will tell you when it's time to leave.

The Comfort Zone
Familiar, warm, and inviting, but not where your wings stretch.

The Comfort Zone is one of the most misunderstood spaces in personal development, and one most often confused with the Safe Zone. Society tends to blur the two, using the words interchangeably. But we can assure you from a Wild Sensitives perspective, they are not the same.

Where the Safe Zone is your private sanctuary, the place where even self-judgment is not allowed, the Comfort Zone is a shared space. It's the emotional living room of your life, where others are welcome to sit beside you. Not everyone will, but they can. And that simple fact shifts the dynamic entirely.

The boundary between the Safe Zone and the Comfort Zone isn't a hard line, it's more of a soft fade. A transition. One moment you're in solitude and deep rest, and the next, you're cooking dinner with someone you love, trading stories, laughter, and light. You're not pushing yourself, but you're not protecting yourself either. You're at ease. You're known. You're seen and you're heard.

This is the Comfort Zone. A place that is predictable, familiar, and there is no risk. It's not about isolating or stagnating, not inherently. In fact, it can be a beautiful, nourishing space that fosters connection, warmth, and slow learning. It's where friendships grow, families share meals, and memories are made without pressure. It's where you feel like yourself, without needing to perform or stretch. Here, you're not required to be brave. You just get to be a little more open, a little more interactive, and a lot more human.

What It Looks Like:

The Comfort Zone typically houses routines and habits that feel natural and effortless. It's where we engage in deep meaningful conversations that are familiar and non-confrontational. These conversations invite emotional sharing.

The Comfort Zone is where we spend precious time with people who "get you," and it requires little to no explanation. It's where we choose entertainment or creative practices that delight but don't challenge. It's where we get to enjoy positive emotions like love, gratitude, awe, joy, and gentle pride.

The Comfort Zone is often where we experience the softer side of aliveness, the steady drumbeat of daily rituals, warm hugs, inside jokes, and cozy evenings. It's where our nervous system isn't under threat, but it's also not being restructured. It's emotionally neutral to mildly positive, and for the Wild Sensitive, that kind of stability can be deeply restorative.

Potential Downside for the Comfort Zone:

As comforting as this zone is, staying here too long also has its costs. Growth is slow or stunted, if at all. Rarely do you take even tiny steps beyond what you already know. Life can begin to feel monotonous, flat, or uninspiring. Boredom quietly builds. You stop seeking. You stop asking what if.

You may resist change, not because you're incapable, but because you've become attached to the familiar or convinced by social expectations that change is risky. Important challenges or transitions get delayed because they can feel uncomfortable, even if they're right. For Wild Sensitives, this can become a conflicted space. The Highly Sensitive part of you thrives here, feeling regulated, loved, and calm. But the HSS part? It starts to itch. To stir. To hunger for something more. That internal tension, left unchecked, can create emotional confusion, irritability, or self-doubt.

How to Use It Effectively
The Comfort Zone isn't the problem, staying there indefinitely is. Use your Comfort Zone as a launchpad, a place where your nervous system is steady enough to plan, envision, and gather confidence. Like coming home at the end of a long day, this zone is your emotional hearth, it allows you to recover, reflect, reconnect, and re-center.

Here, you build your energy. Here, you rehearse your next stretch. And when life inevitably invites you into new terrain, you know you have a welcoming place to return, one that restores your spirit and offers deep meaningful connection without demanding your performance.

Think of it like your emotional home base, not your final destination, but a critical part of your wellbeing. And if you share your physical home with others, a partner, children, roommates, or family, the construction of a Comfort Zone becomes even more essential. In today's fast-paced, overstimulating world, where parents come home emotionally spent from work and children return carrying the invisible weight of social dynamics, peer pressures, and school demands, the Comfort Zone must be intentionally cultivated for everyone's sake.

Imagine a home where the kitchen becomes more than just a place to prepare food, it becomes a ritual of reconnection. Where dinner is cooked together, stories are shared without performance, and cleanup becomes a gentle dance of teamwork and reflection. Where conversation is emotionally present, not just functional, and everyone is invited to speak and to feel. No judgment. No quick fixes. Just listening, witnessing, and honoring each person's experience.

For Wild Sensitives, this kind of collective comfort zone is not just nourishing, it's vital. Because in many families or shared spaces, comfort is unconsciously designed around the needs of the less sensitive. The volume stays loud. The lighting stays harsh. The emotions stay shallow. And the deeper needs of the Wild Sensitive, for emotional depth, quieter connection, sensory balance, and meaningful dialogue, go unseen.

Over time, this creates a disconnect. The HSP-HSS individual may feel like they're constantly adjusting themselves to make others comfortable, while no one adjusts for them. Resentment can build. Loneliness can deepen. And the Comfort Zone, rather than being a source of restoration, becomes another space of quiet self-erasure.

This is why intentional co-creation matters. It means checking in with everyone's emotional and sensory needs. It means asking questions like:

- *What helps you feel relaxed at the end of your day?*
- *What kind of energy do you need right now, quiet or conversation?*
- *How can we make this space feel like home for all of us?*

When done with care and commitment, the Comfort Zone becomes not just a refuge for one, but a haven for many. A living space where connection flows, energy restores, and everyone, including the Wild Sensitive, is welcomed as they are. So, whether you're alone or among others, remember, the Comfort Zone is a tool. A rhythm. A resource. Use it wisely. Share it generously. And trust that when built with love, it becomes the place you, and those you care for, can always come back to.

While the Comfort Zone is a wonderful place to return to and certainly one we can (and often should) spend more time in than the Safe Zone, it is not the most ideal zone for your evolution. That zone is what we as Living Adventurers call the Goldilocks Zone, the place that is just right.

It's where the challenge is real, but not overwhelming. It's where you stretch without snapping. It's where learning feels alive, connection feels courageous, and you meet the edges of your growth with presence, not panic. But before you can reach the Goldilocks Zone, you must understand where you are now.

And if you're here, in the Comfort Zone, you're already on the map. Take a breath. Feel the ease. And when you're ready, take one curious step toward something just outside it. Your next zone is waiting.

The Goldilocks Zone
The zone where rootedness and growth walk hand in hand.

You may remember the childhood story of Goldilocks and the Three Bears? Goldilocks stumbles into a stranger's home and tries everything she finds, chairs, porridge, beds, until she discovers what feels just right. Not too hard, not too soft. Not too hot, not too cold. Not too big, not too small. It's a tale of intuitive knowing, of seeking and sensing until comfort and need align.

For us, as Wild Sensitives, this story holds a quiet wisdom. Because in a world that often demands too much or offers too little, we too are searching for that middle path, the place where we're not overwhelmed, but we're not underwhelmed either. We want to be engaged but not overextended. We want to grow, but not at the expense of our nervous systems. We want to belong, but without abandoning ourselves.

That place? That pulse of balance and resonance? It's what we as Living Adventurers call the Goldilocks Zone, the sweet spot where life feels just right.

What Makes the Goldilocks Zone Special?

The Goldilocks Zone is the ideal state for Wild Sensitives to flourish. It is the fusion point where deep processing meets purposeful stimulation, and where challenge is met with care. In the Goldilocks Zone, we are mentally engaged but not overwhelmed. We are emotionally open but not exposed. We are physically active, but not exhausted. We are expanding but not unraveling.

It holds enough stretch to give us a sense of direction, a reason to move, a sense of purpose. But it also includes spaciousness for reflection and restoration, so we are not living in a constant state of push. In the Goldilocks Zone, you aren't hustling for growth, you're growing with grace. This is not a zone of comfort or challenge alone, it's the zone where comfort supports challenge. Where our sensitivity is honored, and our adventurous spirit is gently activated. It is not a place of perfection. It is a place of alignment. And for the Wild Sensitive, that alignment is everything.

What It Looks Like

The Goldilocks Zone is where we learn new things at our own pace, energized, but not rushed. Where we engage in new experiences while feeling emotionally grounded and supported. It's where we can express vulnerability in spaces that are attuned with care and presence. It's where we share moments of joy, awe, and pride with people who understand your depth.

The Goldilocks Zone is where we can venture intentionally into new territory that aligns with our affirmed beliefs, values, and desires. We can build new skills or habits that stretch our capacity while still honoring our nervous system. It's where we can surround ourselves with people who offer both comfort and inspiration, people who challenge you with love.

The Goldilocks Zone might be working on a creative project that excites you, walking a new trail with a trusted friend, sharing your truth with someone who can hold it, or speaking on a stage after weeks of inner preparation. It might be attending a Wild Sensitive retreat where you learn new routines, have deeper conversations, and explore new activities with likeminded sensitives. The Goldilocks Zone is any place or anything that activates your courage without abandoning your capacity.

Why It Matters

For Wild Sensitives, thriving isn't found in constant risk or perpetual retreat. It's found in the dance between stability and stretch. The Goldilocks Zone is where this dance takes place. Here, you are not hiding. You are not leaping without a net. You're expanding with wisdom, while rooted in your tools, and anchored in your truth. This is the zone where new beliefs get tested in safe ways. Where you build confidence through gentle exposure. Where joy meets meaning, and your growth becomes self-led, not externally demanded.

Here are just some of the positive emotions Wild Sensitives Experience in their Goldilocks Zone. A true Joy from living authentically. A deep gratitude for the tools, growth, and support system they have. Compassionate love through deep mutual, meaningful connection. A lasting sense of pride in how far they've come and the courage it took. Inspiring awe at the subtle beauty unfolding within themselves. Hope in the possibilities ahead and inspiration that fuels their creativity, movement, and momentum into the future. This is being a Wild Sensitive.

Potential Downside for the Goldilocks Zone

In truth? There isn't one. This is not the zone of burnout, nor boredom. It is not too fast or too slow. If it stops feeling just right, it means you've likely moved into another zone, and that's okay. The Goldilocks Zone is dynamic and ever-evolving. The work is not to stay in it forever, but to return to it again and again as your steadying rhythm.

How to Use It Effectively

It is here that a deep awareness of who we are authentically is important. Notice your energy: Do you feel alive, slightly challenged, yet in control? If yes, you're likely in the Goldilocks Zone. Use this zone as a training ground after a brief visit to the Secure Zone. It's where you can integrate your stretch with support and confidence.

Let it be your first destination after advancing from your Comfort Zone. This is your next gentle step, not your leap. It gives you an opportunity to invite novelty in manageable, meaningful ways, like a new class, a heartfelt conversation or exploring new possibilities.

Remember to Celebrate every stretch, big or small. A vulnerable moment matters just as much as a bold move. Most importantly, protect this zone, nourish it. It is your ecosystem for sustainable growth.

This is the zone where your roots and your wings finally meet. You are not shrinking. You are not forcing. You are living from the sweet, steady pulse of aligned aliveness. Here, growth feels kind. And adventure feels true. The Goldilocks Zone isn't about doing more, it's about becoming more of who you really are. And from this space, your life begins to stretch in ways that feel both brave and beautifully your own.

The Secure Zone

Where stretch meets strength, and who you are meets who you could become.

The Secure Zone is the space where true, transformative growth occurs. It's where we stretch our edges, not to the point of snapping, but far enough to discover what we're capable of. Here, we don't step forward recklessly. We step with intention, with preparation, and with trust in the tools, techniques, and skills we've been steadily cultivating.

Unlike the Goldilocks Zone, where growth gently occurs, the Secure Zone is more active. It's the psychological terrain of intentional expansion. You may still feel discomfort here, that flutter in your chest, the tremble in your hands, but you're not overwhelmed. You're engaged. You're alive. You're anchored in your values, and you're open to transformation.

This is the zone where we test our beliefs, validate our core values, and discover our deeper capacity. It's where we reach our growth milestones, whether that's having a demanding discussion, presenting your work to a new audience, opening your heart in a new relationship, or applying for the opportunity that scares you just enough to stretch your limit. The Secure Zone doesn't guarantee success. It guarantees growth.

What the Secure Zone Looks Like

The Secure zone is where we initiate a meaningful conversation with people who don't already know your story. It's where we share selective vulnerability, enough to stretch, not enough to collapse. It's where saying *"yes"* to new opportunities, challenges, or environments expand your perspective.

The Secure Zone is where we can explore new ideas, skills, or possibilities while still feeling emotionally resourced and grounded. It's where we practice boundary-setting in real time or take a bold step toward our goals with intention, not urgency.

In the Secure Zone, you start to see the real-world impact of the inner work you've done. You access courage not through force, but through preparation. You speak your truth without needing to be perfect. You experience challenge as a mirror, not a threat.

How to Use the Secure Zone Effectively

To fully access the Secure Zone, you must have enough internal or external support to feel emotionally grounded while stretching. This is why we always recommend building a strong foundation of self-awareness and regulation tools before pushing too far.

Understanding how to work with the Secure Zone is vitally important but remember, before you venture too far into it, be prepared. This is where the 7P's rule applies. The Secure Zone requires us to prioritize self-awareness. Learn to recognize the Floating Zone, that space of emotional friction where you begin to shift between grounded and overwhelmed.

Develop skills and techniques like practicing the 3-R rule, PERRRing, journaling, somatic grounding, or breathwork to help you stay emotionally tethered even as you stretch outward. Surround yourself with secure people. Not cheerleaders or critics, but steady, emotionally mature allies who can hold space for your unfolding.

Allow your beliefs to be questioned. In this zone, we don't defend our old maps, we revise them. Honor discomfort as a vital messenger. Instead of running from fear, ask what it's trying to show you. Stretch with curiosity, not pressure.

The Secure Zone is where your inner alignment gets tested in the outer world. But when you step in prepared, not perfectly, but consciously, you are better equipped to stretch without breaking, and to challenge without abandoning yourself.

Potential Downside of the Secure Zone

The potential downside of the Secure Zone lies in overestimating your readiness or mistaking external progress for internal stability. While this zone is designed for empowered stretching, it can become risky if you attempt to grow too fast without adequate preparation, tools, or support. This might lead to overwhelm, a drop into the Risk Zone, or emotional dysregulation. There's also a subtler trap in that you might confuse external validation (like success or applause) with genuine inner alignment. If this zone becomes performance-driven instead of intention-driven, it loses its transformative power. The key is to stretch from self-trust, not self-pressure.

Why Tools, Techniques & Skills Matter

The Secure Zone is only as expansive as your preparation allows. If your backpack is limited, if you're missing self-regulation methods, decision frameworks, or supportive reflection practices your Secure Zone will be small. You'll hit emotional edges quickly, and before long, you'll be standing in the Risk Zone, triggered and destabilized.

But if you've developed tools like the 3-R Rule, the PERRR Method, and Somatic Grounding, your capacity grows. Your tolerance expands. Your voice steadies. And your ability to navigate new emotional, relational, and environmental terrain increases with it.

Your Secure Zone is your proving ground, not to prove your worth, but to prove to yourself that you are no longer ruled by fear. This is where you apply the tools you've practiced in the Goldilocks Zone. It's where you walk into life's invitations and say, *"I may not have all the answers, but I'm resourced enough to find my way."*

Here, you're not leaping blindly. You're stepping forward bravely. And as you do, you redefine what you thought you were capable of. The Secure Zone is not for perfection. It's for becoming. And every time you choose to step into it with your feet grounded, heart open, and mind aware, you are choosing to live not just wisely, but fully as an empowered Wild Sensitive.

The Risk Zone

Where overwhelm and burnout takes over, and survival overrides intention.

The Risk Zone is the most destabilizing of the six zones, not because risk itself is wrong, but because here, the challenge outweighs our readiness. In this zone, we take leaps into the unknown without the tools, skills, techniques, or support needed to navigate it, and as a result, our nervous system perceives threat. Even if there's no physical danger, the emotional and psychological pressure can feel crushing. This is where survival instincts kick in. Flight, freeze, perform or fight override thoughtful response, and instead of stretching, we shrink. We shut down, flare up, or emotionally fragment.

For us Wild Sensitives, whose systems are wired for deep processing and heightened emotional awareness, entering the Risk Zone unprepared can be especially intense. What might seem like "just a difficult conversation" or "just a new opportunity" to others, may feel like emotional chaos to someone without enough grounding, context, or capacity in that moment.

What the Risk Zone Looks Like
For us, as Wild sensitives, we find we are in the Risk Zone when we enter a difficult or emotionally charged conversation and quickly feel dysregulated. We are in the Risk Zone when we feel rejection, being shut down, dismissed, or ghosted. It's a feeling of deep emotional vulnerability, like your voice, your truth, or even your presence isn't welcome.

We are in our Risk Zone when we encounter negative judgment, sarcasm, or body language (like eye-rolling or cold withdrawal). It's when we are facing a challenge or environment we're not equipped to handle, lacking tools, support, or internal stability. And we certainly are in the Risk Zone when we feel triggered by past trauma, shame, or overwhelming responsibility.

Real-Life Example
Let's say a Wild Sensitive named Rae has been working on asserting boundaries. After weeks of journaling, practicing in her Goldilocks Zone, and building some confidence, Rae decides to finally speak up in a family gathering about a recurring hurt, something deeply emotional.

This could have been a Secure Zone stretch, but Rae hadn't yet practiced this specific boundary in conversation. She hadn't rehearsed it aloud or prepared for possible reactions. No grounding tools were used beforehand, and no support person was present or reachable. So, when the family responds with sarcasm and defensiveness, Rae's nervous system goes into high alert.

Her voice begins to shake. Her thoughts are scattered. Her body goes numb. Then, she retreats to the bathroom in tears, overwhelmed and flooded with doubt. Rae just dropped, unintentionally, into the Risk Zone. Not because the act of speaking up was wrong, but because the leap wasn't properly supported.

This is where tools like the 3-R Rule (Recognize – Regulate – Reclaim) and the PERRR Method (Pause, Enquire, Reflect, Recognize, Respond) become essential. These tools help you slow down reactivity, interrupt spiraling narratives, and recalibrate in real time. They give your body and mind a framework to begin restoring balance when safety feels far away.

Downside of the Risk Zone
While stepping into risk is sometimes necessary, especially when life presents us with unexpected challenges, lingering here too long can have significant costs, especially for Wild Sensitives. We can quickly experience severe burnout or emotional depletion from prolonged nervous system activation. It can increase our irritability, defensiveness, or shutdown.

Decision-making becomes fear based and we feel a sense of urgency rather than aligned intention. It brings on self-doubt, regret, or emotional hangovers after interactions. We see patterns of withdrawal, people-pleasing, or overcorrecting to avoid future pain. In some cases, boredom and despair take hold when the risk turns into stagnation instead of movement. In essence, the Risk Zone is where reaction replaces response, and where the desire to grow gets hijacked by the need to survive.

How to Protect Yourself in the Risk Zone
You can't always avoid the Risk Zone, although society wants to convince us we can. You can prepare for it, and the more prepared you

are, the less you will find yourself there. Know your Floating Zone signals. That "in-between" feeling, where you're not quite grounded but not fully flooded, is your warning system. Pay attention.

Properly equip yourself. Build emotional tools (like breathwork, grounding techniques, boundary scripts), practice them, and develop real-world skills so they're available when you need them.

Create a re-entry plan. When you're heading into a known challenge, establish how you'll come back to yourself. Who will you call? Where will you go? What will you do? Identify a secure person or team, someone who can help you co-regulate or reflect without judgment. Your safety net matters.

Learn, practice, and apply the 3-R Rule and PERRR regularly, even before you step into risk. Think of these tools as your emotional gear: don't hike the mountain without them.

The Risk Zone isn't the enemy but entering it without preparation is like walking into a storm without shelter. Don't confuse emotional activation with growth. Real growth happens in the Secure Zone, where you stretch with support. The Risk Zone should be brief, intentional, and recoverable. If you find yourself here, recognize it as quickly as you can, without fear taking hold. Regulate your emotions and thoughts and reclaim your ability to think and act (The 3-R's).

Know your tools. Know what skills you possess. Know when to apply a technique. Then step back, not in retreat, but in wisdom, and ask yourself:

What do I need to feel confident again? What did this moment teach me? How can I return stronger?

The Risk Zone isn't a failure. It's a signal. And when listened to with care, it becomes part of your growth story, not the place it ends.

The Floating Zone

The feeling before the shift. The message before the move. The wisdom between breath and action.

The Floating Zone isn't a place. It's a state of internal awareness, a powerful, intuitive signal system that exists between the other zones. It doesn't belong to a single zone because it moves between all of them, and its job is simple, yet profound: to guide you. It exists to protect your nervous system and direct your aliveness.

Unlike the other zones, the Floating Zone doesn't offer stability or safety. It doesn't give answers. Instead, it offers what we Wild Sensitives crave the most: sensation, the whisper in your gut, the tightening in your chest, the flicker of tension in your shoulders. It speaks in somatic language, not logic. And for Wild Sensitives, it is one of our greatest allies… if we learn how to listen.

This zone is often misinterpreted, especially when we've been conditioned to distrust our instincts or override our emotions. If we're unaware, a moment of healthy discomfort can be mistaken for danger. A rising emotion can feel like a red flag instead of a green light. We may brace when we actually need to breathe. That's why the Floating Zone requires not just presence, but discernment, curiosity, and compassion.

The Floating Zone Offers Three Core Sensations
1. **Discomfort that calls for growth**: That inner tug or ache that says: *"This is scary… but you're ready."*
2. **Discomfort that warns to withdraw**: A nervous system signal that says: *"This isn't right. Pull back."*
3. **Pain that signals misalignment or overextension**: A sharper sting that says: *"Stop. You've gone too far."*

These sensations don't tell you where you are. They tell you where you're not. You're not grounded enough to stretch. You're not being true to your values. You're not aligned with your deeper needs. But instead of judgment or urgency, the Floating Zone invites pause and inquiry. It doesn't force. It whispers. It doesn't demand. It informs.

What the Floating Zone Feels Like to us Wild Sensitives

Ever have a "gut Feeling." That strange indiscernible whisper in your gut telling you to *"Stretch but do it with care."* Or that tightness in your chest that says, *"Retreat just far enough to re-center."* How about a sting in your nervous system that says, *"Stop. This path is not for you."*

What about a sudden lack of clarity, like standing at a foggy crossroad, knowing movement is needed but unsure of the direction or the sensation of holding your breath, not from panic, but uncertainty?

The key here is to respond with intention, not to react from fear or conditioning. These feelings, these sensations are levels of un-comfort that are asking us to gently pull back, not all the way into the Safe Zone, but just far enough to land in your Goldilocks Zone again. Or they are saying we should take a brave but calibrated step forward, because your body is telling you it's time.

A Real-Life Example

Let's say Jade, a Wild Sensitive, is invited to speak at a work event. It's an exciting opportunity, one that aligns with her desire to grow. She wants to say yes. But the moment she considers it, her stomach turns. Her thoughts spiral: *"What if I mess up? What if I'm judged?"* Jade mistakes this as a sign she's not ready, retreating to safety by declining the opportunity. But what's really happening is that a limiting belief is overriding her discernment. Her discomfort isn't signaling danger, but expansion. Her body isn't saying no… it's saying prepare. Had Jade paused and used her tools, like the 3-R Rule (Recognize – Regulate – Reclaim) or the PERRR Method (Pause, Enquire, Reflect, Recognize, Respond), she might've realized: *"I'm nervous, but this aligns with my goals. What I need is to prepare my nervous system, not abandon the opportunity."* The Floating Zone showed up to guide her. But the old belief, discomfort equals danger, blocked her path.

How to Use the Floating Zone Effectively

Begin to get curious about discomfort. Is it calling you to grow, asking you to retreat, or warning you to realign?

Track your body, not just your thoughts. Your body will speak before your mind understands.

Practice micro-withdrawals, not full shutdowns. Sometimes, just stepping back a little is enough to restore clarity.

Journal or check in. Ask yourself: *What value is being tested? What belief just got activated?*

Anchor before action. Use breathwork, grounding, or your anchor object to find stillness before making a move.

Know your personal signs. Floating doesn't feel the same for everyone. Learn your unique cues. The Floating Zone is the sacred space between who you are and who you are becoming. It doesn't demand movement, it invites alignment. It is the quiet moment when your body speaks before your mind decides. It is the pause that prevents reactivity, the breath that bridges instinct and intention.

Learn to listen here, really listen. Because the discomfort you feel might not be fear. It might be the threshold of your next becoming. And while your discomfort might tell you it's time to stretch, remember growth doesn't mean dragging others along. True expansion honors both your own readiness and the pace of those around you. The Floating Zone teaches you not just when to grow, but how to grow wisely, and kindly.

This zone doesn't ask for mastery. It asks for mindfulness. And the more fluent you become in its language, the more your life becomes guided by inner truth, not outer pressure.

Chapter 10

The Wild Sensitive Backpack

Learning to work with what strengthens you, not what breaks you.

"Carrying many tools doesn't make you a master, using them does. Mastery lives in the reach, the repetition, the quiet moment when you choose the right tool at the right time. As Wild Sensitives, our power comes not from packing light, but from packing wisely, and practicing until those tools become extensions of our inner knowing."
The Living Adventurers

Every craftsman knows, the quality of the outcome doesn't just depend on their skill, it depends on having the right tools for the task. A master woodworker wouldn't use a hammer to smooth an edge, or a chisel to extract a stripped screw. It's not that a hammer is bad, it's just not the right tool for that job. And yet, in the realm of personal growth, many of us have been unknowingly using the wrong tools in the wrong ways, hoping they'll help us heal, connect, or grow.

What we've often been given, or what we've learned to reach for, are tools like grit, overthinking, suppression, avoidance, perfectionism, and performance. Sometimes, these get us through. But often, they leave us bruised, discouraged, or deeply misaligned. They may be the only tools we've known, but that doesn't mean they are the ones we truly need.

In this chapter, we introduce you to a set of tools that are not only ones we've adopted, but ones we've developed, refined, and lived by as Living Adventurers. These tools were designed for the nuanced and layered life of the Wild Sensitive, the one who feels deeply and seeks boldly. But they are also accessible and powerful for anyone who wants to grow in ways that are both sustainable and sovereign.

Think of this as your personal tool backpack. While anyone can gather tools from books, podcasts, courses, or social media posts, owning a tool doesn't make you a craftsman. The difference lies in how you use it. Using tools wisely, consistently, and in the right context requires practice, not pressure. And that practice can't happen in the chaos of everyday life. It must begin in a zone that offers support, guidance, and manageable environments, where learning is honored and feedback is welcomed.

This is where so many Wild Sensitives go wrong, not because they lack will, but because they were never shown how to apply what they've learned. They read the instructions, feel inspired, and then leap into life expecting mastery. But when the tools don't "work," or worse, when they backfire emotionally, they assume something is wrong with them… or that the method is flawed. So, they toss the tool aside, disheartened, whispering: *"I guess this doesn't work for me."*

But the truth is rarely that simple.

Imagine walking into a gym for the first time. You see a machine you've never seen before. There's no guidance, no coach. You sit down, try to guess your way through it, and suddenly drop the weight, hurting your shoulder. Was the equipment broken? Probably not. You just didn't know how to use it yet. Personal growth is no different. Just like physical tools, emotional and cognitive tools require training, proper orientation, and feedback.

This is why life coaches and life guides' matter. A coach is someone who understands which tools will help you meet your goals. They walk you through how to use them, slowly, gently, and with clarity. A professional life guide, however, goes one step further. They know the terrain you're walking. They've lived parts of it themselves. They don't just show you the tools, they walk beside you while you learn to wield them. They support your practice. They help you discern when to act and when to pause. They hold space for the setbacks and celebrate the steps forward.

As Living Adventurers, we've learned, sometimes the hard way, that when it comes to your mental, emotional, and physical well-being, you are not a project. You are a masterpiece in progress. And the way you care for that masterpiece matters. Deeply.

This is why we strongly encourage you to consider working with a trusted coach or guide. Not because you can't do this alone, but because you don't have to. In a world that tells us to self-help our way to perfection, seeking support is a radical and wise act of sovereignty.

That said, we also honor those who are ready to venture forward independently. That's part of the Wild Sensitive path too, the quiet courage to walk with your own rhythm, to try, to adapt, and to learn as you go. This chapter was created with both in mind: those who walk with a guide, and those who walk by starlight and instinct.

So now, let's return to our craftsman metaphor. Picture a quiet, intentional workspace. A wide wooden table. Tools laid out, each with its own purpose. Some smooth, some strong, some subtle. Some you'll use often. Others, only in specific moments of transformation or tension. But each one matters. Before we dive into the tools themselves, we want to clarify something essential: what these tools actually are and what they are not.

Tools for personal growth are not trendy life hacks. They are not clever scripts or "one-size-fits-all" solutions. For the Wild Sensitive, tools must be regulation companions, extensions of your emotional, mental, and physical awareness. They don't exist to "fix" you. They exist to help you return to yourself, again and again, with more clarity, stability, and strength.

Each tool must be chosen with care. A hammer for structure. A file for shaping. A brush for finishing. You wouldn't try to file down a delicate edge with a mallet and yet, many of us try to force progress with only the tools we know, even when those tools hurt us or others. What you learned growing up, perhaps over-control, self-denial, emotional suppression, may have been survival tools. But that doesn't make them healing tools.

Some people even develop what we might call unconscious tools, such as manipulation, avoidance, shutdown, aggression, often out of fear or trauma. These, too, are tools. But they are not ones that honor our relationships, our bodies, or our deeper selves. They may produce short-term control, but they often leave long-term damage. The tools in this chapter were created to counter that pattern. They are gentle yet powerful. They don't dominate your nervous system, they support it. They've been lived and tested by us, not just as ideas, but as lifelines. Each one was born not from theory, but from necessity, forged in the fires of overwhelm, grief, longing, and awakening.

As you read through this chapter, remember having a tool is not the same as knowing how to use it. Give yourself space. Start small. Try one. Practice. Reflect. Adjust. Try again. This isn't a checklist. It's a conversation between you and your growth. And over time, these tools will become more than methods, they'll become muscle memory. They'll become the way you move through the world.

Because here's the truth, your well-being is not optional. It's not indulgent. It's your foundation. And you deserve tools that honor your sensitivity, your speed, and your sovereignty. Let's open the backpack... together.

The 7-P Rule: The First Tool of the Wild Sensitive

Because transformation requires more than tools, it requires thoughtful preparation.

The 7-P Rule stands for, "Proper Prior Planning Prevents Piss Poor Performance."

This isn't just a catchy saying. It's one of the most powerful tools we've ever used, and the very first one we believe every Wild Sensitive needs to carry into their journey.

The 7-P Rule is your reminder to pause before you leap, to prepare before you perform, and to learn before you launch. It's the foundational mindset that says: Know yourself. Know your needs. Know the terrain you're walking into.

As Wild Sensitives, we live in a world that often encourages fast action and one-size-fits-all advice. But we are not one-size-fits-all humans. Our wiring is unique. We feel deeply, process thoroughly, and seek sensation in ways most people don't understand. That's why proper planning for us doesn't just mean setting goals. It means understanding who we are and why we operate the way we do.

Before we can effectively use grounding techniques, emotional tools, or connection strategies, we must first make a conscious commitment to learning:

- *What are the needs of my sensitive nervous system?*
- *What lights up my sensation-seeking side?*
- *What environments dysregulate me?*
- *What tools or practices actually match my emotional landscape, not someone else's?*

Think of it like this, imagine you've just decided to hike the West Coast Trail, the same journey we shared at the beginning of this book. It's your first backpacking trip, and you meet someone who once camped at a drive-in site for a weekend. They tell you, confidently, what you'll need for your trek: *"A sleeping bag, some granola bars, a flashlight, a cheap tent, you'll be fine."* But they've never hiked 75 km of coastal wilderness. They've never navigated shifting tides, mud pits, suspension ladders, or river crossings. Their advice might be well-intentioned, but it's not equipped for your journey.

The same is true for personal development. Your journey requires your own map, your own gear, your own preparation. That's what the 7-P Rule is really about. It invites you to:

- Learn who you are, not just in traits, but in your lived patterns and emotional cycles.
- Understand what tools fit you, not what worked for your friend, your partner, or your favorite podcast host.
- Practice intentionally, choosing tools that serve your nervous system and emotional rhythms.
- Adapt techniques to your pace, personality, and present capacity.

The 7-P Rule reminds you that poor performance is often not personal failure, it's misaligned preparation. If something doesn't work, it may not be the tool; it may be that you haven't yet found the right fit, built the proper foundation, or learned how to apply it in the terrain you're currently walking through. Preparation isn't about perfection, it's about knowing what you need before you need it, and adjusting as you grow, evolve, and encounter new challenges that ask more of you than the last.

That's why this rule comes before all the others in this backpack. It is the difference between using a map and simply wandering. Between thriving and just surviving. Between following someone else's path and claiming your own with confidence, clarity, and the self-trust that comes from choosing your tools with intention.

The 7-Ps in Practice:

Proper – Learn from multiple sources, especially those that understand HSP-HSS dynamics.

Prior – Don't wait until you're overwhelmed. Prepare before you engage.

Planning – Map out your emotional, physical, and relational needs like you would a trip.

Prevents – Anticipate roadblocks. Plan for recovery, not just performance.

Piss Poor – Don't ignore this part. Without it, the best tools will fall short.

Performance – This isn't about productivity. It's about your ability to stay regulated, resourced, and responsive in the moments that matter.

You're not just hiking a trail. You're building a life, one that matches your depth, your sensitivity, and your adventurous spirit. The 7-P Rule ensures you're not just reacting to life but meeting it with readiness. And that readiness? It's not about doing more. It's about knowing yourself well enough to choose wisely. So, before you dive into the rest of this backpack… take a breath. Then ask: *Have I prepared to meet myself well on this journey?*

That's where real change begins.

Emotional Awareness & Somatic Grounding Tools
Tools that help us notice, name, and regulate internal states.

Before we can grow, we must feel a sense of security within ourselves. Before we can stretch, we must feel rooted. And before we can change our lives, we must first know what we're feeling, where it lives in our body, and whether we can stay with it, without collapsing, avoiding, or reacting. This is where all transformation begins for the Wild Sensitive.

For those of us who are both highly sensitive and high sensation seeking, the world is not just observed or experienced, it's absorbed. We take in more, we process more, and we feel more, and need more, often all at once. Our inner world can become deeply layered, overwhelming, or even chaotic if we are unprepared. We might not always be able to name what's happening inside us, but we can feel its weight: a tight chest, a racing thought loop, a flooded heart, or a sudden retreat from everything.

This is why emotional awareness and somatic grounding are not optional skills, they are foundational. These tools help us do what so few were taught to do: recognize, feel, name, and stay with our internal experience long enough to understand it. Not to fix it. Not to judge it. But to listen to it as valuable, embodied information, the kind only Wild Sensitives can fully access.

When we build emotional awareness, we gain the ability to pause in moments of activation and ask, *"What is this really about?"* We begin to notice that our triggers often have deeper roots than we first assumed. We may recognize that beneath our anger is grief. Beneath our fatigue is overstimulation. Beneath our withdrawal is a part of us that doesn't feel comfortable being seen.

At the same time, somatic grounding brings us back into our body, not as an object to control or change, but as a home to return to. When our nervous system is dysregulated, our capacity to think clearly, respond calmly, and stay present disappears. Our body either revs into survival or shuts down into numbness. Without grounding, even the most effective tools can become inaccessible, and even small stressors can feel like too much.

In our experience, and in the lives of those we've supported, true healing doesn't happen when the mind is running the show alone. It happens when the mind, nervous system, and body are aligned. That alignment begins here.

The tools in this section are designed to help you name and understand complex, layered emotions without becoming overwhelmed by them. Return to your body with gentleness, especially when you've been pulled into stress, disconnection, or overstimulation. Regulate your nervous system so you can access clarity, connection, and choice. Create an inner safety, so your system doesn't shut down every time life gets loud, intense, or uncertain.

Some of these tools are simple enough to use in public spaces, during conversations, or while standing in line at the grocery store. Others are best practiced in quiet moments when you have time to pause, enquire, and reflect. Together, they form a gentle scaffolding for emotional resilience, helping you become more attuned to your needs and more present in your choices. They guide you in building a nervous system that can hold both stillness and sensation, both discomfort and delight.

These are not "tricks" to get rid of discomfort. They are invitations into wholeness, into staying connected to yourself, even when things feel hard. They are the very tools we, as Living Adventurers, return to daily. Because we are building lives that are emotionally rich, somatically secure, and deeply aligned.

Before we can reach for external growth, new relationships, new goals, new environments, we must first become allies to our own internal world. That alliance begins with emotional awareness. It deepens through grounding. And it flourishes through practice.

Let's begin with the tools that help you feel again, bringing with them a deep sense of security, presence, and possibility into your life.

The Wild Sensitives Feelings Guide

Because naming what we feel is the first step in coming home to ourselves.

The Wild Sensitives Feelings Guide is not just a list of emotional vocabulary, it is a deeply attuned tool for naming the layered, paradoxical, and often misunderstood emotions that Wild Sensitives experience. Created specifically for those who feel more, sense more, and process more, this guide helps Wild Sensitives develop emotional literacy, which is essential for nervous system regulation, healthy connection, and personal clarity.

At its core, this guide is about naming the invisible. So many of us were never taught how to identify what we feel, only how to suppress it, justify it, or apologize for it. And for Wild Sensitives, that suppression can be even more disorienting because we experience emotions in layers, not in isolation. We may feel exhilarated and anxious at the same time. We may feel lonely in a crowd or overwhelmed by joy. Without the language to describe these nuances, we often default to saying *"I'm fine"* or *"I don't know,"* even when something significant is stirring inside us.

This guide is useful because it gives your inner experience words, weight, and worth. When you can name what you feel, with accuracy and compassion, you can respond to yourself in ways that bring relief, connection, and choice. Unnamed emotions tend to stay stuck. Named emotions begin to move. They soften. They clarify. They lead you toward your needs instead of away from them.

How to Use the Guide

Use the Wild Sensitives Feelings Guide anytime you feel emotionally overwhelmed, disconnected, uncertain, or stuck. Begin by checking in with your body. Ask yourself:

"Where am I feeling this?"

"What sensation is present, tension, heaviness, buzzing, numbness?"

Then scan the guide to see what emotion most closely fits what you're sensing. You may resonate with more than one, that's normal. Wild Sensitives often feel multiple emotions at once. Choose one or two to begin with and let yourself name them without needing to "fix" or explain anything. Just the act of naming begins the integration.

You can use this guide in journaling, in therapy or coaching sessions, before making a decision, or simply as a quiet check-in with yourself when something feels off. Over time, it helps you create an internal vocabulary that builds emotional trust within your system, the kind of trust that allows regulation, resilience, and connection to flourish.

The Feelings Categories

Below are categories of emotions that frequently arise in Wild Sensitives. Each category includes several nuanced emotional states, along with somatic cues and common triggers, to help you identify what may be happening within you. While feelings can show up differently, what it feels like to one person can be different in another, the following are just a few examples, so feel free to create your own descriptions.

Vulnerability-Based Emotions

These arise when your internal world feels exposed or threatened, whether through beauty, connection, or fear of being seen.

Exposed – Emotionally "naked," uncertain how others will respond
Body cues: fluttery chest, tight throat
  Triggers: sharing something personal, being observed too closely

Tender – Open-hearted, moved by intimacy or beauty
  Body cues: warm chest, watery eyes
  Triggers: acts of kindness, emotional resonance, music, poetry

Fragile – Emotionally thin-skinned, easily impacted
  Body cues: tension in face, quick startle response
  Triggers: emotional fatigue, criticism, overstimulation

Activation Emotions (Drive + Restlessness)

These feelings arise when your HSS wiring is seeking stimulation, novelty, or expression, but can't find an outlet.

Electrified – Buzzing with energy or ideas to the point of overwhelm
Body cues: tingling limbs, quick speech
Triggers: new inspiration, social energy, caffeine, overstimulation

Caged – Confined, blocked, or creatively stifled
Body cues: clenched fists, pacing, fidgeting
Triggers: repetitive environments, lack of freedom or movement

Starved – Emotionally or sensorially, craving meaningful stimulation
Body cues: sighing, screen scrolling, drifting attention
Triggers: boredom, emotional flatness, shallow conversation

Disorientation & Disconnect Emotions

These reflect internal fragmentation or a loss of clarity, often due to overwhelm or emotional layering.

Fragmented – Pulled in multiple internal directions, hard to focus
Body cues: headache, forgetfulness, foggy mind
Triggers: too many tasks, unprocessed emotion, social expectations

Floating – Untethered, disconnected from body or core
Body cues: light-headedness, numb limbs, zoning out
Triggers: overstimulation, conflict avoidance, emotional bypassing

Overfull – Too much to process, can't take in one more thing
Body cues: head pressure, hot face, defensive tone
Triggers: crowded spaces, back-to-back interactions, lack of solitude

Anger & Boundary Emotions

These arise when your space, truth, or time has been disrespected or denied.

Bristled – Irritated, prickly, reactive
  Body cues: jaw clenching, shallow breath
  Triggers: noise, interruption, lack of attunement

Invaded – Unwelcome intrusion into your energy or space
  Body cues: leaning away, physical tension
  Triggers: unsolicited advice, emotional dumping, physical contact

Suppressed – Holding back truth or expression to maintain peace
  Body cues: chest pressure, voice strain
  Triggers: fear of being too much, performance roles, people-pleasing

Grief & Melancholy Emotions
These feelings hold depth and often accompany transition, reflection, or emotional release.

Saturated – Soaked in emotion with nowhere to pour it
  Body cues: heavy limbs, tears near surface
  Triggers: emotional buildup, endings, art, music

Lonesome – Not just alone, unseen or emotionally un-held
  Body cues: low belly ache, aching chest
  Triggers: social disconnection, being in a crowd without resonance

Nostalgic Ache – Bittersweet longing for a time or feeling once held
  Body cues: misty eyes, distant gaze
  Triggers: memory, scent, music, holidays

Elevation & Expansion Emotions
These emotions reflect when you're aligned with meaning, creativity, or connection.

Lit – Bright, turned on, full of insight or energy
  Body cues: wide eyes, alert posture
  Triggers: shared values, creative bursts, new ideas

Aligned – Peaceful, rooted, deeply okay
  Body cues: open chest, smooth breath
  Triggers: congruent action, values-led choices, solitude

Moved – Touched by something meaningful or beautiful
  Body cues: goosebumps, soft smile, deep exhale
  Triggers: music, truth spoken aloud, intimacy, art

Your emotions are not messes to clean up. They are messages to understand. The Wild Sensitives Feelings Guide isn't here to tame you, it's here to help you track your truth. Use it as a compass. A mirror. A language you're learning to speak fluently. The more clearly you name what lives inside you, the more safely and skillfully you can live from it.

Emotional Landscape Mapping
Because knowing where you are helps you know what to do next.

Emotional Landscape Mapping is a self-awareness tool designed by us, The Living Adventurers, to help Wild Sensitives locate themselves in their internal environment, emotionally, mentally, and physically, so they can make informed, compassionate choices rather than reactive or avoidant ones.

As Wild Sensitives, we experience life deeply and dynamically. But when emotions rise or overwhelm hits, we often lose our sense of internal "place." We may not know if we're emotionally secure to stretch, or if we're on the edge of shutdown. We may push too far into stimulation when what we need is stillness. Or we may hide in safety when what we actually crave is engagement. That's where this tool becomes essential.

Emotional Landscape Mapping gives us a framework, a personal navigation system, for assessing our readiness, resilience, and relational openness in any moment. It helps us shift from confusion or collapse to clarity and self-trust. Instead of guessing, it allows us to pause and ask: *Where am I right now? And what does this place require from me or offer me?*

Why It's Useful

Most people move through emotional states unconsciously, reacting based on habit, fear, or pressure. But Wild Sensitives tend to feel first and think second, which means our nervous system may make decisions before our conscious mind has caught up. This can lead to impulsive actions, avoidance, emotional reactivity, or self-doubt. When you know your location on your emotional landscape, you gain access to choice. You can honor your needs instead of overriding them. You can regulate your system before you collapse. You can stretch just enough to grow, not enough to break.

This tool also helps us navigate the paradox of being both sensitive and sensation-seeking. Sometimes we crave stimulation while simultaneously needing stillness. Emotional Landscape Mapping helps us sort through those inner tensions, gently and practically.

How to Use It

At any point during your day, especially before or after a challenging moment, pause and check in. Using the zones below, ask yourself:

"Which zone am I currently in?"

"What sensations, emotions, or thoughts tell me I'm here?"

"What is the healthiest next step from this place?"

You can mentally map this, journal it, or even speak it aloud. Over time, you'll begin to recognize your own patterns and build an internal GPS that keeps you grounded and empowered, even when things feel intense or unpredictable. This practice strengthens trust in yourself and deepens emotional clarity.

The Six Emotional Zones of the Wild Sensitive Landscape

Each of these six zones represents a common internal state. None are "bad" or "wrong," they simply require different strategies for care, connection, and growth.

Safe Zone
Definition: You feel fully regulated, open, steady. This is your reset zone.

Body cues: Calm breath, open posture, soft eyes.

Emotions: Peaceful, present, grounded.

Use this time for: Rest, reflection, nourishment, creative play.

Warning: You may feel tempted to stay here too long and avoid future growth, bore-out, loneliness and depression can be felt.

Comfort Zone
Definition: Familiar and easy, but low in growth energy. You're not challenged, and you're not distressed.

Body cues: Slight stillness, habitual movement.

Emotions: Content, relaxed, fulfilled, accepted.

Use this time for: Connecting with friends and family.

Warning: Staying too long here can lead to emotional bore-out or stagnation.

Goldilocks Zone (Optimal Stretch Zone)
Definition: Stimulated but not overwhelmed. Curious, challenged, capable. You're expanding your edge with care.

Body cues: Heightened energy, tingles, strong breath.

Emotions: Inspired, engaged, clarity, confident.

Use this time for: Practicing new skills, gentle exploration, honest conversations.

Warning: Don't confuse adrenaline with alignment, keep checking in.

Secure Zone (Regulated Risk)

Definition: You're engaging with challenge that pushes your current skills to new levels, while staying regulated through tools or support.

Body cues: Elevated heart rate, steady voice, slight nervous tremble.

Emotions: Excited, alert, challenged, determined.

Use this time for: Coaching, therapy, stretching with supervision or guidance.

Warning: Don't stay too long without rest or recovery, check your energy reserves.

Risk Zone (Unregulated Exposure)

Definition: You're pushing too far or too fast. You feel exposed, scattered, or vulnerable to collapse.

Body cues: Rapid breath, frozen body, flushed skin.

Emotions: Overwhelm, burnout, anxiety, fear.

Use this time for: Brief recognition of your current limits.

Warning: Growth doesn't happen here, injury does. Return to your comfort zone first. If needed step into your Safe zone until you have recuperated.

Floating Zone (Your signal zone)

Definition: The zone that floats between all other zones, your messenger that tells you when to shift zones.

Body cues: When experiencing withdraw discomfort, tight chest, shallow breathing, slumping posture, drooping shoulders, the desire to hide, go silent, or leave a space or conversation. When experiencing growth discomfort, fidgeting, tapping fingers, shifting positions often, feeling trapped in your skin, yawning, even if well rested, sighing repeatedly without full relief.

Emotions: Confusion, uncertainty, uneasiness, jittery, restless, scared, avoidant.

Use this to: Recognize the discomfort, learn to understand its needs.

Warning: Fear, limiting beliefs and past conditioning can override this zone and send false messages. Be mindful if it's a true message or a false message.

The goal of Emotional Landscape Mapping is not to stay in the "best" zone or to force yourself into constant expansion. The goal is to honor where you are and respond from that place with care and curiosity. Each zone offers insight. Each has a purpose and a message. When you learn to map your inner world with compassion, you stop reacting out of habit and start responding from sovereignty, with grounded presence, emotional clarity, and self-trust guiding your next step.

Return to this map as often as needed. Make it your own. Your emotions are not your enemies; they are guides to your next right step. Keep exploring where you are, one zone at a time, with patience, presence, and a willingness to be surprised.

Somatic Grounding & Breathwork

Because you can't think your way to safety, you have to feel your way there.

Somatic Grounding & Breathwork is the practice of using your body and breath to create internal stability, especially in moments of emotional overwhelm, sensory overload, or disconnection. It helps bring the nervous system back to a regulated state by focusing not on solving problems, but on settling the system that's reacting to them.

For Wild Sensitives, dysregulation often happens quickly and silently. A tone of voice, a crowded room, too many open tabs, even someone else's unspoken tension, can send our system into subtle panic, shutdown, or overdrive. In those moments, our thoughts race, emotions surge, or we go numb. We disconnect from our body because it feels like too much. And the deeper truth is, we're not safe to feel until we know we can stay. That's why somatic grounding and breathwork give us the ability to stay.

Why It's Useful

Somatic practices, like breathwork, body scanning, and grounding, are not just alternative wellness trends; they are evidence-backed methods proven to regulate the nervous system and improve emotional resilience. Scientific studies show that intentional breathing techniques can activate the parasympathetic nervous system, lower cortisol levels and reducing symptoms of anxiety, depression, and PTSD. Breath awareness reconnects the mind to the body, a particularly powerful intervention for those of us who live in our heads or carry trauma in our tissues.

This reconnection is vital: it provides a way to self-regulate when stimulation becomes too much and offers access to calm presence when the world feels overwhelming. In our own work and lived experience, somatic practices have often been the doorway, to embodiment, clarity, and authentic power. When we bring our awareness to the body, through grounding techniques, conscious breathing, and mindful presence, we signal to the brain: We're not in danger. We're here now.

For Highly Sensitive High Sensation Seekers, this is especially important. Our sensitivity heightens our reactivity, and our sensation-seeking nature often places us in stimulating or high-energy environments. Without regulation, we either become overwhelmed or we detach. Breathwork and grounding allow us to remain present, emotionally, cognitively, and physically, without collapsing or overextending.

This isn't about forcing calm or pretending we're okay. It's about creating enough internal stability to re-engage from a place of sovereignty and self-connection.

How to Use it

There are many ways to ground and breathe intentionally. The key is to practice regularly, not just in crisis, so your body begins to associate these tools with comfort and security and return.

Practice regularly when you are in your Comfort zone and Goldilocks zones. Practice, especially in your Safe Zone. It is also ok to practice these in your Secure zone. Remember, it is when you are in your Risk zone, these tools help guide you back to one of the other zones. Think of them as your guiding light home.

Below are several tools, each adaptable to different contexts, environments, and levels of activation. You can also find instructional videos on our website at wildsensitive.com

Somatic Grounding Tools

Use these when you feel disconnected, overstimulated, or unmoored in your body.

Rooted Feet

- Stand or sit with both feet flat on the ground. Take a minute to slow down your breathing and become aware of your body.
- Press your feet gently into the floor. Imagine roots growing downward, anchoring you.

- Wiggle your toes. Shift your weight slightly from heel to ball.
- Silently say: *"I am here. I am safe. I belong in this body."*
- Don't rush through it, take 5 minutes to really imagine it, and feel your feet.

Surface Mapping

- Bring awareness to three body parts in contact with your environment (e.g., feet on floor, back on chair, hands in lap).
- Notice temperature, texture, and pressure.
- Describe them silently or aloud: *"My back feels supported. My hands are warm."*
- This returns you to sensory presence and out of spinning thought.

The Holding Wrap

- Cross your arms and gently hold your upper arms or shoulders.
- Apply soft pressure, like a self-hug.
- Breathe slowly and rhythmically, holding for 30 seconds to 1 minute.
- This mimics co-regulation and helps your body feel contained.

Breathwork Tools

These breath patterns support nervous system regulation and emotional reset. Practice in quiet moments and also when agitation arises.

Box Breathing (4-4-4-4)

- Inhale for 4 counts
- Hold for 4 counts
- Exhale for 4 counts
- Hold for 4 counts
- Repeat 4–6 times

Use when: You feel anxious, flooded, or scattered. Creates rhythm and balance.

4-7-8 Breathing
- Inhale through the nose for 4 counts
- Hold for 7 counts
- Exhale slowly through the mouth for 8 counts
- Repeat 3–4 cycles

Use when: You feel wired but tired, overstimulated, or emotionally fragile. Slows the heart rate and calms racing thoughts.

Tension Release Exhale
- Inhale deeply through the nose
- Hold for 2 seconds
- Exhale with a sound — a sigh, hum, or soft moan — through the mouth
- Let your shoulders drop as you exhale

Use when: You need an emotional reset or to release pent-up energy without words.

Putting It into Practice

It is vitally important that you do not wait until you're overwhelmed to use these tools. In fact, they are most effective when practiced regularly, even when you feel fine. Just one or two minutes of breathwork or body connection throughout the day creates a baseline of stability.

Then, when disruption happens, your system already knows the path back to center. If you're unsure which tool to try:
- Use feet or surface grounding when you feel dissociated or mentally unanchored.
- Use box breathing when you're overstimulated or anxious.
- Use holding techniques when you feel emotionally unsafe or exposed.
- Use sound on exhale when emotional intensity is rising fast and needs release.

You can also layer breathwork with somatic grounding for more power: ground your feet while box breathing or hold your shoulders while doing a 4-7-8 breath cycle.

One of the biggest mistakes Wild Sensitives make is trying to analyze or explain what's happening emotionally before the nervous system has returned to regulation. But the truth is: when you're dysregulated, the mind will make meaning from a place of fear, not clarity. This is why PERRRing is so effective. In pausing, we breathe and ground ourselves. Once we have Paused and re-zoned ourselves, we can then Enquire by asking, what am I feeling? What do I need?

From there, the next step becomes more visible, and more self-honoring.

Somatic Grounding & Breathwork won't make you immune to the world. But they will make you sovereign within it. And that changes everything.

Pocket Grounding Tools for Wild Sensitives
Because sometimes, you need to come back to yourself quietly, without stepping away.

Pocket Grounding Tools are simple, sensory-based practices you can use anytime, anywhere to quickly reconnect to your body, calm your nervous system, and re-center your emotional state. They're small in action, but powerful in effect, especially for Wild Sensitives who often find themselves energetically flooded or emotionally raw in everyday environments.

These tools are what we reach for in conversations that feel too sharp, in rooms that feel too loud, or in moments when we suddenly feel the urge to shut down or disappear. Their power lies in discretion and repetition. You can use them in a meeting, at a dinner table, while walking, or on public transit, without needing to explain, pause your day, or retreat from others.

They are quick recalibrations, allowing your body, breath, and awareness to reconnect when intensity rises. Think of them like internal handrails, steadying you quietly so you don't collapse inward or lash outward.

Pressure Pulse
A grounding gesture to signal "I am here. I am secure."

What it is
A subtle, rhythmic finger-press technique that uses tactile sensation to re-anchor your awareness to your body in moments of stress, overwhelm, or dissociation.

Why it's useful
When overstimulated or emotionally flooded, the Wild Sensitive nervous system often starts to detach, floating into mental fog, heightened alertness, or emotional reactivity. Physical pressure, applied gently and with rhythm, activates proprioception (body awareness), signaling security and control.

How to use it
- Gently press your thumb and index finger together.
- Hold for 3–4 seconds. Then release.
- Move to the middle finger. Press. Hold. Release.
- Repeat for each finger, one at a time, both hands if needed.
- As you press, silently say: *"Here. Now. Secure."*
- Complete as many rounds as needed, until you feel tension reduce or focus return.

Ground Through Breath and Word
Pairing breath and intention to calm your system in one cycle.

What it is
A quick grounding technique that combines a conscious exhale with a chosen word (spoken silently or quietly aloud) to restore emotional regulation and redirect inner dialogue.

Why it's useful
When the inner world gets loud, with spiraling thoughts, emotional flashbacks, or external pressure, breath alone may not feel like enough.

Adding a resonant word links the breath to meaning, offering both physiological and emotional support in one.

How to use it
- Inhale slowly through your nose.
- As you exhale through your mouth (or nose, if in public), silently repeat one word. Choose something like:
  - *"Peace."*
  - *"Here."*
  - *"Ease."*
  - *"Soft."*
- Repeat for 2–3 full breaths, each with the word.
- Let your nervous system match the rhythm of the breath and the tone of the word.

Choose your grounding word before stress hits. Keep it simple, soothing, and emotionally resonant. It becomes a touchstone that your body will begin to associate with calm over time.

Three-Point Trace
A somatic mapping tool to bring mind, heart, and body back into alignment.

What it is
A gentle gesture of tracing a small triangle on your palm, symbolically connecting your head, heart, and gut, to restore your awareness.

Why it's useful
In moments of overwhelm, Wild Sensitives often become mentally overloaded or emotionally hijacked, leaving the body behind. This tool helps realign your thinking, feeling, and sensing centers, bringing them back into conversation with one another. It's subtle, portable, and deeply regulating.

How to use it

Open one hand, palm up.

With the index finger of your other hand, gently trace a small triangle. Start at the bottom left corner.

1. As you trace upward: *"Mind — what am I thinking?"*
2. Across the top: *"Heart — what am I feeling?"*
3. Back down: *"Gut — what do I sense or know?"*

- You don't need perfect answers. The act of tracing and asking is the regulation.
- Repeat if needed, slowly and with presence.

Optional: Pair this with a slow breath for each point. Let the triangle become your anchor for realignment in emotionally complex moments.

Why These Tools Work

Each of these Pocket Grounding Tools targets one or more systems:

- **Pressure Pulse** regulates tactile input and activates the parasympathetic system.
- **Breath and Word** bridges the cognitive and autonomic systems.
- **Three-Point Trace** reconnects fragmented awareness across mental, emotional, and somatic layers.

Together, they offer a portable safety net, a quiet way to return to center without needing to explain, withdraw, or pretend you're fine. And over time, as they become part of your nervous system's rhythm, they become micro-acts of self-trust.

These aren't just tricks to calm down, they are practices of belonging to yourself, even when the world is loud, the moment is tender, or the feeling is too big to name yet.

Keep them close. You never know when you'll need to come home to yourself, gently, and without delay.

Mental Recalibration & Reflective Practices

Because your mind isn't your enemy, it just needs better instructions.

For Wild Sensitives, the mind is a double-edged gift. We think deeply, reflect instinctively, and absorb meaning from even the smallest cues. But when we're under stress, this gift can turn into a spiral, racing thoughts, mental replays, or over-analysis that leaves us paralyzed. This is especially true in environments that are emotionally charged, socially complex, or overstimulating.

Mental Recalibration is the art of slowing the mind without silencing it. It's about giving our cognitive system a structure to respond instead of reacting. Reflective Practices help us process events and interactions after they happen, so we don't carry emotional residue or live on mental replay.

These tools help us turn sensitivity into sovereignty, not by reducing how much we feel, but by retraining how we think during and after emotional moments. Used regularly, they become internal mental anchors that keep us from spinning out, shutting down, or giving away our power.

The 3-R Rule: Recognize – Regulate – Reclaim

What it is
A rapid response tool to help you interrupt instinctive reactions and choose intentional responses, especially in emotionally triggering or overstimulating situations.

Why it's useful
Many Wild Sensitives experience "emotional hijacking," where we react automatically from old programming, rather than from current truth. The 3-R Rule helps you create just enough space between stimulus and reaction to regain clarity and self-direction.

How to Use It (Step-by-Step)

Recognize – This is immediate awareness that you're being triggered. It's not asking you how or why, just awareness that it is happening. No action, response or reaction is required, just awareness.

Regulate – Pause and ground. Use a somatic grounding or breath tool to calm the nervous system. This could be a Pocket Tool like Pressure Pulse or a simple deep breath. Again, you are not trying to figure out how or why, you're simply regaining mental control to re-zone yourself. Your goal is to regulate before you make any responses, which are often only reactions.

Reclaim – When you have reclaimed your mental clarity, you can then decide which tool is best suited for the situation. Use the 3-R Rule in conversations, meetings, conflict, or when emotional intensity rises quickly. With practice, it becomes an automatic pause button for alignment.

P.E.R.R.R. Method

Pause – Enquire – Reflect – Recognize – Respond

What it is

A short reflective decision-making framework for effective decision making. This tool is only effective if you are not in conflict, or confused, as high emotional or sensory input makes clear thought difficult. It is used after the 3-R rule, or in situations where we need to apply our careful deep processing.

Why it's useful

Wild Sensitives often feel so much so fast that our decisions can either become impulsive or completely frozen. Once have regained our ability to think, PERRR creates a gentle pathway to appropriate and effective responses after we have converted that intensity into something more manageable. It is here we are giving both the heart and mind a seat at the table.

How to Use It

Pause: Stop what you're doing. No action, no explanation. Create a moment of space.

Enquire: Ask yourself, *what's happening inside me right now? What emotions, sensations, or thoughts are present?*

Reflect: Is this reaction coming from the present, or from a pattern, a past hurt, or a fear of judgment?

Recognize: Notice any mental stories running the show. Is there a belief trying to drive a reaction (e.g., *"I'm not allowed to say no"* or *"I'll be abandoned"*)?

Respond: From this clarity, choose your next step, to control your response in staying true to yourself, and not based on reacting to the situation.

Many believe they need to respond to situations immediately. Although we have experienced this a few times, most do not. While some believe these tools take time, with enough practice they become automatic and lightning fast. It is far better to respond with intention then to react, even if the response isn't accurate, because reactions leave people questioning your emotional management. Try and journal your PERRR's after tough conversations or mentally walk through it before important choices.

Meaning-Driven Decision Filter
Real. Aligned. Necessary.

What it is
A 3-part internal filter that helps prevent burnout, overcommitment, and people-pleasing by aligning your choices with your core values and truth.

Why it's useful

Wild Sensitives often say "yes" too quickly, to avoid discomfort, keep peace, or chase excitement. But decisions made from reaction instead of alignment often leave us drained or resentful. This filter brings your compass back into play.

How to Use It

Before committing to something, ask yourself:

Is this real? - *Is this request or offer rooted in truth, or am I projecting fear, fantasy, or old stories onto it?*

Is this aligned? - *Does this choice reflect my values, needs, or boundaries, or is it a performance or a "should"?*

Is this necessary? - *Is this the right time, energy, and place for this action? Or is it urgency disguised as importance?*

If all three answers are *"yes,"* move forward. If any are *"no"* or unclear, PERRR. PERRRing can protect your energy, deepen your discernment, and prevent emotional or energetic debt.

Reflective Debriefing

What we unpack, we don't have to carry.

What it is

A post-event reflection practice that helps you process and integrate experiences, especially emotionally charged ones, so they don't linger in your system.

Why it's useful

Wild Sensitives are meaning-makers. We often replay moments long after they end, especially when something felt off, unresolved, or emotionally intense. Without conscious reflection, we can internalize guilt, shame, or confusion. This tool helps release, reframe, and reset.

How to Use It

After an event, interaction, or even a full day, set aside 5–10 minutes to ask yourself:

- *What happened - objectively?*
- *What did I feel - and where did I feel it in my body?*
- *What stories did my mind create about this moment?*
- *What part of this feels true, and what part may be old pattern or fear?*
- *What do I want to carry forward, and what can I now release?*

You can journal this, speak it aloud, or reflect quietly. The goal is integration, not self-critique. Your mind is not a battlefield. It is a brilliant, sensitive, meaning-seeking companion. These recalibration tools don't silence your mind, they teach it to trust you. With every pause, breath, and reflection, you rebuild your ability to lead yourself from alignment, not anxiety. And that, dear Wild Sensitive, is what true mental sovereignty looks like.

Boundary Work & Self-Permission Practices

Because protecting your energy is not selfish, it's sacred.

For Wild Sensitives, boundaries are not just about saying *"no."* They are about creating conditions where our nervous systems can stay regulated, our emotions can be honored, and our truths can be expressed.

Boundaries aren't walls. They're containers, and when built with clarity and compassion, they allow intimacy and expansion to occur without us losing ourselves. But for those who feel deeply, think intuitively, and read the room before we read ourselves, boundary work can feel unnatural or even unsafe. Many of us were taught to attune to others, to avoid conflict, or to perform to be loved.

That's why boundary work must begin inside. And that's where self-permission practices come in. They remind us that we are allowed to take up space. To rest. To say no. To be misunderstood without overexplaining. To choose the path that honors our system, not the one that pleases the crowd. These inner boundaries are not rigid walls, they are living agreements with ourselves, rooted in self-respect and evolving with our growth. They are not fixed in place, but flexible and responsive, adapting to different contexts while still anchoring us in truth, clarity, and emotional safety.

This section equips you with tools to create external space and internal freedom. It's for the version of you who is tired of shrinking, silencing, and shape-shifting, and ready to return to sovereignty.

Sensory Boundary Awareness
Noticing your sensory thresholds and protecting your energetic space.

What it is
A practice of learning your personal limits when it comes to sound, touch, light, texture, temperature, and emotional energy, and adjusting your environment accordingly.

Why it's useful
Wild Sensitives don't just feel emotions, we also absorb and react to sensory input at a heightened level. A conversation in a bright café, a loud meeting, or a tag in a shirt can tip us into dysregulation without warning. Without awareness, we may think we're emotionally "broken" when in reality, our sensory boundary has simply been crossed.

How to Use It
- Begin noticing when you feel overstimulated or shut down.
  Ask: *"What just changed in my environment?"*
- Track your personal thresholds: noise, proximity, light, scent.
- Create a *"Sensory Map"* of what environments feel calming, neutral, or activating.
- Make adjustments: noise-canceling headphones, warm lighting, clothing that soothes, quiet recharge spaces, planned breaks during social events.

- Normalize saying, "I need to adjust my environment before I can engage fully."

Boundaries aren't just what you say to others. They're how you care for your system before it cries out in pain. When you practice this before you become overstimulated, making this a habit, you'll become better at recognizing when you are getting overwhelmed. *Asking yourself, "what am I feeling, emotionally and physically, right now, and is it sustainable?" "Am I still choosing this, or just enduring it?"*

Boundary Scripts
Words that protect your peace without guilt or apology.

What it is
Pre-written, emotionally congruent phrases that express your limits clearly, respectfully, and without over-explaining.

Why it's useful
In the heat of the moment, especially when overwhelmed or caught off guard, Wild Sensitives often freeze. We don't want to disappoint or be misunderstood. Having scripts prepared ahead of time helps you stay grounded and express boundaries without spiraling into anxiety or guilt.

How to Use It
Create a short list of "go-to" phrases for different categories of boundaries:
- **Time/Energy:**
  "I'd love to connect, but I don't have the capacity right now."
- **Sensory:**
  "I need a quiet space to reset before I can continue this conversation."

- **Emotional:**
  "I'm not available for this topic right now. Let's return to it later."
- **Touch/Space:**
  "I prefer not to be touched right now, thank you for understanding."

Practice saying these aloud in neutral moments so they're familiar when you need them.

Radical Self-Permission Statements
Rewriting the internal scripts that keep you small.

What it is
A reframing tool that replaces inherited, fear-based beliefs with conscious, compassionate permission to be who you are, without justification.

Why it's useful
Many Wild Sensitives carry internal narratives like:
- *"I have to earn rest."*
- *"If I speak up, I'll be rejected."*
- *"It's my job to keep everyone else comfortable.*

These beliefs are boundary blockers. Self-permission statements create an internal sense of comfort by affirming that you are allowed to honor your limits, without needing someone else's approval or justification. They restore agency, rebuild trust in your inner voice, and remind you that self-worth isn't earned through constant accommodation.

How to Use It
Start by identifying a situation where you feel pressure or guilt. Then write a counter-statement beginning with:
- *"I give myself permission to…"*
- *"I am…"*
- *"It's okay for me to…"*

Examples:
- *"I give myself permission to say no without explaining."*
- *"I am confident."*
- *"It's okay for me to rest even if others are still working."*

Counter statements should be said in an affirming, positive and present tense. Say I am confident, verses I need to find confidence. Saying *"I am confident"* affirms confidence as part of your identity, prompting your mind and body to align with it. In contrast, *"I need to find confidence"* creates a sense of lack, keeping confidence outside yourself and reinforcing hesitation. The words you choose shape your self-perception, confidence is not found, it's embodied. These statements can be spoken aloud, written, or placed in visible areas. Use them daily until your nervous system begins to believe them.

Self-Belonging Practice
The simple but profound mantra: "I belong to myself."

What it is
A centering phrase used to reclaim internal power, especially after experiences of people-pleasing, emotional disconnection, or performance-based self-worth.

Why it's useful
As Wild Sensitives, we are often taught to belong to others, to be palatable, agreeable, accommodating. This creates fragmentation. But when we say, *"I belong to myself,"* we declare that our emotions, energy, and attention are ours first, not something to be bartered or sacrificed for acceptance.

How to Use It
- Say it quietly or internally in moments of overwhelm, decision-making, or self-doubt.
- Place one hand on your chest, breathe in, and say: *"I belong to myself."*
- Repeat until the words begin to soften the inner tension.
- Use it post-boundary, post-conflict, or post-performance to re-anchor in your truth.

Over time, this phrase becomes a homecoming, a signal to your system that safety isn't "out there," it's inside your own alignment.

When you practice boundary work and radical self-permission, you aren't pushing people away, you're creating space to be fully present with yourself first, and then with others. These tools aren't about control, they're about care. They are the scaffolding that lets you live, love, and create without losing your center. Protect your energy. Honor your needs. You don't have to explain why you matter, only believe it long enough for your nervous system to remember it too.

Expansion & Resilience Practices
Tools for growing courageously while respecting your sacred limits.

Expansion is not about constant forward motion. And resilience isn't about "bouncing back," it's about staying intact as you stretch into new experiences, sensations, and expressions of self.

For Wild Sensitives, life is a delicate dance between the craving to explore and the need to retreat. One part of us wants to leap into the world. The other part wants to hide from its noise. Without guidance, we either suppress our growth to stay safe, or we chase stimulation until we burn out.

Expansion & Resilience Practices were created to help us grow wisely, by honoring our unique wiring and learning how to stretch without snapping. These tools are not about forcing bravery or pushing past pain. They are about building capacity slowly, with curiosity, choice, and somatic awareness. This section introduces four key tools, each one designed to help you engage with life more fully while remaining rooted in your emotional, mental, and physical alignment. These practices respect your nervous system, while also reminding you that growth, adventure, and meaning are not just allowed, they are essential to your wellbeing.

Self-Guided Exposure
Growing capacity by micro-dosing discomfort, safely and intentionally.

What it is
A practice of intentionally introducing small, manageable challenges that help you retrain your nervous system to tolerate growth without panic or collapse.

Why it's useful
Wild Sensitives often avoid discomfort not because we're weak, but because our systems were overwhelmed early, without support. This tool helps you stretch your edge on purpose, in secure ways, so that growth doesn't feel like a threat, but a process you control.

How to Use It
Identify an area where you feel called to grow, but fear or resistance stops you. (Examples: speaking up in groups, trying something new, being seen.)

Choose a low-stakes version of that activity.
(Instead of joining a large class, try one conversation. Instead of a bold post online, write it just for yourself.)

Before doing it, breathe and ground. Let your body know it's safe.

Do the thing. Reflect afterward with:
"What did I feel?" "What did I learn?" "What capacity did I just build?"

Repeat. Slightly increase intensity only when your system feels steady. This is not exposure therapy. It's sovereign experimentation, you lead, you pace, you choose.

Micro-Novelty Practices
Feeding your High Sensation Seeking side without tipping into chaos.

What it is

A creative strategy to introduce manageable variety and meaningful change into your life, to prevent bore-out, creative stagnation, and emotional flatness.

Why it's useful

The HSS part of the Wild Sensitive craves newness, but not just for entertainment. We seek depth, beauty, mystery, and aliveness. Without novelty, we can feel depressed, irritable, or creatively starved. Micro-novelty offers safe stimulation without destabilizing the nervous system.

How to Use It

Choose one new thing daily, weekly, or monthly that awakens your senses or engages your creativity.

Keep it small but intentional

- Try a new tea.
- Take a different route home.
- Rearrange a room.
- Read a new genre.
- Listen to a new song or style of music
- Get a piece of clothing or bedding with a new texture."
- Wear something that feels a bit daring.

After each micro-novelty, ask yourself:

"Did this energize me?" "Did this ground me?" "Would I try this again?"

Over time, this practice becomes a gentle thrill for the nervous system, creating a sense of adventure without overwhelm.

Structured Adventure Planning

Creating experiences that balance stimulation and recovery.

What it is

A system for planning intentional, nourishing adventures, from solo retreats to creative projects or life transitions, with built-in cycles of risk and rest.

Why it's useful
Most people plan based on the outcomes. Wild Sensitives must also plan based on our emotional and sensory impact. Without structure, our adventures can exhaust us. With structure, they empower us.

How to Use It
Choose an "experience," something that excites and challenges you.

Ask yourself:
- *"What part of this will light me up?"*
- *"What part may flood me?"*
- *"Where will I need to recover?"*

Build your plan in four phases:
1. **Prepare** — Ground, set intention, clear your space
2. **Engage** — Show up, stretch, allow expansion
3. **Recover** — Rest, reflect, decompress
4. **Integrate** — *"What did I learn?" "What changed in me?"*

Include self-care checkpoints, co-regulation support (if needed), and space for rest after big emotional exertion.

This tool is especially helpful when preparing for:
- Public speaking
- Travel
- Social events
- Creative launches
- Life transitions (moving, ending a relationship, changing jobs)

Daily Integration & Pre/Post-Engagement Rituals
Because real transformation doesn't just happen in big moments, it happens in the everyday.

Change, for Wild Sensitives, isn't just cognitive, it's cellular. Every insight we receive, every risk we take, every stretch we make leaves an imprint on our emotional and nervous systems. But without space to process, integrate, and reset, even positive change can become overwhelming. That's why integration is not just the final step in a growth process, it's what makes the growth last.

Daily Integration Rituals and Pre/Post-Engagement Practices are small but powerful tools that help us anchor the shifts we're making into our bodies, thoughts, and daily lives. They act like bookends around experiences, creating containers of grounding before, and emotional recovery after, high-energy interactions or environments.

These rituals are not about performance. They're about staying in relationship with yourself as you move through the complexity of life. They help prevent emotional residue, burnout, social hangovers, and internal misalignment. They're especially crucial for Wild Sensitives who are often in motion, craving stimulation, but needing deep recovery in order to remain regulated and whole.

Pre-Event Rituals
Preparing your system before stepping into stimulation, so you remain rooted in yourself, not lost in the environment.

What it is
A grounding practice that calms the nervous system and connects you to your values, energy, and emotional state before entering a high-sensory, social, or emotionally demanding space.

Why it's useful
As Wild Sensitives, we often get pulled into the energy of a room. Without a ritual of preparation, we risk shapeshifting, people-pleasing, or becoming emotionally fragmented. Pre-event rituals build a somatic anchor so you can remain yourself, even as you engage with others.

How to Use It

Take 3–5 minutes before your event to:

- Use a familiar scent (The TLA Scented Charm)
- Listen to a short grounding song or soundscape
- Visualize your Safe, Comfort or Goldilocks Zone, imagine your energy protected, yet open
- Say an intentional mantra such as:
  - *"I can be present and protected."*
  - *"I choose connection without abandoning myself."*
- Touch an anchor object you can carry into space (stone, necklace, fabric)

The goal is to enter from self-connection, not performance.

Recovery Rituals & Reflection Time

Because stimulation needs to be followed by relaxation.

What it is

A decompression practice to release tension, recalibrate your nervous system, and integrate experiences after engaging events or emotionally charged moments.

Why it's useful

Wild Sensitives don't just experience the moment we carry it. Without a recovery ritual, emotional intensity gets stored in the body. These rituals help discharge excess energy, prevent emotional hangovers, and allow insights to land more gently.

How to Use It

Immediately after the event, or within the same day, choose a quiet reset space:

- Go outside and place your bare feet on the earth
- Take a warm shower while silently reflecting on what felt good or challenging
- Journal with prompts like:

- ○ *"What do I need to release?"*
- ○ *"What did I learn about myself today?"*
- ○ *"What part of me grew?"*
- Engage in low-stim sensory care (soft lighting, weighted blanket, warm drink, nature sounds)

Recovery is not laziness. It is the nervous system's return to integration.

Anchor Objects or Sensory Tools
Physical items that tether you to yourself.

What it is
Tactile or sensory-based objects that act as emotional landmarks, reminding your body that you're secure and seen, even in unfamiliar or overstimulating settings.

Why it's useful
When words fail or overwhelm rises, the body speaks through sensation. Anchor objects offer physical regulation without needing external permission or explanation.

How to Use It
Choose one or more items that evoke a sense of comfort or empowerment:
- A smooth stone or crystal
- A textured fabric
- A small scent roller or calming essential oil
- Jewelry with grounding weight or personal symbolism

Hold or touch the item when overstimulated. Use it intentionally during breathwork or reflection.
Assign it a phrase or memory that centers you:
- *"This reminds me I'm not alone."*
- *"This brings me back to my breath."*

Over time, your body learns to associate the object with regulation and self-trust.

Somatic Check-Ins
Because the body often knows before the mind can name it.

What it is
A quick, body-based awareness practice that helps you track emotional states through physical sensation and respond with care before misalignment builds.

Why it's useful
Wild Sensitives often push through discomfort until it becomes collapse. This tool builds moment-to-moment attunement, helping you make real-time adjustments that protect energy and restore coherence.

How to Use It
Ask yourself:

"Where am I feeling this in my body?"

"What sensation is dominant, tightness, warmth, buzzing, heaviness?"

"What does this part of my body need right now?"

Place a hand over the area with sensation. Breathe into it. Offer a short phrase like:

"I'm listening."

"You're okay to relax."

"I hear you, thank you."

Use this check-in during transitions, decision-making, or emotional intensity. It trains your system to stay responsive, not reactive.

We don't need more insight; we need more integration. Because it's not what you experience that changes you. It's what you process, ritualize, and return to, that becomes part of who you are. These daily practices, while small, are revolutionary acts of self-tending. They help Wild Sensitives stay rooted in a world that often pulls us off-centre. Anchor into you. Again and again. Because you are the most sacred place you'll ever return to.

Wild Sensitive Communication & Connection Tools
Tools for deepening presence and staying authentic in relationship.

Connection is one of the deepest longings of the Wild Sensitive and often one of the most confusing. We crave intimacy, truth, and resonance. Yet, we can lose ourselves quickly in the noise of others' needs, expectations, and energy. Our sensitivity makes us hyper-aware of emotional nuance, while our sensation-seeking pulls us toward bold engagement, even when we're not fully grounded.

That's why communication must be more than just saying the right thing. It must be a practice of presence, sovereignty, and attunement, not just to others, but to ourselves first. Without that inner tether, even honest words can feel disconnected or draining.

The following tools were developed to help you show up in connection without self-abandonment, deepen relationship without overexposure, and speak with clarity even when emotion runs high. They are not scripts for performance. They are frameworks for staying true in moments that matter, giving voice to your values, and protecting your peace without losing your openness.

L.I.G.H.T. Method
Practicing sovereign connection and emotional safety in conversations.

What it is
A five-part process for engaging in emotionally meaningful conversations while remaining grounded in self-awareness, curiosity, and core values.

Why it's useful
For Wild Sensitives, emotional conversations can become overwhelming quickly, especially if we feel misunderstood or responsible for others' feelings. The L.I.G.H.T. Method offers a gentle structure for staying connected while also protecting your inner clarity, reducing emotional overflow, and anchoring you in self-trust throughout vulnerable moments.

How to Use It (Step-by-Step)

Listen: Tune in, not just to the words, but to your body, breath, and environment.
- *"What's happening in me as I listen?"*

Inquire: Ask before assuming. Stay curious, especially when emotionally triggered.
- *"Can you say more about what you mean?"*
- *"What's your experience of this?"*

Grow: Notice where discomfort or disagreement invites your awareness to expand.
- *"Is there something in this moment asking me to grow?"*

Hold Values: Return to your core principles. Let them guide your responses, not fear, guilt, or approval-seeking.
- *"Does this reflect who I want to be?"*

Transform: Use what you've learned to respond, not react. Choose transformation over reactivity.

- *"Given what I now see, what's a response that honors my beliefs, values and desires?"*

Use this method especially in:
- Conflict repair
- Boundary setting
- Vulnerability hangovers
- Group dynamics

It's a structure that creates secure dialogue without emotional collapse.

Curiosity Over Conformity

Ask before adapting. Stay inquisitive before blending in.

What it is

A simple principle for staying authentic and engaged in unfamiliar social dynamics or group environments, by leading with curiosity rather than automatic adaptation.

Why it's useful

Wild Sensitives are masters of blending in. We've learned to read the room, adjust our tone, and mold ourselves to meet the moment. But too much of this leads to invisible self-abandonment. Curiosity disrupts that reflex. It helps you engage on your terms, instead of defaulting to invisibility or over-performance.

How to Use It

When entering new environments or conversations, pause internally and ask:
- *"What's actually happening here?"*
- *"What do I value, and how do I want to show up in this space?"*

Before adapting your language, style, or tone, try:
"What might happen if I stayed curious instead of compliant?"

Use gentle, curious questions to engage, rather than mirror:
- *"That's an interesting take, how did you come to that belief?"*
- *"I'm curious how others here feel about this too."*

Curiosity builds relational bridges without requiring you to give up your voice.

Permission to Pause
Sensory breaks are sacred, not selfish.

What it is
A self-honoring practice of stepping out of conversations, environments, or interactions temporarily in order to regulate and return more fully.

Why it's useful
Wild Sensitives can become overstimulated quickly, especially in groups, emotionally intense discussions, or when co-regulating with someone in distress. But most of us were never taught that taking space is allowed. Instead, we push through, and end up shutting down, lashing out, or numbing. This tool reframes pausing as a responsible, relational act, not a retreat, but a reset that protects connection, preserves clarity, and honors both your nervous system and the relationship itself.

How to Use It
Recognize signs of nervous system overload:
- Increased heart rate
- Shallow breath
- Irritability or brain fog
- Desire to leave or go silent

Gently state your boundary
- *"I care about this conversation, and I need a few minutes to ground so I can stay connected."*
- *"I'd love to keep talking after I take a short break."*

Step outside, move your body, breathe, journal, or sit in silence.

Return only when your system feels steady and sovereign.

Stepping out = Stepping back in stronger.
This tool also teaches those around you that connection can include care, not just for others, but for yourself.

Authentic connection for Wild Sensitives is not about being perfect, polite, or polished. It's about being attuned, inward and outward. These tools help you create relationships where your sensitivity is not a liability, but a source of depth, care, and transformation.

Let your presence speak truth. Let your boundaries hold kindness.
And let your communication be the bridge between who you are, and how you choose to belong.

Bringing It All Together: The Art of Skillful Practice
Because mastery is not the goal, presence is.

You are not here to master every tool at once. This chapter has given you a rich assortment of tools, for grounding, for navigating emotion, for reclaiming your voice, for expanding with resilience, and for anchoring your growth. But let's be clear: these tools are not assignments. They are companions. They are not proof of your worth. They are invitations to relate to yourself more kindly, more skillfully, and more truthfully.

Some will resonate right away. Others may feel awkward, or unnecessary, or not quite right for where you are. That's okay. As Living Adventurers, we've learned that timing matters. That readiness matters. And that forcing yourself to use a tool when what you really need is rest, is just another form of abandonment.

So, start small. Start gently. Start with the one tool that makes your body say, *"Yes... that feels doable."* Practice it not to be perfect, but to be present. Let the tools support you, not define you. Let them help you listen more deeply to what you need, rather than what you think you should do.

And know this: just because you can walk alone doesn't mean you have to.

There is strength in asking for guidance. There is wisdom in choosing to walk beside someone who knows the terrain. A coach can help you use the tools with precision. A guide can help you map the emotional landscape. A supportive community can remind you, in the moments when you forget, that you are not too much, and you are never alone.

Your growth deserves support. Your nervous system deserves compassion.

And your journey deserves tools that match your sensitivity, your courage, and your pace. Keep your backpack nearby. But keep your heart closer. Because the most powerful tool you'll ever use... is your willingness to return to yourself.

One breath. One choice. One moment at a time.

Chapter 11

The Adventure Triskelion

A New Way to Live Wild and Sensitive

"Most people struggle with lasting change because they focus on just one part of themselves, the mind, the heart, or the body, while the others quietly resist. The Adventure Triskelion brings all three into alignment. When your thoughts, emotions, and physical self move together, transformation becomes not just possible, but sustainable."

The Living Adventurers

We now introduce a Living Adventurers original: *The Adventure Triskelion*, a powerful symbol and methodology for transformational long-lasting change.

At its core lies a powerful truth: real change doesn't happen by forcing one part of yourself to comply, it happens through an intricate alignment between your body, your emotions, and your mind.

This isn't just a nice idea. It's backed up by neuroscience. Your nervous system is a record keeper. Every experience you've ever had, especially those intertwined with strong emotions, gets filed away in your body's nervous system. It shapes your reactions, your preferences, even your beliefs about what's possible. We have over 7 trillion nerves in our body, each designed to react and or respond to physical, emotional, and mindful commands, it's no wonder it holds amazing influence on us.

Most of us have heard of 'Muscle Memory' and we certainly have heard of memories held in the mind. Yet, ask yourself, where do emotional memories reside? Science has proven they live in a delicate network of the amygdala, hippocampus, prefrontal cortex, and insula.

Where the amygdala initiates the emotion, the hippocampus provides the detail, the prefrontal cortex interprets, and the insula brings the body awareness into the picture. Connecting all these together is the nervous system. The nervous system plays a central role in emotional memory, both in how it's formed and how it's re-experienced later. Here's how it works:

When something emotionally significant happens (like a fight, a kiss, or a traumatic event), your sensory nerves quickly carry that information (sights, sounds, smells, taste, and touch) to the central nervous system (CNS), specifically to your brain.

Next, your autonomic nervous system (ANS), which controls automatic bodily functions, kicks in. The sympathetic branch (which is the body's stress response system) prepares you for "freeze, perform, flight or fight" by increasing heart rate, tensing muscles, and flooding your body with stress hormones like adrenaline and cortisol. These physiological responses amplify the emotional intensity of the moment, making the memory more likely to be stored.

Then, the amygdala, part of the limbic system, receives signals from your nervous system about the emotional importance of an event. It "tags" certain memories with emotion, especially fear or excitement, making them more vivid and harder to forget. The hippocampus then uses the nervous system's input to gives meaning to the memory (where it happened, what time, etc.). Over time, this memory is stored in long-term memory, but the emotional "charge" often stays with the nervous system, especially if stress hormones are involved.

When a trigger (like a smell, sight, taste, physical contact, or tone of voice) is similar to the original event, your nervous system reacts automatically. You might feel anxiety, warmth, tension, or joy, even if you're not consciously thinking about the original memory. We call this your autopilot.

This is your nervous system "remembering", not with thoughts, but with sensations, heart rate changes, and emotional waves. This means your nervous system is both the messenger and magnifier of emotional memory by sending sensory and emotional data, triggering body reactions that help you remember things better, while helping to "store" emotional weight in the CNS, ANS and brain which allows reactivation of those feelings when similar events occur.

The Adventure Triskelion recognizes three inter-dependent pillars of being:

- **Mental Clarity** (the thoughts, beliefs, and meaning you assign to your experiences)
- **Emotional Connection** (how you feel and what brings you joy, fear, or fulfillment)
- **Physical Engagement** (the body and its capacity for movement and sensation)

Only when these three are aligned, long-lasting change can begin to take place. When they are not, you'll feel resistance, self-sabotage, confusion, or burnout not because you are weak, or because you don't want to, but because one, two or all three of those inter-dependent pillars of being are out of sync.

Think of your overall wellbeing, as a triangular roof being held up by three main pillars, physical, mental, and emotional. If even one of those pillars is out of balance, collapse can occur. Here is an example:

Let's say you were eight years old, and your parents signed you up for a little league baseball team. You didn't ask to join, they just thought it would help you come out of your shell and learn how to toughen up by connecting with other kids.

When they inform you, *"you're going,"* your nervous system begins buzzing. Because you have no choice, you try your best to emotionally prepare yourself. You're the new kid, small, quiet, and sensitive to loud noises and sharp eyes. The other kids see your vulnerability right away, not in your appearance, rather in you don't know the rules, and this game was new to you. Bravely, yet awkwardly, you put on the uniform and stepped up to the plate for the first time and handed a bat. No coaching, no instructions, just expected to figure it out.

Standing there, heart pounding, your entire body sends a clear signal to the kid standing on the pitcher's mound. He's a little older, and he too has something to prove. He notices your nervousness. He sees the fear in your eyes, the awkward way your hands trembled on the bat, and instead of offering support, he chooses to humiliate you.

With a smirk, he hurled the ball hard at the dirt, aiming not at the strike zone but 4 feet in front of you. The ball bounces wildly into the air 10 feet from you. Startled and panicked, you swung wildly, never having a chance. Then you heard a roar of laughter. It came from other players in the dugout, from the parents standing on the sidelines, even the coach. Not kind laughter, but the laughter that cuts itself through your heart like the sharp knife of shame. You were the punchline, and the world was standing there pointing at you as if you were the joke. You were 8 years old. There was no support from the coach, nor any of the parents. You were utterly alone in the world, and the world had just proven to you, it's dangerous. In that moment, something inside you shifted. Your body locked up, flooded with humiliation and fear. Your heart clenched with shame. Your mind, too young to make sense of what had happened, came to a simple conclusion: There's something wrong with me.

And that's how trauma takes root, not just in the moment, but in the absence of support. Especially for Highly Sensitive children, who process deeply and feel broadly, an experience like this doesn't fade, it embeds. As you grew older, that single moment began to quietly shape your inner world. Emotionally, you carried a vague but persistent sense of embarrassment, a fear of being exposed or laughed at. Mentally, you built beliefs around that day: Trying something new in front of others is dangerous. Being seen means being humiliated.

You began to avoid group activities or new challenges, not because you lacked interest or talent, but because your mind associated visibility with pain. And physically, your body remembers. Every time you faced a group setting, tried to perform, or risked vulnerability, your shoulders tense, your breath shallows, and your posture curls inward. Your nervous system was doing its job: trying to keep you protected by keeping you small. Your mind adopts the belief, people cannot be trusted, watch them closely.

This is what it looks like when the emotional, mental, and physical systems fall out of alignment. You may long for connection, yet fear being seen. You might crave new experiences but feel paralyzed at the edge of action. You might tell yourself, It's fine, while your body screams, I'm vulnerable. That internal conflict doesn't mean something is wrong with you, it means your younger self was never given a place to process what happened. And so, those parts of you split. Misalignment is the echo of trauma that never got resolved or even acknowledged, let alone healed.

For Wild Sensitives, who live with heightened awareness of both threat and beauty, this kind of misalignment is especially painful. We don't just remember with our minds, we remember with our bodies. We carry the moment we were laughed at, dismissed, shamed, or silenced into boardrooms, relationships, creative spaces, and decisions we never fully understand.

Until, one day, we began to realize what happened wasn't weakness, it was wounding. We begin to question the belief: Does that one moment define my worth? Or is there something more truthful beneath it? We then begin to name it, helping us identify it better. Then we start, gently, to reconnect the pieces.

Healing begins when we let our emotional truth be heard, when our body is no longer punished for protecting us, and when our mind is allowed to update the story. Because our destination, the full, free expression of who we are, cannot be reached while dragging behind the weight of unhealed wounds. And yet, those very wounds can become the foundation of our becoming. The place where strength is born, not in spite of the pain, but because we finally turned toward it with care.

Many of our fellow Wild Sensitives have told us when they were taking our programs, how this lived experience, deeply connected to them. Not the baseball team, or the swinging of the bat, but rather the emotional impact of something similar that they deeply recall. They then begin to connect, how one experience can define their entire approach to life. From building a career, making new friends, falling in love, and living a healthy fulfilling life.

You might feel the desire to be in a healthy relationship, but if your emotional system associate's closeness with pain, or your body tightens every time someone gets too near, that relationship will never feel secure or sustainable. This equally applies to any area of life you want to grow in. If all three of the pillars are not aligned, you're in constant struggle to keep the roof of wellbeing held up.

Your nervous system is your narrator. It's always speaking, always listening, always remembering, always on guard. It controls your impulses, your hesitations, your fatigue, your joy. And most of the time, it's not telling today's story. It's retelling an old one. One you didn't write. One often told by an experience early in life, when you didn't have the ability yet to recognize the experience for what it truly was.

Experiences are interpreted through the eyes of a child at a certain age, at age 3 you would not even understand the words, at age 8 you would interpret the feeling only through a certain lens, while as an adult you can look at all the possibilities of the event, not just the one you saw as a child. A story typically cast into you from experiences that told you to be protected, you needed to be small, quiet, unseen.

It sends emotional, mental and physical blocks when we step out of our Safe Zone and try something new. Not because it's wrong, risky or unfamiliar. Rather because it is familiar in a deeply hidden painful memory. Our overall wellbeing, at its core, has been subconsciously trained to survive, not to thrive. Thriving is a conscious action, limited only by our beliefs.

The Adventure Triskelion is about retraining that belief system to over- and re-write those emotional, mental and physical stored memories. Through small, intentional, integrated actions, where your physical self, emotional self, and mental self, get to realign together.

Most people fail at change because they focus only on one pillar. For example, improving one's mental health. They read the book, take the course, make the plan. But if your heart isn't in it, or your body feels unprotected, you'll emotionally and physically resist.

When we focus on our physical health by going to the gym and dieting, our minds and emotions struggle because it's not stimulating due to boring food and repetitive routines that do not see instant results. If we even try to discuss emotional health, our minds and body instant reject us because of the social stigma that any emotional improvement equals vulnerability and weakness.

Change doesn't happen through willpower alone. It happens through integration. And that's what the Adventure Triskelion gives you, a process for alignment, an action for rewriting your memories stored in the nervous system.

As Wild Sensitives, we often carry complexity where others have simplicity because of our sensitive nervous system. Change, for us, doesn't happen in a straight line, it happens in layers: emotional, mental, physical, and energetic. That's why the Adventure Triskelion was developed, not as a rigid formula, but as a living model that brings alignment to our personal growth journeys.

In the pages ahead, we'll explore three powerful examples of how this model can be applied in everyday life. Whether you're navigating the path to a healthier body, recovering from emotional or energetic burnout, or longing to cultivate deeper, more fulfilling relationships, this model will help you move forward not with force, but with sovereignty, and from the inside out.

Each example will show you how to integrate the Adventure Triskelion's three pillars, Emotional Connection, Mental Clarity, and Physical Engagement, alongside supportive tools and reflections to help you stay grounded, empowered, and fully you.

Applying the Adventure Triskelion

Example 1: Losing Weight Through the Lens of the Adventure Triskelion

Let's start by applying the Adventure Triskelion to a very sought-after challenge many have. Losing weight. More specifically, we need to reframe this to become physically healthier in a sustainable, life-affirming way. While many believe they must focus entirely on the physical, the Adventure Triskelion suggests something vastly different.

Weight gain and body image are rarely just physical. They are emotional, mental, and deeply experiential. They are often woven into our history of regulation, shame, craving, and self-worth. The Adventure Triskelion shows us that authentic transformation happens when these three areas work together:

- **Mental Clarity** – What we believe about our body, weight, and worth
- **Emotional Connection** – What we feel and how we cope or numb
- **Physical Engagement** – How our body stores, signals, and metabolizes experience

If these three aspects of our system are out of sync, we'll keep fighting ourselves, no matter how many diets plans or workouts we try. For each of the pillars, we will explore our current beliefs, feelings and preferences we have. Let's explore this by asking key questions to clarify each pillar, how our beliefs, habits, and physical reactions influence the journey.

Questions to explore the pillar of Mental Clarity
- *Do I truly believe weight loss is possible?*
- *Why is it important to me to lose weight?*
- *What message did I hear growing up about weight, food or appearance?*

This seems like a logical yes, but for many Wild Sensitives, weight has become a layer of protection, shame, or fear. Our internal beliefs can quietly say the opposite of what we consciously declare. Risk is not about physical; it's more about judgment and criticism in the gym.

Possible Limiting Beliefs
- *"Every time I try, I fail, why would this time be different?"*
- *"If I go to the gym, I'll be seen more, and that makes me feel vulnerable."*
- *"I'd rather be overweight and unhealthy than laughed at."*

Mental Impact
These beliefs drive self-sabotage. The brain unconsciously creates friction with "healthy choices" because it doesn't trust the process or outcome. You might start strong, then quit quietly, convinced something is broken in you because you caught someone looking at you out of the corner of your eye.

Emotional Impact

Feelings of unworthiness, disappointment, or hopelessness arise before action is even taken. You may feel like change is a punishment, not a pathway. Embarrassment and humiliation rise, even before you begin.

Physical Impact

The body holds tension around movement or eating differently. You might feel heavy, sluggish, or resistant, not because you're lazy, but because your system is bracing against the perceived threat. The pain we feel in our muscles after the first workout tells us everything. The old conditioning is changing, and our bodies are fighting us.

Questions to explore the Emotional Connection pillar:
- *What emotions come up when I think about changing my weight or body?*
- *What am I feeling when I eat?*
- *What role has food played in my emotional life?*

Weight challenges for many, do not begin at the refrigerator. They begin in the moments of being shamed, being ignored, being forced, or judged for how we looked, especially in childhood and early adulthood.

Possible Limiting Beliefs
- *"Food is the only thing that comforts me."*
- *"Exercise is punishment."*
- *"If I'm smaller, I'll lose my identity."*

Mental Impact

Rigid "all or nothing" thinking may develop. We tie our worth to numbers. We over-identify with control or rebellion. Our bodies become battlefields, not a temple.

Emotional Impact

Guilt and shame often follow exercise and eating. Many swings between trying to do it perfect to the "screw it" mode. Food and a sedentary lifestyle become a stand-in for love, regulation, or rebellion.

Physical Impact

The nervous system associate's movement or body exposure with humiliation or rejection. You may feel disembodied, disconnected, or even dissociative when exercising or seeing yourself in mirrors.

Questions to explore the pillar of Physical Engagement:
- *How does my body feel when I think about movement or change?*
- *What movements do I like or enjoy doing?*
- *How do I feel in my body when moving?*

This question touches your emotional truth, beneath the "goals" and "before-and-after" fantasies. What emotions rise when you picture yourself lighter, stronger, more energized?

Possible Limiting Beliefs
- *"I'll never be enough, no matter how much weight I lose."*
- *"Thin people are more lovable and I'm not lovable; that's just the truth."*
- *"If I change, I'll lose who I am."*

Mental Impact

You might idealize weight loss while holding deep fear failure. This inner split causes inconsistency, self-sabotage, and confusion. Better to not try and not fail.

Emotional Impact

You may feel grief, longing, or fear when you imagine transformation, not because it's wrong, but because it threatens the identity you've built to stay protected.

Physical Impact

The body may resist weight loss by retaining water, triggering fatigue and pain, or amplifying cravings, because the emotional terrain underneath isn't being addressed.

Why the Triskelion Model Matters for Weight Loss

When our beliefs, emotions, and physical responses are shaped by fear or trauma, weight loss becomes a war. Our mind may say, *"I want to change,"* but our body and nervous system may say, *"change makes us vulnerable."* That is a misalignment. And it's why many Wild Sensitives feel stuck in cycles of trying, stopping, or dissociating.

Transformation begins when these systems come back into conversation:
- *What am I believing about my body?*
- *What am I feeling around change?*
- *What is my body trying to protect me from?*

Then we offer compassion. We recalibrate, slowly, gently, with effective tools and patience.

Applying the Adventure Triskelion to Weight Loss: One Small Step at a Time

Step 1: Emotional Connection - Feel First, Feed Second

Start by tuning into emotional cues before eating. Ask, *"Am I hungry, or seeking comfort?"* Build tolerance for emotional discomfort by listening to what it is saying before reacting to it through food. This isn't about denial, it's about connecting with your emotional world.

Practice
- Use the *Pressure Pulse* technique before meals to self soothe.
- Keep a journal and record how you feel in these moments, just one sentence before or after eating.

Say to yourself: *"I can feel without feeding every feeling."*

Step 2: Mental Clarity – Awareness Over Willpower

Bring consciousness to your patterns. Use the 3-R Rule when you're triggered to binge, skip a workout, or mentally spiral:

- **Recognize** the impulse
- **Regulate** your breath or environment
- **Reclaim** your choice by naming your value (e.g., *"I choose nourishment over control"*)

Then PERRR:
- **Pause**, even for a moment.
- **Enquire**, what discomfort am I acting from?
- **Reflect** on whether it's out of habit or intention.
- **Recognize** old patterns that lead to the behavior.
- **Respond** with the current truth.

Micro-action: Replace *"I blew it"* with *"I noticed something."* That's growth.

Step 3: Physical Engagement – Move to Come Home, Not to Fix
Begin moving your body in ways that feel restorative, sensory, and self-honoring, not punishing. This can be a walk in nature, dancing in the kitchen, or simply stretching with music.

Practice
Use the *Three-Point Trace* after movement to integrate:
- Head: *What did I think during that walk?*
- Heart: *What did I feel?*
- Gut: *What did I sense about what I need next?*

Over time, your body will stop bracing against movement and start craving it.

Putting It All Together
Let's say you just finished a stressful day and feel the pull to eat an entire bag of chips.
- **Mentally**, you catch the script: *"This will help me feel better, but only for a minute."*
- **Emotionally**, you pause: "I feel overstimulated and alone."

- **Physically**, you breathe, ground, and regulate with a Pressure Pulse.

Then you make a choice. Maybe you still eat some of the chips, but this time, you do it consciously. Without shame. With awareness.

That's not failure. That's alignment in motion.

Example 2: Recovering from Burnout & Overwhelm

Recovering from Burnout & Overwhelm Through the Lens of the Adventure Triskelion.

Let's now apply the Adventure Triskelion to another common challenge faced by many Wild Sensitives: burnout and overwhelm. For many of us, burnout isn't just about doing too much, it's about being out of alignment emotionally, mentally, and physically for too long. The nervous system stays on high alert, while we override its signals out of obligation, performance, or people-pleasing.

The Triskelion invites us to reframe recovery as more than just "rest." It's about restoring internal communication between the systems that have been running on empty. Burnout happens when our emotions, thoughts, and physical actions stop working together.

The Adventure Triskelion reminds us that authentic recovery happens when these three systems realign:

- **Mental Clarity** – What we believe about rest, worth, and performance
- **Emotional Connection** – What we feel and how we acknowledge or suppress emotion
- **Physical Engagement** – How the body shows exhaustion, stress, or shutdown

If these systems are disconnected, we keep pushing or numbing, even while our nervous system begs for reconnection. Let's bring these three pillars into conversation.

Questions to explore the pillar of Mental Clarity:
- *What do I believe about rest and productivity?*
- *What fears come up when I think about slowing down or saying no?*
- *Where did I learn that being exhausted is acceptable or even admirable?*

Possible Limiting Beliefs:
- *"If I stop, everything will fall apart."*
- *"Rest is for people who aren't strong enough."*
- *"My worth is measured by how much I do."*

Mental Impact
These beliefs keep the brain in overdrive. They create chronic tension, guilt around rest, and a mindset of self-abandonment. Even when physically resting, the mind may be racing.

Emotional Impact
Guilt, shame, and internal pressure to "keep going" show up when trying to rest. Emotional numbness or frustration arises, especially in quiet moments.

Physical Impact
The body resists rest, yet shows clear signs of collapse: insomnia, exhaustion, body aches, or wired-but-tired fatigue. Even leisure can feel like pressure.

Questions to explore the Emotional Connection pillar
- *What am I really feeling right now, beyond "I'm tired"?*
- *What emotions have I been avoiding or numbing?*
- *What part of me feels unseen, unheard, or unsupported?*

Possible Limiting Beliefs
- *"If I allow my emotions, they'll overwhelm me."*
- *"No one cares how I feel, so why bother?"*
- *"Feeling things makes me weaker or more unstable."*

Mental Impact
Avoiding emotions takes mental energy, leading to brain fog, overthinking, and emotional detachment. The mind may default to "just push through."

Emotional Impact
Flatness, irritability, apathy, or quiet despair emerge when emotional needs go unmet. Emotional pressure builds until it leaks out as tears, anger, or disconnection.

Physical Impact
Physical signs of unprocessed emotion show up as tightness in the chest or throat, digestive issues, chronic fatigue, or shutdown responses like freezing or zoning out.

Questions to explore the pillar of Physical Engagement
- *How does my body feel when I think about rest or recovery?*
- *What is my body trying to say when I feel tension, fatigue, or tightness?*
- *What physical sensations do I experience when I override my limits?*

Possible Limiting Beliefs
- *"I don't have time to rest."*
- *"Listening to my body is self-indulgent."*
- *"If I slow down, I'll never get back on track."*

Mental Impact
The body becomes a battleground for control, used, ignored, or pushed rather than honored. The mind often overrides the body's need for stillness.

Emotional Impact

The body's signals feel frustrating, anxious or inconvenient. We disconnect emotionally from our physical state, which breeds more resentment and confusion.

Physical Impact

Chronic tension, shallow breathing, sleep issues, and nervous system dysregulation occur. Even when lying down, the body may feel braced or restless.

Why the Triskelion Model Matters for Burnout Recovery

Burnout isn't solved with a weekend off. It's healed when your body, emotions, and mind begin to work together again, with gentleness. Your mind may say, *"Just push through,"* while your heart says, *"Please slow down,"* and your body says, *"I can't keep going."* That's misalignment.

Recovery begins when we ask
- *What am I believing that keeps me stuck in this cycle?*
- *What am I really feeling underneath the numbness or urgency?*
- *What is my body trying to protect me from or communicate?*

Then we meet those answers with kindness, not force.

Applying the Adventure Triskelion to Burnout: One Small Step at a Time

Step 1: Emotional Connection – Name the Feeling, Don't Numb It

Start by acknowledging emotional truth without judgment. Overwhelm often hides deeper unmet needs or grief. Learning to identify and name each emotion gives it true identity.

Practice

- Use Somatic Journaling to write one sentence a day: *"What am I feeling right now?"*

- Try Emotional Naming to say it aloud: *"This is exhaustion. This is sadness. This is pressure."*

Mantra: *"I can name what I feel and process it."*

Step 2: Mental Clarity – Awareness Over Obligation
Begin questioning the internal script. Are you living from survival or personal leadership?

Practice
Use the 3-R Rule
- •**Recognize:** *"I'm about to override myself again."*
- •**Regulate:** Use breath, grounding, or a calming word.
- •**Reclaim:** *"I choose peace over performance."*

Follow with PERRR
- •**Pause**
- •**Enquire:** *"What part of me is afraid to slow down?"*
- •**Reflect:** *"Where did I learn that rest is weakness?"*
- •**Recognize:** *"That's not my truth anymore."*
- •**Respond:** *"It's safe to rest."*

Micro-action:
Change your to-do list to a "Permission List." Add one thing that brings softness or joy.

Step 3: Physical Engagement – Restore Safety in the Body
Shift from performance to presence. Your body isn't a machine, it's your ally.

Practice:
- Use the Three-Point Trace: Head (thoughts), Heart (feelings), Gut (body needs).
- Take a Micro-Movement Pause every 90 minutes: gentle stretching, walking barefoot, or breath + sway.

- Create a Rest Ritual: 15 minutes of nothing. No phone. No input. Just being.

Mantra: *"My body doesn't need to earn rest. It welcomes it."*

Putting It All Together

Let's say it's the end of the day. Your body is buzzing with tension, your brain is foggy, and you feel a wave of sadness you can't quite name.

- **Mentally**, you notice the script: *"I should push through and finish more."*
- **Emotionally**, you pause and name it: *"I feel overwhelmed and disconnected."*
- **Physically**, you ground with breath, stretch your neck, and drop your shoulders.

You step away. You light a candle. You sit for 5 minutes without doing. That's not avoidance. That's realignment in action.

Example 3: Building Relationships

Building Relationships Through the Lens of the Adventure Triskelion

Let's now apply the Adventure Triskelion to another core area of life for Wild Sensitives: building meaningful relationships. Whether romantic, platonic, or professional, relationships are where our sensitivity and sensation seeking most often collide. For many, connection feels both deeply desired and deeply overwhelming.

We long to be seen, and also feel uncomfortable with it. We crave closeness, and then are overwhelmed by it. The Adventure Triskelion can help us understand and overcome these internal contradictions. They are signs of misalignment between the mind, emotions, and body. Healthy connection doesn't happen by forcing yourself to be vulnerable. It happens when your mental clarity, emotional truth, and physical safety are in sync. The Triskelion reminds us that sustainable connection happens when these three systems work together:

- **Mental Clarity** – What we believe about connection, trust, and intimacy
- **Emotional Connection** – What we feel in moments of closeness, distance, or rejection
- **Physical Engagement** – How the body processes and expresses safety, stress, or openness

If any of these pillars are out of sync, we might feel stuck in patterns of avoidance, self-sabotage, or relational confusion. Let's explore this by asking key questions to clarify each pillar, and how our beliefs, feelings, and physical responses influence how we relate to others.

Questions to explore the pillar of Mental Clarity
- *Do I truly believe I'm worthy of real connection?*
- *What messages did I grow up hearing about relationships?*
- *What do I expect from others, and what do I expect from myself?*

Possible Limiting Beliefs
- *"People always leave."*
- *"I'm too much for anyone to stay with."*
- *"Needing people makes me weak."*

Mental Impact
These beliefs create a default mindset of mistrust, control, or withdrawal. The brain becomes hyper-vigilant for rejection or betrayal, scanning even safe connections for danger signs.

Emotional Impact
Hope and dread often arrive together. There may be a deep longing for closeness shadowed by anxiety, fear, or resentment. The heart aches for connection but doesn't feel safe enough to reach for it.

Physical Impact

The nervous system tenses at the thought of intimacy. Common signs include tight jaw, shallow breath, stiff posture, or feeling "on edge" around others, especially in emotionally charged moments.

Questions to explore the Emotional Connection pillar – What do I feel when I think about connecting with others?

Questions to explore:

- *What emotions come up when I think about closeness or vulnerability?*
- *When was the last time I felt emotionally safe with someone?*
- *What past emotional wounds might be shaping how I relate now?*

Possible Limiting Beliefs

- *"If I open up, I'll be rejected or laughed at."*
- *"It's safer to stay guarded than get hurt again."*
- *"No one really understands people like me."*

Mental Impact

The mind begins overanalyzing everything, from what you say in conversations to how long it takes someone to text back. Overthinking replaces presence. Trust becomes conditional.

Emotional Impact

Shame, fear, and grief often surface around connection. You may feel numb or overly emotional in relational settings. There's often a tension between expressing yourself and needing to protect your heart.

Physical Impact

The body may armor up, clenched muscles, tight throat, closed posture. You may feel physically tired or shut down after social interactions, even when they go well.

Questions to explore the pillar of Physical Engagement – How does my body experience connection?

Questions to explore
- *What does safety feel like in my body?*
- *How does my body respond to closeness, attention, or touch?*
- *Can I tell the difference between true discomfort and old protective habits?*

Possible Limiting Beliefs
- *"My body betrays me when I get nervous."*
- *"Physical closeness always leads to pain."*
- *"If I let someone in, I'll lose control."*

Mental Impact
When physical signs of stress (tightness, sweating, fidgeting) appear, the mind may interpret them as proof something is wrong. This deepens avoidance and fear.

Emotional Impact
Your body becomes a source of insecurity. You may feel ashamed of your reactions, even when they're just protective patterns doing their job.

Physical Impact
Fight-flight-freeze patterns kick in. You might withdraw, perform, or go numb. The body reacts to connection as if it's a threat, making true intimacy nearly impossible until physical safety is restored.

Why the Triskelion Model Matters for Relationship Building
For Wild Sensitives, connection isn't simple. It's layered, sometimes loud with longing, sometimes silent with fear. Our minds may crave closeness, while our emotions carry past hurts, and our body resists being seen or touched. That's misalignment.

Relational healing begins when we ask:
- *What am I believing about connection and trust?*
- *What am I truly feeling underneath my reactions?*
- *What is my body trying to protect me from?*

We don't force connection. We create conditions where connection can arise, through safety, presence, and integration.

Applying the Adventure Triskelion to Relationships: One Small Step at a Time

Step 1: Mental Clarity – Rewrite the Relational Script
Interrupt old patterns by becoming aware of what you believe and expect from connection.

Practice
Use the 3-R Rule in social moments:
- **Recognize:** *"I'm shutting down or overexplaining again."*
- **Regulate:** Breathe, step back, and reconnect with your center.
- **Reclaim:** *"I choose curiosity over fear."*

Then apply PERRR:
- **Pause**
- **Enquire:** *"What story am I telling myself about this interaction?"*
- **Reflect:** *"Is this a belief I chose, or one I inherited?"*
- **Recognize:** *"This is an old pattern trying to keep me safe."*
- **Respond:** *"I can try something different, even in a small way."*

Micro-action: After a conversation, jot down one sentence: *"In that moment, I believed ___, and I felt ___."* Track your patterns with kindness.

Step 2: Emotional Connection – Feel the Response, Don't Force the Risk

Before opening up to others, open up to yourself. Let your feelings be valid, even when they're uncomfortable.

Practice
- Try Emotional Naming: In moments of social tension or anticipation, name the feeling: *"This is anxiety,"* or *"This is hope."*
- In safe environments, reflect: *"What did I feel when I was with that person?"* not just *"What did I say?"*

Mantra: *"I can be honest with myself before I ask others to understand me."*

Step 3: Physical Engagement – Build Safety Through the Body

Your body needs to learn that connection doesn't equal danger. Let it unlearn the fear gently.

Practice
- Use the Three-Point Trace before and after a social interaction:
- Head (what I thought)
- Heart (what I felt)
- Gut (what I sensed)
- Try Anchor Objects or Sensory Tools: Sensory-based objects that act as emotional landmarks, reminding your body that you're secure, even in unfamiliar or overstimulating settings.
- Use Pressure Pulse in moments of social stress: press your thumb and finger together for a few seconds to anchor safety in your nervous system.

Mantra: *"I can feel secure in my body, even when I am uncertain."*

Putting It All Together

Let's say you're about to meet someone new or attend a group event. You feel a rush of anxiety, your stomach tightens, and your inner voice says, *"You don't belong here."*

- **Mentally**, you catch the thought: *"I'm assuming I'll be rejected because that's what happened before."*
- **Emotionally**, you pause and name it: *"This is fear. This is old pain rising."*
- **Physically**, you breathe slowly, drop your shoulders, and use Pressure Pulse.

You walk in anyway. Not to perform. Not to force connection. But to stay present with yourself while letting connection become possible. That's not just courage. That's alignment in motion.

The Adventure Triskelion: A Pathway to Lasting Change

Lasting change doesn't happen by willpower alone. It happens when your mind, emotions, and body work together, not in conflict. That's the power of the Adventure Triskelion. This living model offers a framework to approach any life challenge, whether it's building better habits, healing relationships, recovering from burnout, or stepping into a new identity, through the lens of alignment. When you use your values, your goals as compass, and the three core pillars of your inner system are all in sync, change becomes not only possible, but sustainable.

When we ask the right questions within each pillar, we uncover a new way of relating to the area of life we're trying to change. We stop fighting ourselves. We start listening to all parts of who we are and bring them into conversation. This isn't about being perfect. It's about being in alignment.

So, whether you're navigating health, creativity, relationships, career, or self-worth, the Triskelion becomes your internal compass, helping you align with your truth, take meaningful action, and return to yourself in every step of the journey.

When values and goals align across the body, mind, and heart, change isn't forced. It flows.

Chapter 12

Relationships and Leadership of the Wild Sensitive

The Sacred Dance of Sensitivity and Sovereignty

"To love and lead as a Wild Sensitive is to live at the intersection of depth and dynamism. We don't just want connection, we ache for resonance. And in a world that rewards control, our true strength is attunement. The more we honor how we're wired, the more we can lead without losing ourselves, and love without disappearing."

The Living Adventurers

Understanding Relationship Dynamics as a Wild Sensitive

We've learned something crucial on our journey, not all love is created equal. Especially when you are a HSP who is also an HSS. The relationships we build are deeply impacted by how we're wired, how we've healed, and how self-aware we are. And while our traits don't determine our destiny, they do shape the emotional terrain we travel. This is especially true when it comes to partnerships.

There are far too many variations to map every possible relational combination between sensitive and less sensitive, empowered and unempowered partners to write about in this book. (Our next book will be on relationships and the specific tools and skills we need to have harmonious relationships.) The chemistry between an Empowered HSP-HSS and an Unempowered HSP is vastly different than between two Empowered HSPs. Even the same wiring can create wildly different results depending on awareness, trauma history, communication habits, and nervous system capacity. So instead, we offer more general descriptions of a few combinations and the dynamics that show up in relationships that help you orient yourself and your partner in your relationship.

And it all begins with one essential reality:
The more awareness you have, the more clarity you will gain, about your own reactions, your partner's behavior, and the relational field between you. In many partnerships, it's often the more empowered partner who takes the lead in emotional responsibility, communication, and co-regulation. But empowered leadership isn't about dominance, it's about discernment and negotiation.

True empowerment doesn't seek to control. It listens, maps, and collaborates. It notices what's happening beneath the surface and responds with intention. In contrast, dominance, is used by someone who is unempowered, becomes a tool for control, a mask for fear, a way to avoid vulnerability.

Even in relationships where both partners are growing, one may have greater awareness in a given moment. And without awareness, we react. With awareness, we respond. With sovereignty, we negotiate, not just with others, but with the moment itself.

Leading in love isn't about doing all the work or sacrificing your needs. It's about holding a clear map and inviting your partner to help shape the path forward together, while also recognizing when they're not yet able or willing to meet you there.

The Ache to Connect
Many Wild Sensitives carry a deep longing to connect, not just to be

with someone, but to be felt, seen, and understood in their full emotional landscape. This longing often has roots in early experiences where their sensitivity was denied, dismissed, or misunderstood by the world around them. Over time, this creates not only a habit of hiding, but a hunger to be met, not in performance, but in presence. It's not about constant closeness, but about emotional resonance, the kind of bond where unspoken moments speak volumes.

When that kind of connection is missing, especially in a relationship with a partner who is less sensitive or not wired for emotional depth, it can create subtle but growing gaps. While less sensitive partners may bring incredible strengths, steadiness, resilience, and the ability to navigate the outer world with greater ease, they don't always see, or even value, the inward richness that sensitivity brings. They may interpret depth as delay, nuance as overthinking, or emotional insight as intensity.

Something as simple as a nature hike can reveal the divide: the sensitive one may want to pause, absorb the sunlight filtering through leaves, trace the feeling of bark under their fingertips, or reflect on the subtle shift in air, while their partner moves steadily forward, focused on distance, speed, or achievement. Neither is wrong. But without shared understanding, these differences can feel lonely. What begins as a different pace becomes a different presence.

This becomes even more complex when one partner is a Wild Sensitive and the other is not only less sensitive, but also not sensation seeking. Now, not only is there a disconnect in emotional depth, but also in energy, pace, and appetite for experience. One partner may crave stillness, the other intensity. One may need words, the other silence. These differences don't mean the relationship is doomed, but they do require a high level of awareness, emotional management, and honest communication. Without those, the relationship can become a place of quiet grief, two people loving each other, but missing each other completely.

The Art of Emotional Mapping in Relationships

For the Wild Sensitive, relationships aren't just about words or actions, they're an emotional ecosystem. We read subtle shifts in mood and energy the way others read headlines. A sigh, a pause, a glance held just a little too long can register as a full-body signal. This sensitivity can be a powerful gift: it allows us to attune, empathize, and often understand our partner's emotional state before they've even put it into words. But without internal clarity, that same gift can become a trap.

Projection happens when we assume the feeling we sense is about us, when in truth, it might not be. Empathy fatigue builds when we're constantly absorbing another's emotions without grounding in our own. And over-attunement can lead us to adjust ourselves pre-emptively, trying to manage the emotional weather of the relationship instead of letting it move naturally. Especially in a relationship between two HSP's this can become very intricate. The biggest danger is when we don't know what we feel, because we're so busy feeling them. This creates a strange kind of emotional mirroring: one partner senses the other's discomfort and tries to fix it, while the other senses that effort and reciprocates, often resulting in a loop of over-functioning and silent sacrifice.

No one is being dishonest, but both may end up giving what the other doesn't need, while quietly longing for something else entirely. The relationship begins to feel tangled, confusing, even performative, two loving people caught in a cycle of emotional compensation rather than true connection. Emotional mapping is the skill that breaks this loop: the ability to notice, name, and own your internal state before responding to the other's. It's the art of saying, "This is mine," "That is theirs," and "Here's what I truly feel and need." When both partners can do this, the relationship moves from reactive to responsive, from enmeshment to intimacy.

How to Be Yourself When You Can Feel the Other

When you're highly sensitive, especially as a Wild Sensitive, being in a relationship often means feeling the other person from the inside out. Their tension, joy, disappointment, or withdrawal doesn't just register, you absorb it. And if you've learned to survive by keeping the peace or avoiding conflict, your system might instinctively shift to accommodate. You become what they need. What they expect. What makes things smoother. It happens so quickly, you might not even notice. But over time, it costs you something sacred: your center.

You begin to vanish in subtle ways, choosing what they like, softening your tone, ignoring your own needs to preserve connection. You become a relational chameleon, always adjusting to the emotional temperature around you. So how do you stop? Not by shutting down your empathy, but by anchoring into your own truth first. Before you respond to their energy, check in with your own: *"What am I feeling? What do I want right now? What part of this is mine?"* Build that pause into your emotional reflex.

Practice small acts of self-expression, even when they feel edgy. State a preference. Set a boundary. Share a desire without immediately cushioning it with their comfort. Let their feelings be theirs, not problems to solve, but waves to witness. Being yourself in a relationship where you can feel everything means learning to stay inside your own skin, even when someone else's energy wants to pull you out of it. It's not disconnection. It's sovereignty. And the more you practice it, the more honest, resilient, and fulfilling your relationships become.

When Two Wild Sensitives Love

When Wild Sensitives step into their full, integrated self, the relationship becomes nothing short of extraordinary. They bring a rare fusion of emotional depth and dynamic energy, the ability to feel profoundly, yet move boldly through life. In partnership, this looks like someone who can sit with you in your darkest hour with unwavering presence and compassion, then wake up the next morning ready to invite you on an unexpected adventure that rekindles your joy. They listen not just to what you say, but to your silences. They notice what goes unspoken. They sense the tension in your shoulders, the flicker behind your smile. They are often the first to ask the brave question that breaks open a deeper truth.

Their love is intentional. Because they process life so deeply, when they choose you, they mean it. And because they're sensation seekers, they often infuse the relationship with creativity, playfulness, and a desire to co-create meaningful experiences, whether it's a spontaneous road trip, a late-night philosophical conversation, or a quiet moment watching the sky change. They hold the kind of memory that remembers the exact words you didn't say three weeks ago during a difficult conversation and will gently circle back when you're ready.

But the real magic happens when both partners are empowered, no longer shape-shifting, no longer over-adapting to avoid rejection. From this grounded place, they offer not performance, but presence. Not perfection, but truth. There is emotional safety without stagnation, unpredictability in the best way, and a shared journey rooted in curiosity, honesty, and respect. They don't always know which path to take, but they have the security within each other to admit uncertainty. And in that vulnerability, they grow, not apart, but together.

When two Empowered Wild Sensitives love, they create a partnership where each supports the other's evolution. There's mutual permission to change, to feel fully, to stretch beyond old stories. They are not just lovers or companions, they become mirrors, allies, and co-adventurers. Their love becomes a place to land and a launchpad to leap. It's a wild, beautiful thing, rooted not in fear, but in the full-bodied desire to live, love, and expand. Together.

The various relationships we can find ourselves in as a Wild Sensitive. First let us define the terms we will use.

UWS (Unempowered Wild Sensitive) – Unempowered Highly Sensitive Person – High Sensation Seeker
This individual feels the deep pulls of both sensitivity and sensation-seeking but lacks the tools or support to manage either. They may cycle between over-stimulation and under-stimulation, often feeling misunderstood, overwhelmed, impulsive, or stuck in burnout or boredom. They crave more from life but don't yet know how to navigate it sustainably.

EWS (Empowered Wild Sensitive) – Empowered Highly Sensitive Person – High Sensation Seeker
Here, the sensitivity and the craving for novelty work in harmony. This person has developed the emotional regulation, tools, and self-awareness to manage their nervous system and direct their energy intentionally. They're grounded in who they are and channel their intensity toward purpose, creativity, and growth.

UHSP – Unempowered Highly Sensitive Person
A person with high emotional depth and sensory processing sensitivity, but without the support, understanding, or boundaries to thrive. Often overwhelmed by emotions or environments, they may internalize their sensitivity as a weakness or retreat from life to avoid overstimulation.

EHSP – Empowered Highly Sensitive Person
This person has embraced their sensitivity as a strength. They have built resilience, created nourishing routines, and developed emotional clarity. Their empathy becomes a gift rather than a burden, and they know how to protect their energy while remaining connected and open.

UNON – Unempowered Non-Highly Sensitive Person
Typically, less emotionally and sensory attuned, this individual may lean on control, logic, or dominance to navigate the world. They often struggle with nuance, vulnerability, or emotional expression, and may dismiss or suppress sensitivity in others due to their own discomfort or

lack of understanding.

ENON – Empowered Non-Highly Sensitive Person

While not highly sensitive themselves, these individuals have developed strong emotional intelligence, self-regulation, and respect for others' differences. They are balanced, grounded, and often make excellent partners, leaders, or allies to sensitives when they value and honor emotional diversity. Each type exists on a spectrum and can evolve. Empowerment is not a fixed identity, it's a path.

Combinations with the Unempowered HSP-HSS (UWS):

1. UWS + UNON
2. UWS + ENON
3. UWS + UHSP
4. UWS + EHSP
5. UWS + UWS

Combinations with the Empowered HSP-HSS (EWS):

6. EWS + UNON
7. EWS + ENON
8. EWS + UHSP
9. EWS + EHSP
10. EWS + UWS
11. EWS + EWS

Combination #1
UWS + UNON: "The Explosive Mismatch"

This relationship often begins with intensity, attraction, novelty, even chemistry, but quickly devolves into confusion, conflict, and disconnection. The UWS, already struggling with inner fragmentation (craving intensity but collapsing from overstimulation), meets the UNON, who lacks emotional depth and has little tolerance for what they perceive as "drama," "moodiness," or inconsistency.

At first, the UWS may be drawn to the UNON's steadiness, mistaking it for safety or strength. The UNON, in turn, may find the UWS adventurous, wild, unpredictable, and passionate, until that passion becomes emotionally demanding. As soon as the UWS begins to seek deeper connection, ask for emotional attunement, or display sensitivity, the UNON typically shuts down, dismisses, or criticizes.

The UWS, lacking a secure sense of identity, may become increasingly anxious, reactive, or self-abandoning in an effort to "earn" love or regulate the connection. But the more they pursue, the more the UNON pulls away, often retreating into distraction, avoidance, or even control. Over time, this dynamic creates emotional injury for the UWS and emotional exhaustion or irritation for the UNON.

Common Patterns:
- UWS feels unseen and "too much"
- UNON feels confused, annoyed, or burdened
- Frequent emotional misfires and shutdowns
- Power struggles rooted in emotional illiteracy
- Passion without mutual understanding
- Longing without landing

Potential for Growth: *Low*
Unless both parties commit to deep personal transformation. The UNON would need to awaken to emotional literacy and curiosity, while the UWS would need to stabilize their inner world and develop boundaries. Without that, the relationship often becomes emotionally unsafe, volatile, or quietly eroding.

Combination #2
UWS + ENON: "The Grounded Mirror, the Restless Storm"
This pairing brings potential, but not without friction. The UWS is full of depth, intensity, and emotional yearning, but lacks the regulation and tools to manage their dual wiring. The ENON, by contrast, is emotionally steady, grounded, and self-aware, but may not be naturally inclined toward emotional exploration or sensory nuance.

At first, this can feel like a breath of fresh air for the UWS. The ENON's calm energy offers a sense of safety they've rarely known. The ENON, meanwhile, may find the UWS intriguing, even inspiring, captivated by their passion, creativity, and sensitivity. But soon, the imbalance emerges.

The UWS often seeks emotional resonance and intensity, needing to process and connect at a deeper level. The ENON may offer kindness and listening, but not the intensity or mirroring the UWS craves. When emotional waves hit, as they often do for the UWS, the ENON may try to "solve" or "calm" the storm instead of holding space for it, unintentionally leaving the UWS feeling misunderstood or emotionally dismissed.

In turn, the ENON can feel overwhelmed or even emotionally manipulated by the UWS's volatility, especially when their need for stimulation or connection becomes erratic or ungrounded. The ENON wants harmony, while the UWS is often living in emotional and existential flux.

Common Patterns:
- UWS feels safe but unseen
- ENON feels responsible but confused
- Moments of beauty punctuated by emotional crash cycles
- ENON offers structure, UWS resists feeling "managed"
- Emotional intensity meets practical containment

Potential for Growth: *Moderate to High*
If the UWS begins the journey of self-regulation and emotional empowerment. The ENON can be a stabilizing force, offering consistent care and grounded presence, but only if they don't become the default emotional regulator for the relationship. With coaching or guiding, communication tools, and a shared commitment to growth, this relationship can become surprisingly solid, but only if both respect and

learn each other's wiring.

Combination #3
UWS + UHSP: "The Echo Chamber of Emotion"

This relationship is rooted in shared depth and emotional sensitivity, but when both partners are unempowered, it often leads to emotional enmeshment, overwhelm, and stagnation. The UWS brings intensity, volatility, and an insatiable hunger for experience, while the UHSP brings emotional depth and fragility, but lacks the boundaries or resilience to stay regulated in the face of strong emotion or change.

At first, these two may feel like soulmates. They recognize one another's inner worlds. They both "feel everything." They may bond over shared wounds, mutual sensitivity, and a longing to be seen. The problem arises when neither partner has the capacity to hold the emotional weight they're inviting in. Their shared sensitivity becomes a kind of emotional echo chamber, intensifying instead of soothing.

The UWS often tries to move, chasing novelty, connection, or growth in erratic ways. The UHSP, however, may resist this movement, needing predictability and calm. The UWS partner may push forward without awareness, overwhelming the other. The UHSP partner may retreat, shut down, or spiral, triggering guilt, frustration, or rejection in both directions. Instead of balancing each other, they flood each other. Emotional reactivity, overprocessing, and shared dysregulation can dominate the relationship. What might feel magical in the beginning, all that understanding and vulnerability, slowly becomes draining, unstable, or even co-dependent.

Common Patterns:
- Over-identification with pain or sensitivity
- Emotional co-regulation without boundaries
- Inconsistent pacing (UWS drives, UHSP resists)
- Burnout from overstimulation, isolation from under-stimulation
- Intimacy without direction, safety without growth

Potential for Growth: *Low to Moderate*

This relationship can become healing if both partners commit to emotional regulation and self-development. But without those shifts, it often remains locked in cycles of emotional overwhelm, romantic idealization, and mutual withdrawal. Shared wounds don't automatically equal shared healing, especially without skillful tools.

Combination #4
UWS + EHSP: "The Seeker Meets the Sanctuary"

This dynamic can feel like salvation for the UWS, and like a sacred challenge for the EHSP. One partner is in constant motion, emotionally hungry, overstimulated, and searching for meaning. The other is grounded in emotional clarity, boundaries, and self-awareness. The EHSP has done the work to turn sensitivity into strength. The UWS, by contrast, is still caught in the paradox of craving more while feeling too much.

Early on, this pairing can feel magnetic. The UWS may feel deeply seen for the first time, not judged for their contradictions, but gently mirrored by the EHSP's calm, contained presence. The EHSP may feel purpose-driven: here is someone who needs their emotional wisdom, someone whose depth mirrors their own, even if it's still in chaos.

However, this pairing can quickly fall out of balance if the UWS begins to rely too heavily on the EHSP for emotional regulation, grounding, or decision-making. The empowered partner may unintentionally step into a caretaker or therapist role, especially if their empathy is still entangled with responsibility. Meanwhile, the unempowered partner may idolize, resist, or unconsciously sabotage the very stability they crave.

The EHSP values slowness, sanctuary, and truth. The UWS wants fire, change, and intensity. If not bridged through conscious communication and pacing, these needs begin to clash. The EHSP may begin to feel drained or manipulated. The UWS may feel restricted, unseen in their bolder longings.

Common Patterns:

- UWS idealizes or clings to the EHSP's stability
- EHSP becomes the emotional anchor, sometimes at their own expense
- Growth potential exists, but power dynamic must rebalance
- Emotional depth is shared, but rhythm is misaligned
- One partner is moving inward, the other trying to leap outward

Potential for Growth: *Moderate to High*

If the UWS is willing to take responsibility for their inner world, this relationship can become transformational. The EHSP can model regulation and presence, while the UWS can reawaken creativity, courage, and expansion in the EHSP. But boundaries must be strong, and roles clearly defined, otherwise, love turns into labor.

Combination #5

UWS + UWS: "The Wildfire Without a Compass"

When two UWS individuals come together, the initial energy can feel electric. Both partners understand the inner paradox, the hunger for stimulation, the depth of emotion, the quick overwhelm. There's a shared recognition: "Finally, someone who gets both the thrill and the fragility." At first, this feels like liberation.

But without empowerment, structure, or self-regulation, the relationship often spirals. Both partners are emotionally intense, sensation-hungry, and prone to dysregulation. There is little grounding. Instead, they may amplify each other's impulsivity, emotional volatility, or avoidance of stillness. Passion runs high, but so does chaos, creating a cycle of thrill and rupture that can feel addictive, confusing, and ultimately unsustainable without conscious intervention.

These two might dive headfirst into new experiences, projects, or dreams, only to crash from overstimulation or unmet expectations. Their deep sensitivity means every perceived rejection or misunderstanding cuts deeply. Their High Sensation Seeking means they're both prone to chase novelty instead of stability. Emotional support becomes inconsistent, or even competitive: *"Who's hurting more?" "Whose need matters now?"*

Conflict tends to escalate quickly and resolve poorly. Because neither partner has cultivated the tools to slow down, reflect, or emotionally regulate, disagreements often lead to shutdowns, dramatic exits, or mis-attuned reconnections that don't address the root.

Common Patterns:
- Mutual emotional overwhelm and burnout
- Sensation seeking without stability
- High chemistry, low clarity
- Intimacy laced with inconsistency
- Escalating cycles of passion and withdrawal
- Avoidance of responsibility, blaming external circumstances

Potential for Growth: *Low to Moderate*
This pairing has enormous energy, but energy without direction creates friction, not firelight. If both partners begin the work of self-awareness and emotional mastery, they can become allies in healing. But without individual empowerment, they often become mirrors of one another's instability. What feels like wild love can become an uncontained blaze.

Combination #6
EWS + UNON: "The Wild and the Wall"
This is one of the most challenging pairings. The EWS brings emotional depth, energetic complexity, and a life designed around meaningful experience, embodiment, and alignment. The UNON, on the other hand, operates largely from conditioning, control, and surface-level function. Where the EWS is expansive, the UNON is often closed. Where one seeks resonance, the other avoids emotional exposure. This creates a dynamic in which the empowered partner may constantly feel muted, dismissed, or unseen.

In the early stages, the EWS might feel intrigued by the UNON's apparent steadiness, a contrast to their own internal intensity. The UNON might be drawn to the EWS magnetism, creativity, or presence. But soon, the gap becomes clear: the EWS craves emotional reciprocity, intellectual and sensory exploration, and a deep, embodied life. The UNON often lacks the willingness, or tools, to engage on that level.

Conflict can emerge around vulnerability: the EWS wants truth, transparency, emotional growth. The UNON wants comfort, control, and minimal disruption. This can trigger old wounds for the EWS: being "too much," "too emotional," "too complex." If unaddressed, the empowered partner may shrink to maintain peace or erupt when ignored. The UNON, unwilling or unable to meet them in that space, may respond with shutdown, criticism, or withdrawal.

Common Patterns:
- EWS feels stifled, unseen, or invalidated
- UNON feels overwhelmed, judged, or annoyed
- Misalignment in emotional fluency and desire for growth
- Disempowered avoidance meets empowered presence
- Risk of repeating old patterns: over-functioning, under-responding

Potential for Growth: *Low*
Unless the UNON begins a process of emotional awakening. The EWS has done the work and needs a partner who can meet them, not mute them. Without mutual growth, this relationship can become a source of frustration, depletion, or identity distortion for the empowered partner. Sometimes the most empowered act is leaving, not out of rejection, but in devotion to one's truth.

Combination #7
EWS + ENON: "The Anchor and the Flame"
This is a powerful and complementary match when built on mutual

respect and curiosity. The EWS brings emotional depth, sensory richness, and a hunger for meaningful experience. The ENON offers steadiness, grounded logic, and resilience, often thriving in the practical or external world. While they operate differently, their values can align beautifully if they hold space for one another's ways of being.

Early in the relationship, the EWS may feel relieved to meet someone who doesn't get overwhelmed easily, someone who can hold ground when life gets intense. The ENON often feels invigorated and inspired by the EWS's passion, insight, and vibrancy. They appreciate the emotional intelligence, even if they don't naturally mirror it.

The key dynamic here is difference without distortion. The EWS doesn't need the ENON to feel everything, only to honor what they feel. And the ENON doesn't need the EWS to be less intense, only to remain self-responsible and not project unmet needs. When this mutual understanding is in place, the relationship becomes a dance of grounded movement: one partner creates waves, the other builds the container.

Challenges can arise when the ENON seeks simplicity or action while the EWS wants to process or explore nuance. The EWS may need more emotional dialogue than the ENON is naturally wired to give. But if the ENON stays open, and the EWS stays self-aware, the two can find a rhythm that enriches both.

Common Patterns:
- ENON stabilizes, EWS energizes
- Conflict handled with emotional insight and practical clarity
- Depth meets direction; intensity meets containment
- Mutual respect for different processing styles
- Requires ongoing communication to bridge inner vs. outer world

Potential for Growth: *High*
This relationship can thrive when each partner honors their strengths

without trying to become the other. The EWS learns to trust stillness and structure; the ENON learns to feel more, stretch more, and grow beyond surface living. Together, they create a partnership rooted in presence, possibility, and respect.

Combination #8
EWS + UHSP: "The Awakener and the Withholder"

This relationship often begins with a strong emotional pull. Both partners are sensitive, and feel deeply, but they express and navigate that depth very differently. The EWS is a fully embodied, dynamic presence: bold yet sensitive, emotionally intelligent, and grounded in their unique rhythm. The UHSP, in contrast, often struggles with emotional overwhelm, self-doubt, and a fear of being too much for the world.

In the early stages, the UHSP may feel awe and comfort in the EWS's self-possession. *"You live the way I wish I could."* They may feel inspired, supported, even cracked open by the empowered partner's capacity to feel deeply without drowning. The EWS, in turn, often feels drawn to the softness and sincerity of the UHSP, sensing both a shared inner world and an opportunity to guide or uplift.

But here lies the risk: the relationship can slip into a rescuer–rescued dynamic. The EWS, if not vigilant with boundaries, may overextend themselves emotionally, constantly holding space or encouraging the UHSP to grow, often more than the UHSP is ready for. The UHSP, meanwhile, may idealize the empowered partner but also fear being left behind, feeling unseen or "less evolved." This can lead to subtle patterns of withdrawal, comparison, or emotional dependency.

The empowered partner thrives in a life of growth, movement, and expansive honesty. If the unempowered partner resists their own healing or avoids responsibility for their emotional reactivity, the relationship becomes lopsided, one expanding, the other retreating, creating emotional distance, unmet needs, and a growing tension that words alone can't bridge.

Common Patterns:
- EWS becomes an emotional or motivational guide
- UHSP alternates between admiration and insecurity
- Growth gap creates emotional misalignment
- High empathy, but unequal emotional capacity
- EWS may suppress their fire to protect the other's fragility

Potential for Growth: *Moderate*
This can be a profoundly healing relationship if the UHSP is willing to step into their own empowerment. The EWS can model what's possible but cannot drag their partner into wholeness. Without mutual growth, this dynamic can become quietly draining, a mismatch between sovereignty and hesitation.

Combination #9
EWS + EHSP: "The Still Flame"
This relationship brings together two emotionally attuned individuals who've each done the inner work, but who express their sensitivity in different ways. EWS is dynamic, exploratory, and sensation-seeking, yet grounded in deep emotional wisdom. The EHSP is spacious, steady, and inwardly rich, oriented toward sanctuary, nuance, and sustainable connection.

At its best, this pairing is a dance between stillness and motion, tenderness and boldness. The EHSP provides depth, patience, and the kind of emotional presence that nourishes the EWS like water to fire. In turn, the EWS brings vitality, movement, and inspired challenge to the EHSP's well-structured inner world.

These two often connect through shared values: authenticity, meaning, emotional honesty, and growth. Both are self-aware, emotionally literate, and willing to name their needs. The EHSP may prefer ritual, rhythm, and predictability. The EWS may prefer variety, adventure, and stretch. When honored consciously, these differences create complementarity, not conflict.

However, challenges can arise if pacing isn't explicitly navigated. The EWS may crave novelty or stimulation just as the EHSP needs restoration. The EHSP may misread the EWS's appetite for movement as restlessness or dissatisfaction. The EWS may misread the EHSP's love of calm as emotional passivity. Bridging these interpretations is essential.

Common Patterns:
- Shared emotional fluency and inner richness
- EHSP offers anchoring; EWS offers expansion
- Strong communication, potential for co-creation
- Need to negotiate stimulation vs. spaciousness
- Mutual respect is high; pacing needs conscious design

Potential for Growth: *Very High*
When both partners remain in honest dialogue about needs, energy, and boundaries, this becomes a deeply generative relationship. Together, they build a life that is emotionally resonant and vibrantly alive, a sanctuary that moves, a fire that listens.

Combination #10
EWS + UWS: "The Embodied Guide and the Inner Storm"
This is a relationship full of recognition and resonance, and it can either catalyze transformation or collapse into imbalance. Both partners share the rare and complex trait combination of high sensitivity and high sensation seeking. But only one has learned to navigate it with clarity, self-regulation, and ownership. The EWS has done the inner work. The UWS is still caught in contradiction, longing, and dysregulation.

At the beginning, this match may feel like destiny. The UWS often feels seen for the first time. The empowered partner validates their intensity, emotional depth, and craving for life, not as flaws, but as features of their unique wiring. The EWS, in turn, feels a kinship: "You are like me. I know this fire." But quickly, the gap in integration begins to show.

The UWS may idealize their empowered partner, seeking emotional safety and direction, but also fearing judgment or abandonment. They may lean on the EWS for regulation, inspiration, or identity. The empowered partner, if not careful, may fall into over- functioning, managing the emotional swings, anchoring the connection, or playing therapist. Without boundaries, resentment builds.

The relationship can become a mirror of "what is" and "what could be." The empowered partner sees the unempowered one's potential. The unempowered partner sees who they want to become but may collapse under the pressure of comparison. If the EWS tries to pull the other into growth, the result is emotional resistance or relational fatigue.

Common Patterns:
- Empowered partner becomes a guide, sometimes a crutch
- High resonance, but unequal regulation
- Shared craving for depth, but different capacities to hold it
- One partner inspires, the other idealizes (or resists)
- Possibility of transformation or emotional dependency

Potential for Growth: *Moderate to High*
If the UHSP-HSS takes ownership of their journey. This can be a sound relationship when both partners remain sovereign. The EHSP-HSS cannot carry the healing, but they can model it. If the UHSP-HSS steps into their own power, the relationship becomes electric, meaningful, and wildly alive. Otherwise, it risks draining the very fire it seeks to hold.

Combination #11
EWS + EWS: "The Wild, Wise Mirror"
This is the rarest, and potentially most powerful, pairing of all. Two EWS individuals in relationship are like meeting your reflection: depth meets depth, intensity meets intensity, and both have done the work to hold it all. This connection often feels instantly alive, awake, and aligned. It is filled with movement, magic, and meaning, but also demands

constant honesty and intentional pacing.

Because both partners are wired for emotional depth and stimulation, the energy between them can be expansive and fast-moving. They may dream together, create together, adventure together, all with a shared understanding of nuance, complexity, and nervous system care. This relationship is not for the faint of heart, but for those who want to live fully. There is no hiding here.

When balanced, these two can co-regulate and co-elevate, each knowing how to tend to their own system while respecting the other's rhythm. They bring curiosity to conflict, creativity to constraint, and compassion to every inner edge. Their lives may look unconventional, but they are consciously chosen, not unconsciously reactive.

In a truly empowered relationship, both partners meet as equals, not in perfection, but in presence. They don't dominate or defer; they co-create. Each brings awareness, emotional responsibility, and a willingness to grow not just for themselves, but with each other.

When both remain empowered, something remarkable happens they help one another notice when the fire is burning too hot, when momentum becomes overwhelming, or when one of them is overextending. There's no blame, only shared noticing. No rescue, only reflection.

This kind of partnership is rare, and deeply powerful. They share drive. They value boundaries. They understand the importance of values and honor each other's deep desires without judgment. They don't just make space for one another's truth, they affirm it.

Together, they hold a living map of their pasts, their beliefs, and the evolving story they're writing. And if either partner temporarily dips into an unempowered state, as we all do from time to time, the relationship doesn't break. It bends with grace, waits with compassion, and gently invites a return to center.

This is what we call a sovereign partnership, one where love is not about fixing, controlling, or saving, but about seeing, supporting, and co-evolving.

Common Patterns:
- Shared hunger for growth, depth, and adventure
- Mutual self-awareness, high respect for complexity
- Can create together, lead together, stretch each other
- Deep, mutual awareness of themselves and each other
- Potential for spiritual, creative, and relational evolution

Potential for Growth: *Extremely High*
This is the Wild Sensitive dream pairing, while both partners remain self-responsible, regulated, and attuned to pacing. When they do, the relationship becomes not just a home, but a launchpad of affirmed beliefs, values, desires, and goals, where creativity meets adventure. It's a sacred union where both fire and flow belong.

Complexity as a Gift, Not a Flaw
Our complexity is not a flaw, it's a gift, and when embraced, it makes us incredible colleagues and friends. As Wild Sensitives individuals, we bring a rich inner world to every relationship and collaboration. We don't just skim the surface; we notice the details others miss, feel the energy in a room, and intuitively understand unspoken dynamics.

This depth allows us to show up with empathy, insight, and care. At the same time, our sensation-seeking side brings innovation, spontaneity, and a readiness to dive into new ideas or experiences. We're the ones who can hold space during a tough moment, then spark laughter or creativity when it's needed most. In friendships and teams, our ability to hold paradox, stillness and momentum, emotion and strategy, makes us steady, dynamic, and deeply loyal. We may not always be predictable, but we are profoundly engaged. When we're allowed to be all of who we are, we help create spaces that are more human, inspired, and alive.

Contribution and leadership

Empowered Wild Sensitive individuals often make remarkable leaders, creators, and catalysts, not despite their sensitivity and complexity, but because of it. With their deep emotional intelligence and attunement to subtle dynamics, they naturally sense what's unsaid, what's needed, and what's possible. Their high sensitivity gives them empathy, foresight, and relational wisdom, while their sensation-seeking drive fuels courage, innovation, and bold thinking. They're the ones who ask the deeper questions, hold space during conflict, and bring vision that includes both purpose and people. In a world that too often prizes speed over substance, Wild Sensitives offer a new kind of leadership, one rooted in awareness, integrity, and resonance. They're not here to dominate; they're here to elevate, to lead not from the top, but from the heart, co-creating environments that are more emotionally honest, creatively alive, and deeply human.

Redefining Leadership for the Sensitive Soul

For too long, leadership has been defined by volume, dominance, and control, by the ability to command a room, push through resistance, and always have the answer. But for the Wild Sensitive, true leadership looks nothing like performance. It is presence, rooted, attuned, and deeply embodied. Sensitive souls lead not by overpowering others, but by empowering them by noticing the invisible, and creating spaces where authenticity can thrive. Their strength is in their resonance, the way their presence calms nervous systems, invites truth, and gives permission for vulnerability. This is leadership as emotional clarity, not ego. As integrity, not intensity. When a Wild Sensitive leads from their empowered self, they don't have to prove anything, they become the invitation. And in doing so, they help shift leadership itself from command-and-control to connection-and-coherence, showing that the softest voices can create the deepest impact.

The Invisible Strengths of the Wild Sensitive Leader

The Wild Sensitive leader is a rare and valuable asset to any organization. They lead from the heart, while consistently assessing the needs of the organization. They carefully observe the spaces others miss. Their strengths aren't loud, but they are profound. With empowered high sensitivity comes deep observation, empathy, and a strong internal compass guided by integrity. They feel the emotional currents in a room before words are spoken, often naming what others sense but can't articulate.

Paired with their High Sensation Seeking drive, they don't just sit with what is, they see what could be. Their desire for stimulation and novelty becomes innovative vision, propelling them toward creative expansion and diverse thinking. Their sensitivity keeps that vision ethically grounded, ensuring that what they build serves something deeper than just success. While Wild Sensitive leaders recognize patterns others overlook and lead through resonance rather than force, they often encounter challenges from less sensitive leadership who lack these innate skills.

Traditionally, leadership was granted to the stoic and unemotional, keeping a hard line at the cost of the emotional wellbeing of others. This archaic philosophy is rapidly diminishing as the mental health impacts are being realized. While some organizations move towards more and more automation, removing the human component, many require a more effective leadership approach. Countless studies have proven compassionate leadership outperforms aggressive leadership. Wild Sensitive leaders focus on proactive management rather than reactive management which bridges intuition with action. Their leadership is nothing less than sound, effective, respected, transformational, born of courage, insight, and a deep desire to move the world forward without losing what makes it human.

Challenges in Traditional Systems

For some Wild Sensitives traditional systems like corporate workplaces, hierarchical organizations, or rigid institutions often feel like wearing clothes that never quite fit. The environment is typically fast-paced, overstimulating, and saturated with unspoken power dynamics. While others may tolerate this by pushing through, the Wild Sensitive is often doing double the labor, navigating not just tasks, but emotional undercurrents, interpersonal tensions, and their own internal processing.

Their natural empathy can lead them to pick up what others ignore, often making them the quiet holders of emotional labor in a system that doesn't see or value it. Many Wild Sensitive leaders find themselves over-giving, under-supported, and chronically questioning their value, not because they're incapable, but because the system wasn't built with their nervous system or strengths in mind. To thrive, they don't need to toughen up, they need spaces that honor depth, flexibility, and emotional intelligence as leadership assets, not liabilities.

The Zone-Aware Leader

The most powerful leaders don't just manage tasks, they manage energy. For Wild Sensitives, understanding and embodying the Six Zones of Life becomes an essential leadership skill. The Zone-Aware Leader knows how to lead from the Goldilocks Zone, that sweet spot where grounded presence meets just enough stretch to thrive, engaged, and inspired. They aren't running on urgency, nor stuck in overwhelm. They know their own nervous system intimately and recognize when they're drifting into burnout, boredom, or false safety.

Most importantly, they lead without defaulting to people-pleasing. They don't micromanage to control discomfort or over-accommodate to avoid conflict. Instead, they bring clarity, curiosity, and emotional steadiness into the relational field. Because they've done the work of understanding their own zones, they can also help others recognize theirs, creating team cultures that are psychologically secure, creatively energized, and sustainable. This is leadership as attunement, not sacrifice. It's how Wild Sensitives guide with integrity, by modeling wholeness, not hustle.

Below are a few examples of leadership characteristics in today's world.

1. Unempowered Less sensitive Leader (UNONL)

Leadership Style: Directive or hierarchical

Workplace Behavior: Values structure, control, and efficiency over nuance. Tends to lead from authority rather than empathy. Often dismisses emotional input or sees it as weakness.

Strengths
- Jovial and pleasant during normal operation
- Accommodating and agreeable
- Often, not always, compliant with rules and policies

Challenges
- Reactive under pressure disguised as decisiveness
- Emotional turbulence triggers reactionary management styles
- Uses the 'Fake it till you make it'

Shadow Pattern: Dominates instead of collaborates; equates productivity with worth.

2. Empowered Less Sensitive Leader (ENONL)

Leadership Style: Practical, grounded, results-focused

Workplace Behavior: Confident and balanced. Not emotionally driven, but more emotionally aware than the UNONL. Strong boundary-setter. Values clarity and functionality.

Strengths
- Sound stabilizer in teams
- Fair and clear communicator

- Can manage sensitive personalities with respect

Challenges
- May miss deeper emotional or intuitive cues
- Needs reminders to slow down for process-oriented collaborators

Shadow Pattern: May unconsciously prioritize output over culture.

3. Unempowered HSP Leader (UHSPL)

Leadership Style: Withdrawn or over-accommodating

Workplace Behavior: Often avoids leadership altogether or leads through quiet approval-seeking. May overthink decisions, fear conflict, and struggle with boundaries.

Strengths
- Deeply empathic with team members
- Attuned to emotional undercurrents
- Observant and thoughtful

Challenges
- Avoids confrontation
- Easily overwhelmed by demands or overstimulation
- Struggles to make decisions under pressure

Shadow Pattern: Martyrdom, people-pleasing, or silent burnout.

4. Unempowered Wild Sensitive Leader (UWSL)

Leadership Style: Charismatic but inconsistent

Workplace Behavior: Oscillates between visionary energy and collapse. May overcommit, chase stimulation, or burn out quickly. Can inspire others but struggles with follow-through.

Strengths
- Big ideas, contagious enthusiasm
- Willing to take creative or interpersonal risks
- Reads emotional energy in teams

Challenges
- Disorganized, reactive under stress
- Prone to identity crisis or self-doubt
- May crave validation from achievements

Shadow Pattern: Starts fires but doesn't build the hearth. Uses activity to avoid stillness.

5. Empowered HSP Leader (EHSPL)

Leadership Style: Quietly transformational

Workplace Behavior: Leads by example, presence, and values. May not seek leadership roles, but when present, becomes a culture-shifter. Creates security and trust in teams.

Strengths
- Strong ethical compass
- Attuned to unspoken group dynamics
- Deep integrity and vision

Challenges
- May need help asserting authority
- Sensitive to team conflict or fast-paced environments
- Can take too much responsibility for others' emotional states

Shadow Pattern: Self-silencing to preserve harmony.

6. Empowered Wild Sensitive Leader (EWSL)

Leadership Style: Visionary and integrative

Workplace Behavior: Thrives in creative or mission-driven roles. Bold and emotionally intelligent. Balances intensity with insight. Motivates through meaning and momentum.

Strengths
- Deep feeler + bold mover
- Builds emotionally aware, high-performing teams
- Passionate about impact, innovation, and authenticity

Challenges
- Needs spaciousness and autonomy to thrive
- Can stretch too thin without systems
- May get frustrated with conventional, rigid systems

Shadow Pattern: Burns bright and risks bore-out unless sustainability is honored.

The Empowered Wild Sensitive Leader:
"The Visionary Bridge Between Depth and Drive"

When an EWSL steps into leadership fully resourced, using their tools, nervous system wisdom, emotional intelligence, and somatic awareness, they become a rare and luminous force. They lead not from domination or ego, but from embodied alignment, relational presence, and inspired action. They are bridges: between people and possibilities, between feeling and function, between vision and execution.

Unlike traditional leaders who push forward at all costs, the EWSL leads from wholeness, recognizing that sustainable progress must include emotion, integration, and humanity. Their sensitivity becomes their superpower, allowing them to read the emotional climate of a team, intuit when something's off, and bring compassionate truth to the surface before it becomes dysfunction. Their High Sensation Seeking becomes fuel, allowing them to spark change, invite innovation, and courageously lead others through uncertainty.

What sets the EWSL apart is not just what they do, but how they do it. They model nervous system literacy in real time, staying regulated under pressure, pacing their teams with attunement, and holding emotional intensity without collapse. They cultivate environments where creativity and vulnerability are not just allowed but appreciated. Feedback is welcomed, not punished. Their questions go deeper than deliverables: not just *"What's the goal?"* but *"What's the cost? What's the impact? What aligns with our deeper why?"* And perhaps most powerfully, they embody quiet courage, leading with fierce compassion and a willingness to grow, stretch, and evolve in public. Their presence becomes a permission slip: to feel, to speak, to belong, and to rise.

In a world that often rewards speed over sensitivity, the EWSL is a revolution. They challenge the binary of softness vs. strength by being both. They invite the people around them to not only perform but belong. And in doing so, they don't just build teams or businesses, they cultivate cultures of meaning.

Chapter 13

The Wild Sensitive Wayfinder
No Longer Just Sensitive—Wise, Ready, and Called

*"Life.. Is not just the passing of time! It is the collection of experiences.
Their frequency and intensity define who we are and what we are capable of."*
The Living Adventurers

Throughout this journey, we've explored the paradox and potential of living as a Highly Sensitive Person (HSP) who also carries the fire of High Sensation Seeking (HSS). We've named the contradiction that so many of us have carried for years, the desire for calm wrapped around a hunger for experience. For many, this has felt like a lifelong tug-of-war. But what if that inner paradox was never meant to be solved or silenced? What if it was never a flaw, but rather, the seed of something rare, radiant, and deeply needed in the world?

This chapter is about what comes next. It's about the moment we stop framing our sensitivity and craving for aliveness as enemies and instead begin to train them into allies. When we take the best parts of being a Wild Sensitive, our empathy, intuition, creativity, and depth, and fuse them with a genuine desire to grow in knowledge, acquire meaningful tools, refine emotional and mental skills, and learn how to guide others through life's terrain, we step into something new. We no longer shrink ourselves to fit into old models of success.

An empowered Wild Sensitive is not simply someone who has overcome struggle; they are someone who has transmuted their struggle into strength, and their inner tension into guidance. They are not defined by their sensitivity alone, but by what they do with it. These are individuals who no longer ask, "What's wrong with me?" but instead inquire, "What is this moment asking of me, and how can I meet it with clarity, courage, and care?"

Think of it this way: an unempowered Highly Sensitive Sensation Seeker might resemble someone who spends most days stuck in inertia, sitting on the couch, indulging in drama, scrolling endlessly through social media to avoid discomfort, eating whatever's closest, reacting impulsively to the world, and feeling lost in emotional cycles. They sense their depth, but it overwhelms rather than empowers them. They crave more from life, but they lack the motivation to break out of the conditioning and habitual cycles they are in, believing access to what they need is just out of reach.

An empowered Highly Sensitive Sensation Seeker, by contrast, has begun the climb. They try to eat a little better. They take walks. They've found a good job, a few real friends. They've started listening more deeply to their intuition and practicing occasional emotional boundaries. They aren't masters, but they are in motion. They've stopped trying to "fix" their sensitivity and have started befriending it. They still get flooded, but they recover faster. They still crave novelty, but they're learning to pace it with presence.

And then there's the Wild Sensitive Wayfinder.

The Wayfinder doesn't just try, they train. They don't dabble in emotional growth, they devote themselves to it. They may not be perfect eaters, but they nourish their body because they understand it's part of their sensory intelligence. They exercise their mind and nervous system with the same commitment they give to their physical health. They read voraciously, 12 books a year, maybe more, because their IQ craves insight. They meditate, journal, and reflect because their EQ needs space to breathe and integrate. They manage their mindset, not through toxic positivity, but through the ongoing art of Positive Intelligence. And their SQ? Their sensory intelligence is embodied. They know how their breath affects their nervous system. They know how sunlight lifts their mood, how stillness grounds them, and how certain environments drain them. They make conscious, aligned choices based on this awareness.

Wayfinders are often CEOs, but not always of companies, sometimes of classrooms, creative collectives, small teams, healing spaces, or even their own households. But wherever they are, they lead. Quietly. Powerfully. Humbly.

What makes a Wayfinder truly rare is not simply their embodiment of the four foundational intelligences of the Wild Sensitive, IQ (the clarity to think), EQ (the capacity to feel), PQ (the power to choose), and SQ (the wisdom to sense), but their unwavering commitment to continuous learning. They understand that having intelligence is not enough. Application matters. Integration matters. They aren't just collecting knowledge, they're applying it, refining it, and turning it into wisdom through lived experience.

They study their reactions, not to shame themselves, but to understand. They face challenges not to prove something, but to stretch into who they're becoming. They develop tools. They refine techniques. And then, they share. They teach. They lead by example, not from a place of ego, but from a genuine desire to see others rise.

What's more, Wayfinders are often those who have faced trauma. Not once, but many times. And not only have they survived, they've mined those experiences for meaning. They've asked, again and again, "What strength is being called forth in me through this?" They've developed resilience by walking through fire, not to burn, but to forge. They revisit their wounds not to dwell, but to understand. Not to relive the pain, but to extract the lesson. They put themselves in challenging experiences, not for the adrenaline, but for the emotional education. They seek out their vulnerabilities, not to wallow in them, but to learn how to manage them, protect them, or transform them into strengths. They willingly enter discomfort to better understand their adaptability. Their growth is not accidental; it is intentional, embodied, and sustained.

And though they may appear rare, they are everywhere. In fact, most Wayfinders do not even know they are Wayfinders. They don't announce themselves. They do not seek attention, applause, or fame. Their sensitive nature remains deeply humble. They do not lead to be seen, they lead to serve. And because they see society for what it truly is, divided, disconnected, and often performative, they choose instead to observe. To learn. To quietly influence change at the roots rather than clamor for the crown.

But imagine this: what if the world shifted? What if society stopped rewarding noise and speed and started honoring wisdom and presence? What if performance gave way to purpose, and the wise were once again welcomed to the center of the cultural fire? Then, the Wayfinders would emerge, not to dominate, but to guide. Not to conquer, but to connect. And we would realize they were always among us, gently lighting the way.

Wayfinders walk beside us in boardrooms, classrooms, studios, clinics, and kitchens. They see through even the most carefully applied mask, not to judge, but to understand. Their intuition notices what words cannot say. They feel the unshed tears in a smile, the hesitation in a yes, the fear in a polished performance. They lead not with charisma, but with coherence.

When they speak, they do so with clarity. When they act, it is with care. They hold space for growth. They foster belonging. And in doing so, they reweave the fabric of the world. To become a Wayfinder is not to arrive at perfection. It is to walk with intention. To meet every moment with presence, to sharpen your tools with care, and to choose again and again to grow. It is to declare that your depth is not a burden, but a compass. It is to turn your inner complexity into outer contribution. It is to say:

"I will no longer just navigate my sensitivity. I will navigate with it. I will grow, I will serve, and I will lead, not just for myself, but for those still learning to find their way."

The Path to becoming a Wild Sensitive Wayfinder

Becoming a Wild Sensitive Wayfinder is not a gift bestowed upon a chosen few, it's a path available to every Highly Sensitive Sensation Seeker, whether they currently feel empowered or overwhelmed. Just as anyone can improve their physical health through better nutrition, movement, and support, any Wild Sensitive can strengthen their internal life through intentional learning, daily practice, and meaningful guidance. The potential is already within you. What changes everything is how you cultivate it.

Think of this journey as a holistic wellness plan, not for your body alone, but for your mind, heart, and nervous system. Just as someone might hire a personal trainer to build physical strength, the Wayfinder path calls for mentors, tools, and techniques that shape emotional resilience, mental clarity, and embodied sensitivity. This is where our Adventure Triskelion comes in, our model for whole-self growth. It weaves together Emotional Connection, Mental Clarity, and Physical Engagement, forming the sturdy tripod on which Wayfinding wisdom rests. With this framework, we begin to recondition our inner landscape. We build not just capacity, but courage. Not just insight, but integration. Every Wild Sensitive already carries the spark. Becoming a Wayfinder is how we choose to light it.

Here are the 13 challenges a Wild Sensitive must overcome to reach the Wayfinder status.

Own Your Sensitivity + Sensation Seeking

Acknowledge the full paradox of who you are: a deeply feeling person with a hunger for rich experience. Stop trying to fix or mute either side. Instead, honor both. Your inner tenderness and outer adventurousness are not enemies, they are the raw ingredients of your purpose.

Cultivate Self-Awareness Daily

Wayfinders observe themselves with clarity and compassion. Begin tracking your patterns, emotional, mental, physical, and energetic. Use journaling, body scans, or emotional mapping to identify what environments support you and which ones drain you. Awareness is your compass.

Balance the Four Intelligences (IQ, EQ, PQ, SQ)

Grow in all four areas:
- **IQ:** Commit to lifelong learning, books, podcasts, courses.
- **EQ:** Deepen your emotional literacy and regulation.
- **PQ:** Strengthen your mindset through practices like mental fitness reps.
- **SQ:** Reconnect with your body and senses as a source of wisdom.

Process, Don't Bypass, Your Pain

Trauma is not your identity, but it holds keys to your strength. Instead of pushing it away or endlessly reliving it, work with it. Seek the support and guidance you need to learn the lessons, and patterns that lead to the resilience and adaptability you need. Wayfinders use every wound as an opportunity to grow more capable, not more cautious, more open-hearted, not more armored.

Build and Refine Your Backpack
Gather tools that support your nervous system, your mind, and your emotions. This might include somatic grounding techniques, conflict resolution strategies, meditation, creative outlets, or cognitive reframes. Practice these tools until they become second nature.

Train for Adaptability
Place yourself in new experiences, ones that stretch, not stress, you. Travel. Learn new skills. Practice discomfort intentionally. The more you train for change, the more resilient you become. Wayfinders welcome challenge because they know growth lives there.

Know When to Lead, and When to Listen
Wayfinders aren't always at the front, but they are always aware. Learn the art of discernment: when to speak and when to hold space. Learn to feel the energy of a room, of a person, of a decision. Your leadership is most powerful when it's responsive, not reactive.

Re-evaluate your Belief
Examine the beliefs shaping your life, many of which were formed in response to pain, misunderstanding, or outdated expectations. Ask yourself: Are my beliefs empowering me or keeping me small? Limiting beliefs like "I'm too sensitive to lead" or "My needs are too much" can be rewritten into affirming truths such as "My sensitivity is my greatest strength" or "My needs are valid and worth honoring." It's not just about repeating affirmations, it's about acting from them. When you align your behavior with these new, empowered beliefs, you begin to live not from fear, but from freedom.

Align Your Life with Your Values
Design a life that reflects your truth, not society's noise. What do you stand for? What energizes your soul? From your work to your relationships, shape a life that supports your sensitivity and purpose. Integrity is your anchor.

Establish Core Desires

Core desires are not far-off fantasies or abstract dreams, they are the deep, tangible longings that enrich your life from the inside out. They are the experiences, feelings, and connections that bring you into alignment with your true self. These might be a sense of inner peace, meaningful work, deep companionship, creative expression, or physical vitality. Unlike fleeting wants or societal "shoulds," core desires are steady and soul-rooted. When honored, they become guideposts, reminding you of what truly matters and helping you shape a life that feels both nourishing and real.

Make your Map with Milestones

Establishing key goals means translating your core beliefs, values, and desires into clear, measurable actions. These goals aren't about external achievement alone, they're about living in alignment with who you truly are. When grounded in your inner truth, goals become meaningful and motivating. Start by identifying what matters most to you, then define specific milestones that reflect progress: weekly habits, monthly check-ins, or visible shifts in your life. Whether it's setting boundaries, launching a passion project, or deepening your relationships, these milestones keep your journey accountable, intentional, and anchored in authenticity.

Share What You Learn

Once your tools are embodied, your voice becomes valuable. You don't have to be a coach or public speaker to be a Wayfinder. You simply need to share the light you've earned. Whether through art, mentorship, parenting or even conversation, learn to guide others gently.

Lead with Heart, Again and Again

Being a Wayfinder is not a title, it's a commitment. Every day, recommit to your growth, your truth, and your service. This is not a linear path. Some days you'll lead. Some days you'll need rest. But every day, you choose to live on purpose.

Yes, Wayfinders cultivate the four core intelligences. They sharpen their intellectual intelligence (IQ) to think critically, solve problems creatively, and navigate the complexities of life with grounded clarity. They deepen their emotional intelligence (EQ) to understand, regulate, and respond to emotions with wisdom and empathy.

They build their positive intelligence (PQ) to recognize the sabotaging voices in their minds and redirect them with resilience and presence. They expand their sensory intelligence (SQ) to stay attuned to the body, to subtle shifts in energy, and to the messages whispered through sensation. But what sets a Wayfinder apart is not the possession of these intelligences, it is how they are lived, integrated, and continuously expanded.

Wayfinders know that these gifts are not static traits, but dynamic capacities that grow through experience. They don't wait until they're "ready" they start where they are. They stumble, reflect, adjust. They learn by living. The world becomes their classroom, their relationships become their mirrors, and their body becomes their compass.

They don't just gather information. They turn insight into practice, and practice into transformation. They test what they've learned in real life: in a tough conversation, a moment of fear, a leap toward a new dream. They use their tools not just to survive, but to stretch. To choose courage over comfort. To return to their center again and again.

And as we build this embodied wisdom, something remarkable happens. We stop trying to prove our worth. We stop asking for permission to feel, to speak, to rest, to leap. Instead, we begin designing lives that reflect our truth. Lives that honor our rhythm, our voice, and our capacity to contribute meaningfully to the world. This is not just personal development, it's personal sovereignty.

But the Wayfinder doesn't walk this path for themselves alone. A defining quality of a Wayfinder is the desire to turn their inner work outward, to share, uplift, and guide others. We carry torches, not to shine the light on ourselves, but to illuminate the path for those still finding their footing. We don't posture as perfect. We say, "Here's what I've learned. Maybe it will help you, too."

The Wayfinder's journey is marked by humility, generosity, and a deep understanding that growth is never linear. We fall. We pause. We tend to the wounds. Then we rise with new insight. Again and again.

Becoming a Wayfinder is not about mastering life. It's about being mastered by life in the most intentional and empowering ways. It's about asking bigger questions:

- *What did this moment come to teach me?*
- *Where am I still outsourcing my power?*
- *What tool or technique can help me hold this discomfort with more strength?*
- *Who else could benefit from what I've just learned?*

We practice. We gather. We pass it on.

Wayfinding requires commitment, not to perfection, but to practice. We come back to the same truths, the same questions, with new eyes. We revisit old wounds with gentler hands. We stop treating the process like a ladder to climb and start relating to it like a garden to tend.

It's also about learning to apply the right intelligence in the right moment. A Wayfinder knows when to use IQ to create structure, when to let EQ soften a moment, when to call on PQ to interrupt a mental spiral, and when to trust SQ to feel what's not being said. It's this refined dance, knowing which intelligence to lead with and how to blend them, that makes the Wayfinder so impactful.

Wayfinders choose, often consciously, to stay unseen and unheard for reasons, not out of fear, but out of intention. To observe. To learn. To prepare. They know that real wisdom comes not from reaction, but from reflection. And when they speak, they speak from a place that is rooted, resonant, and real.

If you're reading this and wondering if you are a Wayfinder, the answer might be yes. Not because you've mastered everything. But because you care deeply. You're devoted to your growth. You feel the pull to serve in ways that matter. You've weathered storms and come out with seeds of wisdom in your hands.

Wayfinding is a calling. One that starts with a whisper and becomes a rhythm. A sacred invitation to stop surviving and start leading, from your depth, with your heart, for the world.

So, continue to nurture your intelligences. Hone your tools. Refine your skills. Move gracefully through your zones. Let experience be your greatest teacher. And most importantly, when you rise, help someone else rise, too. Helping others become Wayfinders doesn't take away from your own light, it deepens your wisdom, sharpens your compass, and strengthens the path beneath your feet.

Because that's how Wayfinders multiply. That's how the world changes from the inside out.

Claiming Your Identity

You are allowed to be all of you. There is no longer a need to fragment yourself to fit in or dim your light to make others comfortable. Being a Wild Sensitive Wayfinder means reclaiming your whole identity, not just surviving as a sensitive soul in a loud and chaotic world, but thriving as an aware, wise, and empowered being. It means allowing your emotional depth to be seen as strength, your intuition to serve as guidance, and your inner complexity to be your compass.

It means your pain becomes your path. Your depth becomes your direction. Your contradiction becomes your wisdom. Instead of viewing your sensitivity and sensation-seeking as traits to be managed or hidden, you begin to recognize them as your greatest assets. You stop asking for permission to feel, to speak, to lead. You begin showing up in your relationships, your career, and your creativity with integrity and intention.

If you're still wondering what a Wild Sensitive Wayfinder might look like in the real world, look to those who quietly but powerfully shape the world with their presence. Look to Maya Angelou, who transformed her pain into poetry and activism, carrying truth like a lantern into dark places. Her voice echoed not just in literature but in the social consciousness of generations. Her Wayfinding was not loud, but profound, guiding countless souls toward dignity and courage.

Consider Robin Williams, a man whose humor lit up lives while masking an oceanic sensitivity. His boundless energy, rooted in empathy and deep emotional insight, reminded the world that laughter and pain are intimately linked. Though he often stood center stage, his truest power lay in his capacity to connect hearts, making the lonely feel seen, and the hurting feel understood. His Wayfinding was in his compassion, even when he struggled to find it for himself.

Think of Brené Brown, who brought the study of vulnerability into mainstream conversation, daring to speak about shame, courage, and worthiness in ways that resonated globally. She didn't just research human connection, she embodied it. Her work gave countless people permission to be seen in their truth. Her Wayfinding is academic, yes, but also deeply human.

Then there's Keanu Reeves, whose quiet demeanor, respectful boundaries, and consistent acts of kindness have made him a modern icon of integrity. He doesn't speak loudly, but his presence is unmistakable. Through his actions, he demonstrates the power of humility, calm, and quiet resilience. He is a Wayfinder for those who lead not through command, but through calm presence.

Toko-pa Turner, whose work in dreamwork and belonging invites us to reclaim the forgotten, the exiled, and the intuitive within. She guides people back to their inner landscapes, creating space for transformation through remembering. Her Wayfinding is spiritual and somatic, poetic and practical. She speaks to the soul, reminding us that we are never as far from home as we think.

And consider others throughout history whose Wayfinder qualities shine brightly. Albert Einstein, whose deep thoughtfulness and intuitive insights reshaped science and philosophy. He sensed what others couldn't, not just in numbers, but in the nature of reality itself.

Carl Jung, whose sensitive soul explored the depths of the unconscious and bridged mysticism with psychology. His Wayfinding was in mapping the inner world so others could follow.

Harriet Tubman, whose courage and intuition led her to guide hundreds to freedom. She sensed danger before it arrived and acted with fierce grace. Her leadership was born from resilience and spirit.

Leonard Cohen, poet and musician, channeled emotion, longing, and wisdom into his words. His music didn't shout, it resonated, slowly, deeply, permanently.

Alan Watts, philosopher and teacher, helped bring Eastern wisdom into Western consciousness. His sensitivity allowed him to translate ancient truths into modern clarity.

Jane Goodall, who gave voice to the voiceless with her groundbreaking work in primatology, rooted in respect and empathy. Her Wayfinding lies in her advocacy and deep bond with the natural world.

Frida Kahlo, who painted pain and passion into art that has become immortal. Her bold, raw expression became a mirror for generations of sensitive creators.

Mister Rogers, who gently entered homes and hearts, teaching kindness, self-worth, and emotional intelligence. His quiet presence was revolutionary.

James Baldwin, who wrote with both fire and tenderness about identity, justice, and belonging. His sensitivity gave him clarity, his intellect gave it voice.

Virginia Woolf, whose introspection and literary brilliance challenged norms and gave voice to inner landscapes previously unspoken.

These individuals may walk very different paths, but they all share a Wayfinder's heart: a commitment to truth, a willingness to feel deeply, and the courage to live from that depth. They are not perfect, and they are not trying to be. What makes them powerful is their honesty, their integrity, and their ability to transform their inner world into guidance for others.

And here's the truth: each and every one of us who holds the traits of a Highly Sensitive Sensation Seeker holds this same potential. But only a few will rise to become Wayfinders. Why? Because it takes motivation. It takes courage. It requires support, education, and guidance. It's like learning to live a physically healthy life: anyone can do it, but not everyone does.

The Wayfinder rises early. They feed their body and mind with nourishment. They read, reflect, and refine. They not only heal, they integrate. They don't just seek personal peace, they carry light for others. They know that their wounds were not just theirs, but doorways to wisdom. They serve not because they're trying to prove worth, but because they can't not.

Wayfinders are born at the intersection of personal empowerment and collective purpose. They are the ones who choose not to shrink away from their emotional intensity, sensory depth, or intellectual curiosity, but to work with it. They seek growth not out of inadequacy, but because they know what's possible. They are the ones who say: "I want to understand more, so I can live more. I want to master the tools, so I can be of service."

Being a Wayfinder means learning to strengthen your nervous system without hardening your heart. It means anchoring into self-awareness so deeply that you can hold space for others without losing yourself in the process. This inner mastery is what makes their leadership so quietly powerful. It is not reactive, but responsive. Not controlling but containing. Not dominating but deeply rooted.

Wayfinders do not hide from life. They embrace it fully and intentionally. In the workspace, they may blend in, but never because they are trying to disappear. They are listening. Observing. Processing. Their inner world is rapidly decoding tone, energy, alignment. Their superpower is translating these subtle cues into actionable wisdom. They sense the emotional undercurrents others miss, the fatigue in a colleague's voice, the fear behind a team's resistance, the quiet disconnect between spoken goals and lived values. And when they act, it is with clarity and care.

They can see through even the most carefully applied mask. No matter how polished the performance or convincing the persona, they sense the dissonance beneath it. It's not judgment, it's keen intuition. A felt knowing that something doesn't quite align. They read the forced laugh, the tight jaw, the energetic pullback. While others may take things at face value, Wayfinders feel the deeper layers. They may not always speak it, but they always know it.

Yet when it matters, they do speak. They guide. They hold the line. In a world that often mistakes loudness for leadership, Wayfinders move with deliberate grace. Their presence reorients chaos. Their steadiness calms rooms. Their quiet conviction opens space for truth to emerge. They know when to speak, and they know when stillness says more.

To step into the identity of a Wild Sensitive Wayfinder is to declare that your depth is not a limitation, but a direction. It is to lead not in spite of your sensitivity, but through it. It is to become someone who studies their reactions, refines their tools, and chooses again and again to grow. Not for applause. Not for ego. But for the simple truth that this world needs more people who can hold contradiction, translate chaos, and lead with heart.

It all begins the moment you decide: I will no longer just navigate my sensitivity, I will navigate with it. And not only that, I will help others navigate too.

We've Lived This

We, Randy and Annet, didn't arrive at this understanding through theory. We arrived by falling apart. By burning out. By feeling lost in systems that didn't see us, and by hearing again and again that we were "too much," or "too quiet," or "too complicated to love." We know what it means to feel like a contradiction. We've sat in the floating zone, uncertain if we'd ever find stable ground. But we didn't give up. We listened, to our nervous systems, to our patterns, to the quiet wisdom within. We gathered tools, we asked for guidance, and we kept going.

The frameworks we now offer, The Adventure Triskelion, The Six Zones, The Wild Sensitive Wayfinder, were not built in a lab. They were forged in the fires of real life. These are the tools that helped us stay. Stay present. Stay curious. Stay alive to ourselves and to each other. We didn't "fix" our sensitivity, we finally learned to honor it. And that changed everything.

This is what we want for you. Not to live like us, but to live like you, fully, boldly, gently, wildly. To stop shrinking. To stop trying to "normalize" your depth. To stop apologizing for your clarity, your hunger, your emotion, your truth. Because the Wayfinder life doesn't mean perfection. It means practice. It looks like this:

You plan for rest and adventure equally, because both are sacred.

You recognize your warning signs before collapse and respond with compassion.

You meet your triggers with curiosity instead of judgment.

You no longer chase chaos to feel alive, you choose growth with intention.

You trust your emotions, your intellect, your body, and your intuition, and you use them in harmony.

You stop hiding. You stop apologizing.

You guide others, not because you have all the answers, but because you've learned how to come home to yourself.

This chapter, and this identity, is not an ending. It's a beginning. The world is calling for deeper leaders, quieter wisdom, and more Wild Sensitive Wayfinders. You... Yes, YOU...may be one of them. And if you are, your path doesn't have to be walked alone. We're here. Others are here. A Wild Sensitive community is rising.

Your contradictions are not a curse. They're a compass. Welcome, Wayfinder. The path ahead is yours to walk.

Chapter 14

The Living Adventurers How we can Help

Together, We Rise: Creating a Home for the Wild Sensitive Heart

"We are not here to be fixed. We are here to be found. And once we find ourselves, we become the ones who light the path for others, not with noise or force, but with the quiet, steady brilliance of knowing who we are."

The Living Adventurers

The Lived Experience of Randy and Annet

As empowered Wild Sensitives ourselves, we have lived through a great many challenges. We've stood in the chaos of overstimulation and the ache of underwhelm. We've questioned our worth in rooms that felt too loud, and felt our hearts race toward new horizons that others said were too risky. We've walked through confusion, pain, and deep loneliness, but never without curiosity. That spark, that hunger to understand, to feel more, to become more, never left us.

It's what led Annet to crawl into that concrete pipe as a child, seeking stillness in the unknown. It's what carried Randy across fifty-six countries, chasing meaning with a backpack and a question that wouldn't let go. It's what brought us together, from the Netherlands and Mexico, across distance, fear, and old beliefs, into a life of raw connection and adventure. From that sacred convergence, we evolved into Wild Sensitive Wayfinders, not a method, but a way of living. A path forged

313

from real stories, real stumbles, and rising again. We don't teach theory. We teach what we've lived. We've taken every insight, every heartbreak, every moment of magic and crafted it into tools, techniques, and skills. We've learned to respond instead of react. To choose stillness without shame, and to leap when the moment is right. Every day, we learn more. And every day, we teach others how to start living the life they long for, deep, rich, aligned.

You may be wondering: *"How do I go from an unempowered HSP-HSS, barely surviving, to an empowered Wild Sensitive, fully alive?"*

The answer isn't a single step, it's many, carefully and incrementally placed with honesty that are deeply doable. We walk with you through each one. We invite you to begin where we once stood: unsure, hopeful, yearning. And we show you what we've found on the other side.

We lived the pain. We lived the paradox. And now, we live the freedom. And we want that for you, too. Because you were never meant to live small. You were meant to live fully.

Strengths, values, and contributions to the world
When we, as Wild Sensitive Wayfinders, step into our empowered state, we become something the world deeply needs, visionaries, connectors, and bridge-builders. Our sensitivity allows us to sense what others overlook. Our sensation seeking drives us to explore what others fear. This rare blend gives us the ability to see problems not as obstacles, but as opportunities. We perceive nuances in conversations, in systems, in relationships, and from that clarity, we craft solutions that others miss. We sense pathways when others see dead ends. We offer fresh perspectives, compassionate leadership, intuitive innovation, and heart-centered action.

Now, you may ask, does this make us better than others? In some ways, yes. In the same way a lighthouse is better at illuminating the dark than a hammer is. But we are not better as people, we are simply uniquely gifted for a particular kind of light work. Every person brings something essential to the world, and this is ours. Our strengths are not louder, they are deeper. Not more forceful, but more attuned. In a noisy world that often praises power over presence, what's missing are voices like ours. Voices that say: there is another way.

When we are empowered, we bring empathy where there was judgment, creativity where there was conformity, and wisdom where there was noise. We bring connection. Innovation. Healing. Wholeness. And perhaps most importantly, we bring vision, what the world could be, if we dared to live aligned. We are not here by accident. We are here to make a difference. To be the ones who see the way forward and light the lantern for others. As Gandhi said, *"Be the change you wish to see in the world."* And as Wild Sensitives, we don't just wish it. We become it.

Inspiration, courage, and community

What we want to offer you now is more than information, it's inspiration. The kind that stirs something ancient and true inside you. The kind that whispers, *"You were always meant for more."* This is your moment to rise, not as someone who needs fixing, but as someone finally ready to claim the fullness of who they are. With every tool you've learned in this book, with every skill you've developed, with every technique you've practiced, you've been preparing for this. With time and intention, these tools won't just sit in your memory, they will live in your muscles. They will become second nature, guiding you not through reactivity, but through creation. You won't just survive the moments life throws at you. You'll shape them. Sculpt them. Turn them into something beautiful and real and uniquely yours.

This path isn't about perfection. Life will still bring storms. But now, you will meet them not as a victim of circumstance, but as a Wild Sensitive Wayfinder, with knowledge in your mind, tools in your hands, courage in your chest, and community at your back. Because while self-discovery begins alone, true transformation happens together. You can only go so far on your own. That's why we've created a living, breathing space for

Wild Sensitives like you, a place of support, understanding, and connection. A place where you don't have to explain your paradox because we already live it too.

In this community, we learn from one another, grow beside one another, and remind each other that we belong, not by changing who we are, but by becoming more of who we've always been.

You're not walking this path alone. We're right here with you. And together, we are not just changing lives, we are changing the world. One wild, wonderful, unapologetically sensitive step at a time.

What we offer as resources through the Living Adventurers.

Through The Living Adventurers, we offer more than a book, we offer a way forward. A living, evolving sanctuary for Wild Sensitives who are ready to walk the empowered path, not alone, but together. At the heart of what we do is community. We've created a space where Highly Sensitive High Sensation Seekers can gather, not to fit in, but to belong. In this space, we host regular live gatherings, virtual campfires where real conversations happen. These aren't lectures or performances; they're deeply held spaces of mutual learning, where we share breakthroughs, process challenges, and explore new tools side by side. These meetings are where resonance becomes connection and where the quiet knowing that you are not alone takes root and grows.

We also offer guided webinars that dive deeper into the emotional and practical aspects of the Wild Sensitive life, topics like boundary-setting, navigating overstimulation, living in alignment with your values, and creating sustainable adventure. Our workshops go further still: interactive, focused, and experiential, they give you the chance to not just learn but embody new skills in real-time. And for those ready to step more fully into their leadership and service, our comprehensive Living Adventurers Coach Training equips you to guide others through this journey with integrity, insight, and heart.

But perhaps the most transformative offering we share is our retreats, immersive, soul-nourishing, and life-expanding experiences designed specifically for the Wild Sensitive. Held in wild, beautiful, energetically resonant locations, these retreats offer a chance to unplug from the noise of the world and drop fully into yourself. Through movement, nature, guided reflection, creative exploration, and community rituals, you'll return not only rested but reconnected to your own wisdom and power.

This is more than personal development. It's a reclamation of your wholeness. And it's all here for you, when you're ready to take the next step.

Here you will find access to the
Wild Sensitive
book page

Where we offer additional materials mentioned in the book, such as videos, audios, and assessments.

or visit us at **wildsensitive.com**

The Wild Sensitive Wayfinder Manifesto
For Those Who Feel Deeply and Live Fully

We are the ones who feel with depth and move with boldness.
We carry both gentleness and fire, presence and passion.
We were made to sense the subtle and seek the extraordinary.

We are Highly Sensitive. We are High Sensation Seeking.
We are beautifully wired for wonder.

Our emotions are intelligence.
Our restlessness is curiosity.
Our paradox is power.

We honor reflection and pursue expansion.
We choose stillness that heals and adventure that awakens.
We live from the center of our truth, curious, conscious, and clear.

We bring compassion to conflict.
We offer insight where others see confusion.
We create beauty, connection, and meaningful change.

Our path is one of awareness and intention.
We move forward with determination, clarity, and deep inner knowing.
We grow through practice, through presence, through purpose.

We live by values that root us and visions that lift us.
We step forward with steady hearts and strong instincts.
We embrace challenge as a teacher and emotion as a compass.

We walk this journey together, in community, in kindness, in celebration.
We support each other's brilliance and rise through shared wisdom.
We are mentors, creators, soul-guides ... Wayfinders.

Scientific & Psychological
Terms Used in the Book

1. **Mirror neurons -** Brain cells that help us understand and feel what others are feeling by mirroring their emotions.

2. **fMRI Scan (functional Magnetic Resonance Imaging)** - A brain scanning method that shows which parts of the brain are active while you're thinking, feeling, or doing something. It works by measuring changes in blood flow, helping researchers see how the brain processes things like emotions, sensory input, or decision-making, especially useful in studying traits like high sensitivity.

3. **Nervous system regulation** - Managing the body's stress and calm responses to stay balanced.

4. **Sympathetic arousal** - The 'fight or flight' response that prepares the body for action.

5. **The Sympathetic and Parasympathetic Nervous Systems** are two branches of the autonomic nervous system that work together to regulate the body's internal state. The sympathetic system is like the body's gas pedal, it prepares you to respond to stress or danger by triggering the "fight, flight, or freeze" response. It increases heart rate, sharpens focus, and floods the body with energy through adrenaline and cortisol. In contrast, the parasympathetic system acts like the brake, it helps the body calm down and recover after stress by slowing the heart rate, aiding digestion, and promoting rest and healing.

6. **Sensory Processing Sensitivity (SPS)** - A natural trait where a person's nervous system takes in and processes more information from their surroundings. People with SPS notice subtle details, feel emotions deeply, and often need more time to rest and recharge.

7. **Neurodivergent** - A term used to describe people whose brains work differently than what is considered "typical." This can include unique ways of thinking, feeling, sensing, or learning. It's not a disorder, just a different way of experiencing the world.

8. **Amygdala activity** - The amygdala is a small part of the brain that helps process emotions, especially fear and danger. When it's active, it alerts you to threats and prepares your body to react, like making your heart race or helping you stay alert in stressful situations.

9. **Cortisol** - A hormone your body releases when you're stressed. It helps give you energy to deal with challenges, but if you have too much for too long, it can make you feel tired, anxious, or overwhelmed.

10. **Freeze, Fawn, Flight, Fight** - These are the four common ways people respond to stress or danger:
- **Freeze** – You feel stuck or unable to move or speak.
- **Fawn** – You try to please others to stay safe or avoid conflict.
- **Flight** – You want to run away or escape the situation.
- **Fight** – You get angry or confront the threat to protect yourself.

Each is a natural survival response for the Highly Sensitive, often triggered by the nervous system.

11. **Prefrontal cortex** - The part of the brain just behind your forehead that helps you think clearly, make decisions, solve problems, control impulses, and understand your emotions. It's like your brain's "wise guide" that helps you act with awareness instead of just reacting.

12. **High Sensation Seeking (HSS)** - A personality trait where someone craves new, exciting, and intense experiences. They often enjoy adventure, variety, and deep exploration. For people who are also highly sensitive, this drive can create a push-pull between wanting excitement and needing calm.

13. **Highly Sensitive Person (HSP)** - Someone born with a more responsive nervous system, which means they feel things more deeply, notice subtle details, and need more time to process and recharge. It's not a weakness, it's a natural trait found in about 20–30% of people.

14. **D.O.E.S. model** – Model created by Dr. Elaine Aron describing the characteristics of a Highly Sensitive Person (Depth of processing, Overstimulation, Emotional responsiveness, Sensory sensitivity)

15. **Rejection Sensitivity** - A strong emotional reaction to the possibility of being rejected, criticized, or left out. People with rejection sensitivity may worry a lot about what others think and feel hurt easily, even by small signs of disapproval. It's often linked to past experiences and a deep desire to feel accepted and safe.

16. **Attachment styles** - Patterns of how we connect with others, especially in close relationships. These styles are usually shaped by early experiences with caregivers and affect how we handle closeness, trust, and conflict. The four main types are:

- **Secure** – Comfortable with intimacy and trust.
- **Anxious** – Craves closeness but fears being abandoned.
- **Avoidant** – Struggles with closeness and values independence.
- **Disorganized** – A mix of wanting connection and fearing it, often linked to trauma.

Understanding your attachment style can help improve relationships and emotional well-being.

17. **Developmental trauma** - Emotional or psychological wounds that happen during childhood, often from neglect, abuse, or inconsistent caregiving. These early experiences can deeply affect how a person feels about themselves, relates to others, and handles stress later in life. Unlike single-event trauma, developmental trauma happens over time and shapes the foundation of emotional development.

18. **Self-regulation** - The ability to manage your thoughts, emotions, and behaviors in healthy ways, especially during stress or strong feelings. It means calming yourself when upset, staying focused, making thoughtful choices, without getting overwhelmed.

19. **Co-regulation** - The process of calming or stabilizing your emotions through a safe connection with someone else. It often happens through gentle presence, tone of voice, eye contact, or physical touch. Especially important for children (and sensitive adults), it shows that we don't always have to regulate emotions alone, sometimes, we need others to help us feel safe and grounded.

20. **Resilience** - The ability to recover from stress, challenges, or setbacks and keep going. It's like emotional strength, bouncing back after hard times, learning from struggles, and growing stronger through them. Resilience doesn't mean never feeling pain; it means moving through it and finding your way forward.

21. **Introversion/Extraversion spectrum** - A scale that shows how people get their energy and process the world:
  • Introverts feel recharged by quiet time, reflection, and deep conversations.
  • Extraverts feel energized by being around people, action, and external stimulation.
Most people fall somewhere in between, and your position on the spectrum can shift depending on your mood, environment, or stage of life.

22. **Sensory Perception Quotient (SPQ)** - A questionnaire used to measure how sensitive someone is to sensory input, like sounds, lights, textures, or smells. It helps identify people who may notice subtle changes in their environment more easily than others, often linked to traits like high sensitivity or sensory processing differences.

23. **Highly Sensitive Person Scale (HSP Scale)** - A self-assessment tool developed by Dr. Elaine Aron to measure how sensitive a person is. It includes questions about how deeply you process things, how easily you get overstimulated, your emotional responsiveness, and your awareness of subtle details.

24. **Zuckerman Sensation Seeking Scale** - A questionnaire created by psychologist Dr. Marvin Zuckerman to measure how much a person craves excitement, variety, and new experiences. It looks at four areas: thrill and adventure seeking, experience seeking, disinhibition (letting loose), and boredom susceptibility. It's often used to understand people with high sensation-seeking traits.

25. **Intelligence Quotient (IQ)** – A test that reflects how well someone can think, solve problems, and understand complex ideas compared to others their age, based on standardized tests.

26. **Emotional Quotient (EQ)** - A questionnaire designed to measure how easily and deeply a person understands and feels what others are going through. It looks at emotional awareness, compassion, and the ability to pick up on social cues. A higher EQ score often means someone is naturally more empathetic and emotionally in tune with others.

27. **Positive Intelligence (PQ)** – An assessment developed by Shirzad Chamine to measure your strength of your positive versus negative mental muscles. Which measures your mental fitness.

28. **Behavioral Inhibition System (BIS)** - A part of the brain that helps you pause, reflect, and stay cautious, especially in new or uncertain situations. It notices potential risks and helps you slow down before acting. In Highly Sensitive People, this system is usually more active, leading to careful thinking and strong awareness of what could go wrong.

29. **Behavioral Activation System (BAS)** - A part of the brain that pushes you to take action, seek rewards, and go after what excites you. It drives motivation, curiosity, and the desire for new experiences. In High Sensation Seekers, this system is often very active, creating a strong urge to explore, create, and engage with life.

30. **Threat detection** - The brain's ability to sense when something might be dangerous, physically, emotionally, or socially. Highly Sensitive People often have stronger threat detection, which helps them notice subtle signs of tension, conflict, or discomfort that others might miss. It's a natural way the nervous system tries to keep us safe.

31. **Somatic Grounding and Breathwork** - A body-based therapy that helps release stress and trauma stored in the nervous system. Instead of just talking about difficult experiences, it focuses on noticing physical sensations to gently process and heal them. It teaches the body how to return to a sense of safety and calm.

32. **Mindfulness-based practices** - Activities like meditation, deep breathing, or gentle movement that help you focus on the present moment with calm awareness. These practices can reduce stress, improve emotional balance for the Highly Sensitive Person.

33. **Mindfulness-Based Cognitive Therapy (MBCT)** - A type of therapy that helps you identify and change unhelpful thoughts and behaviors. It teaches practical tools to manage stress, anxiety, and negative thinking by replacing them with more helpful and realistic ways of thinking and responding.

34. **Trauma-informed care** - An approach to support and healing that understands how trauma affects people's emotions, behavior, and nervous systems. It focuses on creating safety, trust, and empowerment, especially for those who have experienced past harm, by being gentle, respectful, and sensitive to their needs.

Our Research Sources

While many dream of writing a non-fiction book, we can honestly say, it's a monumental journey. Our first book, The Emergence, wove fiction and fact into a soul-stirring guide for younger Highly Sensitive readers. But The Wild Sensitive asked more of us. It pulled us into the depths of both lived experience and science. With over 3,000 hours of dedicated research, we sought to understand, validate, and illuminate what it means to be both Highly Sensitive and High Sensation Seeking.

The result is not just a book, but a body of work grounded in personal exploration and supported by academic rigor. We drew from neuroscience, psychology, leadership, and somatic wisdom, alongside a lifetime of navigating the wild adventure of our dual traits. Below are just some of the resources that helped shape The Wild Sensitive: Unlocking the Power of the Highly Sensitive Sensation Seeker.

Books

1. **Elaine Aron, Ph.D** – The Highly Sensitive Person (1996)
2. **Elaine Aron Ph.D** – The Highly Sensitive Person in Love (2001).
3. **Elaine Aron Ph.D** – Psychotherapy and the Highly Sensitive Person (2011)
4. **Tracy Cooper, Ph.D** – Thrive: The Highly Sensitive Person and Career. (2015)
5. **Tracy Cooper, Ph.D**– Thrill: The High Sensation Seeking Highly Sensitive Person. (2016)
6. **Tracy Cooper, Ph.D** – Empowering the Sensitive Male Soul (2020)
7. **Marvin Zuckerman** – Sensation Seeking, Beyond the optimal level of arousal (1979)
8. **Randy Grasser** – Facing Fear Through Adventure; An HSP's Story (2021)
9. **Bianca Acevedo** – The Highly Sensitive Brain, Research, Assessment, and treatment of Sensory Processing Sensitivity (2020)
10. **William Allen** – Confessions of a Sensitive Man (2020)

11. **William Allen** – On Being a Sensitive Man (2022)
12. **Tom Falkenstein** – The Highly Sensitive man (2019)
13. **Esther Bergsma** – The Brain of the Highly Sensitive Person (2021)
14. **Bessel van der Kolk** – The Body Keeps the Score (2014)
15. **Gabor Maté** – When the Body Says No (2011)

Research

1. **Aron & Aron** – Sensory-Processing Sensitivity and its relation to introversion and emotionally. (1997)
2. **Acevedo et al.** – The highly sensitive brain: an fMRI study of sensory processing sensitivity and response to others' emotions (2014)
3. **Pluess, M. & Belsky, J** – Vantage sensitivity; Individual differences in response to positive experiences (2013)
4. **Belsky, J. & Pluess, M.** - Beyond diathesis stress: Differential susceptibility to environmental influences. (2009)
5. **Zuckerman, M** – Sensation seeking and anxiety, traits and states, as determinants of behavior in novel situations. (1976)
6. **Zuckerman, M**. - Sensation seeking - Dimensions of Personality (1978)
7. **Zuckerman, M., et al.** - What is the sensation seeker? Personality trait and experience correlates of the Sensation Seeking Scales. (1972)
8. **Smolewska, K., McCabe S., Woody E.** - A psychometric evaluation of the Highly Sensitive Person Scale: The components of sensory-processing sensitivity and their relation to the BIS/BAS and "Big Five." (2006)
9. **Greven, C. U., Lionetti, F., Booth, C., Aron, E. N., Fox, E., Schendan, H. E., … & Homberg, J**. - Sensory processing sensitivity in the context of environmental sensitivity: A critical review and development of research agenda. (2019)
10. **Acevedo, B. P., Aron, E. N., Aron, A., Cooper, T., & Marhenke, R.** - Sensory processing sensitivity and its relation to sensation seeking. (2023)

Websites

1. https://hsperson.com – By Elaine Aron
2. https://sensitivityresearch.com – by Prof. Micheal Pluess and others
3. https://drtracycooper.org – Dr. Tracy Cooper
4. https://www.thesensitiveman.com – William Allen
5. https://www.positiveintelligence.com – Positive Intelligence Shirzad Chamine

Podcasts

As part of our journey, we've conducted a multitude of in-depth interviews on our podcast with leading experts in the fields of High Sensitivity and High Sensation Seeking. These conversations have included pioneers like Dr. Elaine Aron, Dr. Tracy Cooper, Michael Pluess, Tom Falkenstein, Esther Bergsma, William Allen, Bianca Acevedo and other renowned voices in psychology, neuroscience, and embodied healing. Each interview offered fresh insights, practical tools, and deeply human reflections, contributing to the rich foundation of this book and the work we now share through The Living Adventurers.

1. **Sensitive and Strong Podcast (Annet van Duinen)** – Interviews with HSP/HSS experts. https://sensitiveandstrong.buzzsprout.com

2. **Men with S.T.Y.L.E. Podcast** – Hosted by Randy Grasser and William Allen – Interviews with HSP/HSS experts. https://menwithstyle.buzzsprout.com